Advance Praise for
**AMERICAN DOOM LOOP**

"For the past half-century, journalist Dale Maharidge has been an indispensable voice on America, bearing witness to what is now widely recognized as an empire in decline, warning us about the fall long before it was fashionable to do so. In *American Doom Loop*, he revisits the 1980s, the start of both his reporting career and so much of our present dysfunction. For anyone seeking to understand the violence endemic to modern America, this is essential, eye-opening reading, a reminder of how we got here—and the human toll that comes with forgetting."

—**Jessica Bruder**, author of *Nomadland: Surviving America in the Twenty-First Century*

"An ode to journalism, the old-fashioned kind, by a working-class kid driven by idealism, by a desire to make America a better place. He rides the rails with hobos, helps young Salvadorans flee the violence, talks to cops, steel workers, and sharecroppers; and has endless hours and empathy for victims of rape and violence. He bears and bares the demons and PTSD. A beautiful book."

—**Raymond Bonner**, author of *Weakness and Deceit: U.S. Policy and El Salvador* and *Waltzing with a Dictator: The Marcoses and the Making of American Policy*

# AMERICAN DOOM LOOP

# AMERICAN DOOM LOOP

## DISPATCHES FROM A TROUBLED NATION
### 1980s–2020s

### DALE MAHARIDGE

New York ♦ Nashville
regalopress.com

Published in the United States of America
1  2  3  4  5  6  7  8  9  10

For Judith Haynes

# Contents

"I think we're an aggressive nation.
We were fighting the British for our freedom.
We fought the Indians to take their land.
We fought the Mexicans.
We wanted California from the Mexicans; we took it.
We've been fighting all of our existence....
We are aggressive—let's face it."

—**Tom Price**, member of L Company, Third Battalion,
Twenty-Second Marines, Sixth Marine Division,
who fought with the author's father in the Battles of Guam
and Okinawa in World War II

# Prologue

Successful feature films and novels have a multidimensional central character shaded with complexity who drives the narrative. These come quickly to mind: Joe Christmas, Tom Joad, Charles Foster Kane, Port and Kit Moresby, Luke in *Cool Hand Luke*, Nathan Zuckerman, Cliff Booth—characters and their worlds providing a truth via the backdrop of a house burning in Mississippi, California's iconic Central Valley, the "Rosebud" sled, the vast Sahara beneath its sheltering sky, a prison chain gang ("What we've got here is a failure to communicate"), a declining industrial city and a glove factory in New Jersey, a wife-killing sidekick to a washed-up actor who is crazy enough to pick a fight with Bruce Lee. Seldom does nonfiction have an avatar that provides universal meaning. Most journalism isn't even one-dimensional—at best it's one-quarter or one-eighth dimensional. It isn't that we as journalists are ignorant of or choose to ignore complexity; many characters simply don't have the ability to get one thousand feet above their place on Earth and share that vision of what they see of their lives, or they can but refuse to allow their psyches to be probed. The vast majority of people in real life never let their guard down for us to get close even in the most nonjournalistic of situations. I recall a conversation in a New York City bar in the 1980s with a Pulitzer Prize–winning novelist: he told our group that he was sleeping with as many women as possible as he researched a certain fiction (one of those women he was attempting to bed was present with us over drinks for this exchange), for when one is naked, one can get closest to another person's secrets. His aim was to learn as many secrets as possible from these unclothed women. This research and/ or thought process, beyond being cringeworthy even in the 1980s, appears to have led to work that this novelist published in the 1990s. He, however, was wrong. One repeatedly realizes, if they have lived a long life of attempted intimacy, that one can have sex with someone for a year or more and never really know them.

The key for the narrative long-form journalist is to identify those rare characters with the ability to ascend to the heights and view themselves one thousand feet below, and then spend a lot of time with them. Slow journalism. Research means patient immersion with people on the receiving end of violence or injustice, who are generous enough to share their experience so that others can learn from it. It's as close as one can get to the veracity of a novel or film character.

This book is about some of those people. Their stories are centered in the 1980s, a decade that has many things to tell us today. I reconnected with central figures in my work from that era and bring their stories forward to the present—in one case forty-one years after I first interviewed her. Through it all, my job description has been to listen.

About the listener:

Memory is not to be trusted; that's reason enough for being a packrat. The stories in this book are drawn from the contents of footlockers that I've lugged through the years: tens of dozens of notebooks, printouts of journals, memos to and from editors, cassette tape recordings, credit card receipts, original newspaper stories, and other material.

In immersing in the dust of this archive, I was transported back in time to the events that gave me PTSD. While writing, without consciously realizing it, words emerged in present tense as some scenes were relived. And with this came a return of the nightmares. Even though use of that tense clashes with the overall voice of this book, I've let it stand in those places for this reason: the traumatic past is an enduring present.

## PART ONE

# "Go for the Fucking Throat"

# River Styx Road

We are told that when we dream of watching a person climbing out onto the rotting branch of a towering, barkless dead tree one hundred feet off the ground, we are really looking at ourselves. We are that person who is upside down, koala bear style, slowly shimmying toward the fragile bone-white tip. The branch is surely going to break, and that person is going to plunge to their death. We try yelling, "Turn back," but no sound comes from our throat. This kind of mirror may pervade our waking hours and explain the dream: what we are drawn to pursue is a reflection of what troubles us.

Riding my Yamaha motorcycle on ice-slick roads in the shoulder seasons of that Ohio winter of 1976, sometimes in sleet storms, wasn't risk. For me, risk is rooted in something ultimately far more dangerous: my desire to learn all that I can about others—their secrets, what motivates them—and to write about it. I'm especially drawn to understand the dark side of human nature, as well as the wounded in heart and soul, and what Jack London called "The People of the Abyss." I wanted to focus on fiction. But a more realistic goal for telling stories, one that actually might put dough in my wallet, was to become a professional journalist.

Bored with college, at the age of nineteen, I began training at the bottom, "stringing" for reporters at the *Cleveland Press*, a big afternoon paper. I covered meetings. There was plenty of work. Some forty suburban cities—all with their own mayors, town councils, and school boards—surround Cleveland. I was kept busy two and even three nights a week. Each morning I phoned in my notes to Sarah and Stephanie, the reporters who would craft them into stories. There were no bylines. But I simultaneously freelanced to get writing clips.

School boards and city councils are populated with the best members of humanity, and also the worst—the petty and conniving. I learned a lot. How to detect bullshit. How to observe. I saw a fight coming between two council members in one meeting long before fists were thrown. I became skilled at getting people to talk. Most of all, I discovered how to listen. Sarah and Stephanie paid me five dollars for the first hour, a buck sixty per hour thereafter. Time hunched over the handlebars didn't count on the clock. I throttled the Yamaha hard between meetings.

In the fall of 1977, I rode the motorcycle to apply for a full-time job at a small daily newspaper, the *Gazette*, located in a city twenty-five miles south of Cleveland with a population of eleven thousand. Settlers in the early 1800s wanted to call it Mecca, but the name had already been taken by another Ohio town. So they chose Medina for both the city and the county. None of the pioneers were Muslim, yet they somehow knew about the two ancient metropolises sacred in Islam, in what would become Saudi Arabia. Gross pay for the job was $125 per week, $103.39 take-home.

I was assigned to a bureau office in Brunswick, a suburb of tract homes at the northern edge of the county. It was a fast-growing enclave for the solid middle class that then still existed, composed largely of blue-collar factory workers and front-office suits. When I was hired, Medina County was nearly 100 percent White. I would never see a person of color in all my time there. It was a White-flight destination for people running from the old Cleveland neighborhoods.

Two weeks after I showed up, Michael Swihart, age eighteen, came back from his freshman year at Miami University to his home at 101 Westchester Drive, on a one-third-acre lot in the Forest Hills subdivision off Boston Road. Michael and his father, Donald, had an argument. The father, forty-one and a front-office worker for Hilti

Fastening Systems, Inc., which sold industrial steel products, was displeased by his son's sports-playing ability. Donald stood in front of Michael holding a baseball bat and asked if he would ever learn how "to use one of these." Michael grabbed the bat and beat Donald to death. When his mother, Sue, age forty, came into the room screaming, he whacked the life out of her too. His brother, Brian, age sixteen, tried to take away the bat, and Michael hammered him to death as well. His nine-year-old brother, Russell, was outside. Michael took Russell to the store to buy him candy. He also purchased gasoline. When they got back to Westchester Drive, Michael beat Russell to death. At 7:40 p.m. that Sunday night, Michael poured gasoline all over the house, walked to the front entrance, and lit a match. The blast shattered the windows of a neighbor's house. Flames leaping into the sky were visible a mile away.

Fellow staffer Ed Noga and I teamed up, scooping reporters from the big dailies in Akron and Cleveland and the out-of-town press. That Monday our stories were splashed across the front page of the *Gazette*. It also happened to be my twenty-first birthday.

Cleveland in those days, with its smoking steel mills, was rife with violence and riven with various ethnic factions of mobsters. In 1975, Shondor Birns, a Jewish gangster with a lengthy murderous history, left Christy's Lounge on Detroit Avenue on the South Side and got in his Lincoln Continental. When he turned the key in the ignition, the car exploded. His body, cut in half, was blown through the roof. The ensuing gangster war was intense: in 1976, there were thirty-seven mob-related bombings. In October 1977, the Italian Mafia took out Irish mobster Danny Greene, who always wore green clothes and wrote in green ink. After leaving a dentist's office in an eastern suburb of Cleveland, he got in his green car. The vehicle parked next to his contained explosives; one of Greene's arms was blasted a hundred feet across the parking lot.

Those killings among mobsters didn't affect ordinary citizens, and in a way, kind of made sense. Michael Swihart's massacre didn't.

I went back to reporting on school boards, sometimes working in the main newsroom. One day, a priest came into the office and asked the receptionist to speak with the religion editor. "Go to Hell and fry," he thought he heard her say. The cleric was outraged.

Helen Fry, the religion editor, had been at the paper forever. Her hair was tied back so tightly that it appeared painful, and she looked ancient. She would thunder with disgust if other reporters sneezed. Helen hated bodily secretions. We lived in fear of catching colds.

Most of the time, however, I worked out of the Brunswick bureau. After my colleague Ed left the paper, the city editor sent in a woman named Jo to fill the spot. That editor wanted to get Jo out of the main newsroom, and as an enticement, he named her Brunswick bureau chief. Every morning, Jo hung a huge American flag out in front of the bureau, inserting the pole into a metal cup that I'd never before noticed. It appears that she'd hired someone to drill holes in the brick and affix the bracket. Jo loved the title of bureau chief—and the power that came with it. I'd be doing an interview, phone cradled in my ear, furiously taking notes, and she'd bark: "Young man, get your feet off that desk! This is a professional office!"

Jo had been a school board member at the same time as she wrote searing unsigned editorials against teachers. After the start of a meeting in that district, a board member, face red with rage, ran up to me. He jabbed a finger in my chest, admonishing me for not reciting the Pledge of Allegiance. I'd stopped in Catholic grade school after a lay teacher's fiancé was killed in action in Vietnam. I didn't bother to explain. According to this board member, I was "un-American and a disgrace to the country." He phoned the city editor to complain.

On another occasion, when Brunswick teachers went on strike, the school superintendent lunged at me, swinging a coffee mug and threatening sexual mutilation. "I'm going to cut off your ying-yang!" he screamed. Aides had to restrain him. I didn't do well with school boards.

There were the old-timers like Jo, and those of us in our twenties. The primary duty of us young staffers was covering high school sports, which was the sole reason most readers plunked down fifteen cents for the paper. Donald Swihart was a typical subscriber—crazy about high school sports. I hate sports. A motivating factor for me to cover them: the twenty dollars of extra-duty pay.

When Steve, the sports editor, assigned me to a football game the first time I worked a Friday night, I confessed knowing nothing about football. I typed out the story on a Royal manual typewriter, using paper cut from the castoff end rolls of newsprint from the printing press that shook the building. After reading my effort, Steve announced: "You're right. You don't know anything about football." After that I became a photographer.

The only good thing about those Friday nights was learning how to shoot and develop Kodak Tri-X black-and-white 400 ASA film. We also drank a lot of twelve-year-old Chivas Regal. As one reporter said about being in that newsroom: "If you were there, you were on your way up or on your way down the ladder of journalistic success."

I covered everything: chamber of commerce events, ribbon cuttings, and "check passes" by donors giving money to an official at a school or an organization. These headlines ran over my stories: "Brunswick boy is budding thespian," "Hinckley girl finalist in pageant," "Pumpkin patrol rides in Brunswick again," "Service unit lends a hand," "Her yarns knit a tale," "Highland sex education book gets parents buzzing at Board session." And I wrote a lot about crime: "Investigation into McNeil stabbing death continues," "Youth okay after accidental shooting," "Ammunition taken from county home," "Shotguns stolen from Brunswick home," "Bad checks spree ends in Brunswick," "Christmas thieves are stirring locally," "Brunswick youths arrested for burglary," "Brunswick pizzeria robbed Thursday."

But the fiction embraced by many residents was that nothing bad ever happened in Brunswick—even after Michael Swihart. One suspects the citizens who were paying fifteen cents for the *Gazette* to see pictures of their sons throwing and catching balls didn't read these kinds of stories, or that if they did, there was a subconscious disconnect. They chose to see only the budding thespian, the girl in the pageant, the service unit, the grandmother spending thirty hours knitting afghans to supplement her Social Security income. Bad things weren't supposed to happen, and if you ignored them, maybe they didn't happen. Yet if everyone felt so secure, one wondered why so many homes had firearms.

If you dropped into this place, you were supposed to salute the flag and pledge allegiance to it. You were supposed to write flattering stories about school boards and ignore the fact that teachers were paid so poorly that some qualified for federal food stamps. Parents were supposed to go to high school games and scream with bloodlust at their sons and their opponents on the court or field. Your children weren't supposed to have sex, and they were not supposed to burglarize the neighbors. Your son was not supposed to come home from college and kill you.

One fogbound night in the winter of 1978, I was driving on River Styx Road south of the main office. I may have been leaving a party at Helen Fry's house. Her husband, "The Colonel," drank whiskey by the tumbler and expected visitors to do likewise. Or I may have been coming back from an assignment. All I recall for certain: visibility was near zero and I was depressed. I'd already outgrown the *Gazette* and was worried about how to next advance my career. The rusting Buick Skylark I drove when not on the motorcycle had a dented front fender that caused one light to skew toward the heavens. Blinding white mist caught in that headlamp came at the windshield that night.

The road led to a hamlet called River Styx, named by uncheerful pioneers in the 1820s because there was a nearby dismal swamp. I'd dropped out of college to work at the paper and didn't know much about Greek mythology. But I knew about the river in the ancient story: it flowed into a desolate marshland. The River Styx formed the border between the living and the dead. Charon, the ferryman, carried the newly deceased across its waters to the underworld.

I soon quit. I'd lasted about eight months. It would be the first of three newspaper jobs that I would quit in anger.

I'd wished that the *Gazette* would be my first and last newspaper gig. I wanted to be a writer, and a real writer wasn't a newspaperman. Now I realize that the newspaper years were the best training. Not to be a writer, but to know America. And knowing America means understanding violence, which means understanding high school sports, school boards, police, crime, war, empire, patriotism, money, and power. They're interconnected. Medina County was a good microcosm for beginning a pilgrimage into the 1980s and what Philip Roth called "the indigenous American berserk."

I write of a time that seems idyllic in comparison to the present day—a time when it was easier to obtain certain books than guns in some states, a time when abortion was legal everywhere in the United States, a time when the word "homeless" infrequently appeared in print. I write of the 1980s, a pivotal decade that was the start of a "doom loop," which is a cycle of negative events that feed off each other, making things progressively worse. Examples: gun sales soar after mass shootings on the belief that access to firearms will be restricted, thus putting even more weapons in circulation. The antiabortion movement has been active for years, with some extremists bombing clinics. Even the overturning of *Roe v. Wade* wasn't enough. States like Texas moved further away from rationality by immediately proposing legislation to limit access to contraception.

The doom loop is especially seen with homelessness. I began covering the unhoused in 1981, before the crisis had a name; the vast majority of the relatively small number of people living on the street were pejoratively deemed "winos." I witnessed the emergence of the "new" homeless that began with the severe recession of 1982. I became immersed in their lives and in places like the necropolis of Youngstown and its shuttered steel mills. One man's story illustrates my point: up to the 1970s, he had driven a truck for the mills. He lost his job in early middle age. He ended up in Houston and, after a series of menial jobs that didn't pay enough to cover his rent, began living in the woods. He was sane then. By 1995, he'd become a man who babbled. Over the past four decades of documenting the homeless, I can attest to one certainty: that after one lives on the street for a year, or two or three years, there is a strong probability that one will become mentally ill. And many by this point will start drinking or using drugs to self-medicate.

Fast-forward to 2023 in doom loop America: conservatives have increased calls to kill the decades-old federal Housing First approach to fighting homelessness. The program is limited in how much it can accomplish, but as its name implies, housing is what those without homes need—it does good work.

Republicans, backed by conservative think tanks, got behind a bill introduced in the US House of Representatives in early 2023 that would mandate treatment for mental illness and drug use before anyone could receive help through the program. This is far from being a humane policy; proponents want to further demonize the homeless by denying them services via onerous hurdles to surmount. A podcast by the right-wing Cicero Institute suggests that instead of calling people "homeless," words like "vagrants," "bums," and "tramps" should be used. This justifies ignoring them.

This vilification is proved wrong by the fact that Mississippi, the second-most poverty stricken state in the union, has relatively few homeless people. Los Angeles County has six times the number of the unhoused per capita compared with the metropolitan area of Jackson, Mississippi. The reason? An average apartment in Jackson rents for around $800, compared with $2,200 in Los Angeles.

In 2023, a study came out from the Benioff Homelessness and Housing Initiative at the University of California, San Francisco, billed as the most comprehensive in decades. It involved surveying hundreds of the unhoused, and found that seventy 70 percent said a monthly rental subsidy of $300 to $500 would have kept a roof over their heads; 90 percent believed that landing a Housing First voucher would have saved them from the street.

Cheaper housing, not subsidies, is the real answer. Mississippi makes it easy to build. California does not. So-called liberal communities in the Democratic stronghold of the Golden State have for decades made it very difficult to construct affordable housing—the inhumane result condemns many of the poor and working class to live in tents and under bridges.

The problem of homelessness could have been addressed early on, with better wages for low-income workers and the construction of affordable housing. Instead it gets more difficult to solve with each passing year.

The most succinct way to sum up the definition of a doom loop: the worse it gets, the worse it gets.

One can trace much of the contemporary crazy to the 1980s. We were a country shimmying out onto the dead branch. Things both noticed and unnoticed began occurring. Ronald Reagan, who started his political career in Sacramento as governor of California, was elected president, with the message that government was the problem. Perhaps not coincidentally, on October 14, 1984, Rush Limbaugh launched a show on KFBK in Sacramento. Simultaneously, a cell of angry right-wing White men began meeting in Sacramento; there were cells like this emerging around the West.

I had a front-row seat for the 1980s, documenting it as a newspaperman, writing about cops, homicides, serial killers, white nationalists, war and its aftermath. I was embedded with that Sacramento group of angry White men. I was immersed in seemingly disparate but connected worlds of worsening violence. When in 1989 Patrick Purdy opened fire at an elementary school in Stockton, California, killing five kids and wounding thirty others, I covered the story. A school shooting was rare then, so rare that it actually prompted Congress to do something. The Stockton shooting led to the Federal Assault Weapons Ban of 1994, which outlawed "semiautomatic assault weapons" and "large-capacity ammunition-feeding devices."

Congress allowed that law to expire in 2004.

What followed is a classic doom loop: in 2000, there were three "active shooter" incidents in the United States, the FBI reports. In 2006, twelve; 2010, twenty-seven; 2020, forty. As I write this, the average is now one every six days in public settings. The FBI does not define "mass shooting." But by the measure of the Gun Violence Archive, a mass shooting is one with four or more victims, not counting the shooter. By its calculation, there were 383 in 2016, 417 in 2019, and 647 in 2022—over one dozen per week in that latter year.

Many mass shootings involve "large-capacity ammunition-feeding devices." These devices, with up to one-hundred-round drum magazines, are legal. Yet it's now a felony punishable by up to five years in prison for teachers to have some books deemed "woke" in Florida classrooms. Amid this, Florida and other states are making it easier to purchase and carry the firearms used in school shootings. And because of "stand your ground" gun laws—which have fueled an attitude of "shoot first and ask questions later"—innocent people are getting shot for simply knocking on the wrong door or pulling a car into the wrong driveway.

Now it's a time of the psycho du jour, with mass shootings so common that many no longer make national news. Ninety-eight percent of the time, it's a dude with a gun. Details conflate. AR-15. Young, alienated male. Loner. Thirty-shot clip. One-hundred-shot drum. Bump stock. The parents knew something was wrong. Screams of children. He was suicidal, hated women, hated Jews, hated gays and trans people, did reconnaissance. Attack was livestreamed. Motive was unclear. The sites of shootings—schools, malls, grocery stores, nightclubs, synagogues, cities—also conflate. Columbine. Virginia Tech. Sandy Hook. Uvalde. Parkland. Highland Park. Greenwood Park. Monterey Park. Pulse Nightclub. Aurora. El Paso. Fort Hood. Las Vegas. Tree of Life. San Ysidro. Nashville. The shock is no longer from the events themselves but from the indifference, which is more horrifying. We've allowed these massacres to become part of the ordinary background noise of American life.

When I walk to my dentist's office in Manhattan, several synagogues are along the route. Each has a police officer or two standing in front, on protective duty.

I take the war correspondent's seat in restaurants: back to the wall, eye on the door. Maybe it's because I have PTSD. Or I simply expect bad shit to happen. It's America, after all.

I've been an unwilling student of violence. I grew up in a house of rage. My father had a traumatic brain injury from a blast concussion during the Battle of Okinawa in World War II. His temper was explosive. It wasn't the "good war" for my father.

One wonders if rampant gun violence is connected to the fact that we as a nation love war. Since 1776, we've been at constant war, save for just fifteen to seventeen years, depending on who does the calculating.

The US defense budget was $266 billion in 1996; in 2024, $836 billion. Simply by paying taxes, even a pacifist supports the American war machine.

One thing this book is not: a definitive academic study. It's about what I've witnessed. I've been the Forrest Gump of journalism, stumbling into the wrong places at the right time. Yet much of what I've documented was planned. If you worked the street in the 1980s, you could see a lot of what was coming. You didn't have to be all that smart to notice.

By default, this volume is also about newspapering. The erosion of the media is part of the story of America's descent. In 1980, there were just three major television networks; cable news was in its infancy. Along with strong regional and national papers, and network radio, these allowed most Americans to be exposed to the same fact-based reality. Today, citizens spend time in thousands of fragmented silos of information. At best, this reinforces what people already believe; at worst, it nurtures conspiracy theories from disinformation spewed on X, formerly Twitter, and other social media.

Those days of print hegemony were a unique time to be a newspaperman. Some legacy journalists are nostalgic about the final days of the "golden era" of daily print, when Sunday editions rolled off the presses so fat with advertisements that they weighed as much as newborns. I'm gravely concerned about the loss of local reporting and its impact on our democracy, but I won't glorify those years. In numerous ways, they weren't so golden. This book isn't a hagiography, yet news then was crafted in an entirely different journalistic ecosystem. There was no posting on social media. Reporters would sometimes spend weeks or months immersed in a project. My last newsroom in Sacramento had over two hundred editorial employees—over one hundred of us were writers and photographers. The editors didn't want something from us every day—it wouldn't fit into the product, the newspaper, that was thrown upon 243,000 driveways and front stoops in the early weekday morning hours.

Newspapers were a curious shorthand. I never felt satisfied when writing for them. In the 1980s, my shop was one of the twenty largest

US metropolitan dailies in terms of Sunday circulation. It barely made that list with 297,000 subscribers, but it was big enough for editors to occasionally send you to wars and around the country. But those assignments were never freely dispensed—you had to fight for them. I fought. In the first eight years at this last newspaper job, I was out of the office for about four of them. That made it a good newspaper job.

# Copshop

When I worked at the *Gazette*, the head cop for the city of Brunswick was Chief Clayton M. Crook. I never brought up the incongruity of his last name, because I figured he'd been kidded about it his whole life. Anytime he smiled, which was rarely, it was when asked something he didn't want to answer. He was a cop's cop. Crook was suspicious of everyone—especially reporters. Especially a kid who was twenty years old and appeared to still be in high school. Crook always looked at me out of the corner of an eye. I dreaded each visit to the front counter at the police station to study the crime reports. He made it clear that this was a huge favor to the *Gazette*, even though what came across that counter was by law in the public record.

I didn't like cops, though this dislike wasn't based on any negative interaction with them growing up. I was a "good" kid. I spent a lot of time alone in the woods. I didn't sell weed, didn't drag race a 1967 Trans Am with a 350-cubic-inch V8 engine or a souped-up Mustang, like the greasers. But I was friends with some of those kids. One sergeant hounded them and made their lives miserable. Selling grass or racing a car at three in the morning on the empty Metroparks road flanked by woods didn't seem all that criminal to me.

I hated authority. It started with the nuns in first grade at St. Albert the Great. Maybe it was partly due to the influence of my father, who churned through the Pacific War as a grunt Marine, landing on the beaches of Guam and Okinawa; he distrusted all authority and political systems. With these ingredients, as I moved up in the grades, the threat of being drafted into the Vietnam War looming, my animosity toward power structures only grew more acute. The papers and television news were filled with images of cops beating protesting hippies. We were a two-newspaper household. The *Cleveland Plain Dealer* arrived in the morning, and the *Cleveland Press* in the afternoon. The *Press*'s Dick Feagler covered the Chicago Democratic Convention in 1968. He was among the few journalists who correctly called it a police riot. I believe he received more than a few billy club whacks from Mayor Richard Daley's cops. Then came Kent State. By the time I showed up at the counter of the Brunswick Police Department in 1977, I was primed to be wary of Chief Crook.

After leaving the *Gazette*, I learned that when a Black family finally moved to Brunswick, they woke up one morning to find their garage door covered with spray-painted hate graffiti: "KKK," the N-word, and a swastika. Crook told a reporter that the father's fear was "foolish…I really don't see it as that important."

I was happy to be done with cops. I turned to freelancing for the *Cleveland Plain Dealer*, writing for the paper's weekly Friday entertainment magazine as well as features for the *Sunday Magazine*. In my best year, 1979, I earned $8,000 plus cash from grinding industrial cutting tools in my father's business. I was now twenty-three and in need of a real income. I'd driven to California earlier that year, in part to land an interview with Governor Jerry Brown for a friend who edited a politics magazine aimed at college students. I didn't get Brown, but I liked Sacramento. The *Sacramento Bee* was doing some bold and creative journalism; there was a story by a reporter who took a Greyhound bus across the nation and reported along the way. It was exactly the kind of work that I wanted to do.

When it became clear I wasn't going be hired for a staff position at the *Cleveland Plain Dealer*, I began a job search with a focus on California, sending a cover letter, clips, and a résumé to some dozen newspapers that had advertised openings in the trade magazine *Editor & Publisher*. Those attempts were futile. No one was going to hire me from two thousand miles away. I hatched a plan to drive my Datsun pickup to California and live out of it while seeking a newspaper gig. How could editors not agree to meet if I was close at hand? I believed that with face time, it would be possible to talk my way into a job.

In August 1980, I loaded the covered bed of the Datsun with all of my belongings and drove west on Interstate 80. My first stop was the *Sacramento Bee*. I had a long meeting with city editor Robert Forsyth. He asked me to return the next day with a critique of that day's *Bee* compared with its rival, the *Sacramento Union*. I wrote my analysis, being unsparing of the *Bee*, on an Underwood manual typewriter that night while camped at Folsom Lake State Park. When I returned with the essay the next day, Bob pointed to a waist-tall stack of four hundred applications in a corner of his office. Out of all of them, he said, he wanted to hire me. But there were no openings. He told me to keep in touch. I used payphones. We talked every week, usually on Friday.

The Datsun was home. I slept in national forest campgrounds, state parks, and secret places used by the homeless with cars and vans. I wangled meetings with newspaper editors up and down the state. In late October, an editor for the *San Bernardino Sun* rejected me because I didn't have a college degree. A few days later he changed his mind. Maybe he was a swell guy, or maybe he couldn't get anyone to work in the Barstow bureau. Other prospective hires might have been repelled by its desolate location in the Mojave Desert, in an area where hit men for the Las Vegas mobsters dumped corpses. But it was a job with benefits, and I was prepared to take it—except that afternoon, the *Riverside Press-Enterprise* asked me to come in for a three-day tryout on the general-assignment night shift.

Riverside had several zoned editions covering the county, which stretched two hundred miles east to west. Forest fires were raging, and that first night a murdered girl's body was discovered in an orange grove. At one point, I had a telephone receiver balanced on each ear as I typed on a computer, updating each edition. It was like working for the wires. On the third night when I entered the newsroom, city editor Jim Bettinger walked up to me, smiling. In his hand was a message from Bob Forsyth. I'd told Bob in a phone call where I was.

Jim knew the deal. He pointed me to an empty office. I closed the door and phoned Bob, who said there might be an opening. He was engaged in some delicate negotiations, vaguely referring to someone he was trying to get moved to another position. "Some people don't like me here, and I'm trying to make a deal," he said. "You can't tell anyone or it might blow it." He brought up pay. I had four years of experience. He proclaimed that if things worked out, he would credit me with five. Because it was a Newspaper Guild shop, meaning its journalists belonged to the union, with a defined wage scale. I'd earn $469 per week. I almost fell over. That was more money than existed in the world. Bob told me to stall Riverside. "CYA," he said. I didn't know what this meant. ("Cover your ass.") If the gig he was trying to create didn't happen, Bob didn't want to see me jobless.

I hung up and went back to my tryout desk. Soon after, executive editor Norman Cherniss called me into his office. Norm was a balding, short man who appeared far older than his fifty-four years, and he had a face and lips that looked like he was always smoking a big fat cigar— but there was no cigar. He sat behind his desk, brow furrowed, and announced I'd "done okay" in the first two days of my tryout. I smelled negotiations mode. He held up my résumé and peered at it through reading glasses. He paused for a long, well-rehearsed moment. The offer: $220 per week. All the while I thought of Bob's offer: $469! But Norm pushed me to say yes, so I said yes. I'm a bad liar, and I wanted to simply get out of Norm's office.

Bob told me to call him for an answer the morning after Election Day 1980. I splurged for an expensive campsite at Doheny State Beach. I wrote letters to friends on the Underwood and took long walks along the surf line. On the appointed day, I phoned.

*Bob:* I've got good news and bad news.

*Me:* What's the bad news?

*Bob:* Reagan's president.

He told me I had the job. And I thought: "Please, please, please don't let it be the police beat."

*Bob:* You'll be covering police.

*Me:* Great!

*Bob:* You're going to replace a guy who's had the beat for decades.

He said my predecessor was an apologist for the cops. He never came into the newsroom, had his checks delivered by courier to the press office in the police station. The guy didn't have a press pass—he had some kind of police ID. My job description was "attack dog:" "I want you to go down there, kick ass, and go for the fucking throat," Bob instructed. He told me to come straight to Sacramento to get the paperwork underway.

Rather than phone Norm Cherniss, I felt the proper thing was to tell him in person. I went to Sacramento via Riverside and walked into the newsroom. Norm's jaw dropped when I told him I wasn't accepting the position. "You have to take the job!" he said. When I politely said I couldn't do that, he shouted, "You'll never work in this state again!" He vowed to undertake a campaign to blacklist me. He called me all kinds of bad names. I yelled back. I remember these words: "They're going to pay me more than twice as much!" Norm was now full-bore screaming. I was screaming. Our invectives blended: "Fuck you!" "Fuck you!" "Fuck you!"

In the next year and a half, I would experience a half-century's worth of life on the police beat. I also learned a lot concerning what would come into public awareness only decades later with the Black Lives Matter movement and police abuse of power. I met and got to know some really bad cops. I also met and got to know some pretty damn good ones. On the police beat, it became clear how difficult the job is, especially for the good cops. But I also learned that a police department represents what its community wants its officers to do. Police accountability is not really about the police. It's about us. Bob Forsyth understood all of this, and he had a great sense of societal justice. This passion had been the foundation of those words when he hired me to "go for the fucking throat." Bob, now long deceased, was ahead of his time.

Everything one needs to know about what I was walking into is contained in this paragraph of the obituary for the reporter I replaced:

In 1947, Warren was hired on by the McClatchy Company as a picture editor for the *Sacramento Bee*. After a short stint in the position he began his three-decade tenure as a crime reporter. Warren's desk was located at the old Sacramento Police Station at 6th and H streets, where he developed a long, trusting relationship with both the Sacramento Sheriff's Department and the Sacramento Police Department. Affectionately called "Scoop" by many officers, Warren was given an honorable Sheriff's Badge and numerous plaques of gratitude for his service upon his retirement in 1984.

## PART TWO

# "In Dreams Begin Responsibilities"

# Snapshots: 1980–1982

My start date at the *Sacramento Bee* was Monday, November 17, 1980. My predecessor took me around to all the detective divisions that first day on the job. Among those he introduced me to was Lieutenant Hal Taylor, head of the homicide unit for the Sacramento City Police. Taylor, balding, looked at me with the same sideways stare as had Chief Crook back in Brunswick. The second time we met was on the morning of December 9, 1980. Taylor was gleeful—John Lennon had been shot dead the previous evening in New York City. Taylor pointed to the headline of the newspaper on his desk and guffawed. I thought he might just be trying to rattle me. But he continued being jubilant, as if he'd just scratched a winning $1,000 lottery ticket.

By then I'd learned from one of the detectives that Taylor had once hung a poster of Adolph Hitler on the outside of his office door. After complaints from officers, a captain ordered him to take it down. Some detectives despised Taylor, and they talked freely to me on background, meaning I couldn't quote them by name. I learned from others that the unit was botching homicide investigations—and that Taylor was part of the problem. I began investigating.

~~~~~~

**Headline in the *Sacramento Bee* on Sunday,
December 21, 1980:
"The Agonizing Wait for a Deputy."**

I covered two major law enforcement agencies: the Sacramento City Police and the Sacramento County Sheriff's Department. The first worked inside the ninety-two square miles of the incorporated city limits. The second worked within the much larger unincorporated county, with 880 square miles. Each agency had the same number of officers, but the sheriff had to cover an area nine times as large, plus staff the jail, which meant fewer officers in patrol cars. I found my first big story in data about response time.

If someone was being beaten, robbed, or raped in a large swath of unincorporated eastern Sacramento County, with its 160,000 residents, the response time after someone called 911 averaged 16.7 minutes in 1980, up from 11.6 minutes five years earlier. In the city it was nine minutes. Some people in crisis waited two hours for a Sacramento County sheriff's deputy. As few as three deputies covered the whole area at night. Some nights, there were periods when no deputies were on duty. I used the sheriff department's own data to discover these facts, and I'd already developed some sources. Deputies were frustrated that they couldn't do their job, that they'd get a priority call about a domestic assault in progress and be a half-hour drive away from it.

When I called Sheriff Duane Lowe for comment, he said that if my two-part series ran, crooks would realize they could run amok. People with bad intentions already knew this, but the public didn't. Newspaper heiress Patty Hearst wrote in her book *Every Secret Thing* that when she and the Symbionese Liberation Army went to rob two banks in 1975, they chose them in the county outside of Sacramento's city limits, because they knew the sheriff's department was understaffed.

It wasn't the fault of the line officers. And only part of the blame rested on the shoulders of Sheriff Duane Lowe. It was a matter of allocation of resources. There wasn't funding to hire more deputies. Ultimately, the question was, how much in taxes did the suburbanites want to pay for better service? They could not make this decision unless they knew that if their spouse were to threaten to stab them to death, they would be a corpse long before a deputy showed up.

No matter. Lowe was pissed about the story. He said I was anti–law enforcement.

~~~~~

THAT FALL OF 1980, two first-year students, both eighteen, were involved in a blossoming romance at the University of California, Davis. Sabrina Gonsalves had moved to Davis that summer from Germany, where she had graduated from high school early that year. Her father, Army Lieutenant Colonel George C. Gonsalves, was stationed there. John Riggins had grown up in Davis—his father, Richard Riggins, was a UC professor. John had long blondish hair that fell straight; the cut resembled that of the then-popular musician John Denver. Sabrina had long dark hair and a wide smile. The two had met two summers earlier while working for the parks department in Davis, but they had become close only just before school started that September. John was Episcopalian, and Sabrina a devout Catholic. John adored his mother so much that he had personalized license plates for his van: "3S MUM," a reference to his mom having three children.

Sabrina and John were inseparable. On the Saturday night before Christmas, they volunteered at the Veterans Memorial Center in Davis, doing cleanup after a performance of *The Nutcracker*. They left hand in hand and got in the van to make two stops. One was Sabrina's apartment, to pick up some presents for her sister's surprise birthday party later that night. The other was a shopping center near the intersection of Covell Boulevard and Anderson Road, to purchase cider for the party. It's unclear which came first.

There was a thick tule fog—named by the Spanish colonists centuries earlier for the winter fogs that erupt from the Central Valley's wetlands; they set in for days on end. At 8:30 p.m., Sabrina and John went to the Chandelier Inn, a restaurant in the shopping center. They picked up a menu. "You should have seen them," chef Robert Mazza said. "They were giggling and laughing. I asked them what they were laughing about, and they said they were laughing because the menu was so big." The couple then left to go to a nearby Chinese restaurant to look at the menu there. Mazza went outside into the dense fog to do something, and he saw a man dressed in black, with a dark cap, hanging out near the couple's van. "When he saw me, he looked away, like he didn't want me to see him."

The couple never made it to the birthday party. They vanished. Family and friends spent all the next day, Sunday, scouring Davis trying to find them.

On Monday, the bled-out bodies of Sabrina and John were found some twenty-five miles to the east. They lay in a dry creek bed, amid a grove of oak trees shrouded in the fog, off Folsom Boulevard near the Aerojet company's vast land holdings. Their wrists were bound with gaffer's tape, and their throats had been slit.

～～～

THE NAKED BODY OF Leah Schendel, age seventy-eight, was discovered beneath a mattress in her apartment, in Sacramento's Meadowview neighborhood, during the third week of December that same year. The killing happened right after an attack on an eighty-eight-year-old man and a ninety-year-old woman. "I counted off forty-eight steps from where the couple was attacked to the front door of the woman who was murdered," Lieutenant Taylor said in our third and penultimate in-person meeting.

Next: David Weaver shot dead Mariano Nito Gray, whom Weaver discovered inside his house stealing a $100 tape deck on January 6, 1981. Weaver fired his .357 Magnum pistol when Gray lunged at him with a screwdriver, he said.

One day later: a White girl named Deborah Leeders, age eighteen and a high school senior, was shot dead in a hail of bullets when she came home at night from her job at Weinstock's department store. The girl lay dead in the driveway of her Elk Grove home. Her former boyfriend, Patrick Hill, age seventeen, was arrested after a forty-minute standoff with sheriff's deputies.

Just over one week later: the nude body of Mary London, a seventeen-year-old Black girl, was found in North Sacramento, stabbed to death. A few days earlier, six blocks from her home downtown, an unidentified undocumented Mexican man had been stabbed to death. I noted this in my story about Mary, because I remembered that victim. But the two killings were unrelated. The paper might have run a one-paragraph brief, but I don't recall our publishing anything about the murder of the immigrant until Mary London was knifed to death.

～～～～

I WAS IN THE NEWSROOM at 2 a.m. writing a Sunday "situationer" on the murdered Davis sweethearts. It was two days after Christmas in 1980. My day had started fifteen hours earlier at their memorial service. I was deep into immersing myself in the slayings, which had haunted my dreams in the few hours of sleep I'd had all week. I'd been out to the oak grove where the bodies were found, amid the continued thick and creepy tule fog; I talked with family members, friends, witnesses.

The last of the editors had cleared out, and the floor was empty. I'd been writing for two hours and had eighteen inches of text: the mainframe computer system packed into a big room down a hall measured the words in this manner. The system was fickle. Computers had been in use in most newsrooms for only a few years. I'd worried about this while in Cleveland—what if an editor who wanted to hire me asked if I could use a computer? Judith Haynes, my *Plain Dealer* editor, had let me practice on a computer in the *Sunday Magazine* office.

It wasn't that our system at the *Bee* was complex. It just didn't work well, always crashed. It was wise to hit the store command a lot while writing. On this night, I had not done this, because it would take three to six minutes or more to save, and during this time the page would be locked. Sometimes I'd hit print when the system was slow, but I hadn't done that either. I was exhausted and focused on putting words on the screen, which suddenly froze. Three mango-size domed warning lights of different colors that hung from the ceiling near the photo desk began flashing.

I turned around and stared at the lights blinking red, yellow, and blue. The computer screen went blank. Poof. Several hours of work gone. Tears streamed down my face. All the emotion poured out. I had been at the paper for five weeks, and most editors barely knew my work. I had to rock with this huge story. I had just turned twenty-four and was living in a new state where I didn't know anyone, and the only people I was dealing with were cops, crime victims or their kin, and people in the newsroom—the vast majority far older than I was and not friend material.

The newsroom had harsh fluorescent lighting as bright as a hospital's operating room. I went to a remote stairwell and curled up in a dark corner to nap for two hours. Upon awakening, I went to my desk. The domed lights had ceased blinking. I recrafted the story, working until well past dawn. I went home and slept a bit.

I returned hours later and continued reporting by phone. I remained in the newsroom until the Blue Star early edition, for circulation in far-flung counties, rolled off the presses sometime after eight that evening. We'd had a story every day in the paper since Tuesday. I was guaranteed page one and most of the back page. I went to the pressroom to get the still-hot copy when the papers came down a conveyor belt.

~~~~~

## Headline in the *Bee* on Sunday, January 11, 1981: "Law Officers Who Use Big Bad Bullets."

My first day on the job, I'd noticed something that appeared very odd: the officers had spare bullets held by loops on waist harnesses, and the tips of the bullets were visible—they were hollow-point—which had been banned in warfare by the 1899 Hague Declaration. They weren't used back East; I confirmed this by making phone calls to numerous big-city police departments. But they were the ammunition of choice by cops in California and other western cities.

"You've got a bunch of cowboys out there," Dennis Hill, a spokesman for the Baltimore Police Department, said. American Civil Liberties Union attorney Amitai Schwartz said of these bullets: "If the person lives, they're calculated to cause unnecessary maiming."

To illustrate this fact, I purchased both solid and hollow-point bullets and drove into the Sierra foothills with a .357 Magnum, and I shot bars of Ivory soap with both. Those soap bars were on the front page: the solid bullets made a tiny hole in the soap upon exiting; the hollow-point ones blew out the back side, nearly cutting the soap bar in two.

When I phoned Sacramento County sheriff's spokesman Bill Miller to ask for an interview with Sheriff Lowe, he told me: "You're not going to put the sheriff on the spot. He's not going to debate philosophical things."

I wasn't talking philosophy—I was focused on the fact that bullets banned in war were being fired on the streets of the county. Miller then announced that I would not be allowed to "play inspector general."

~~~~~

County of Sacramento
Inter-Department Correspondence

Date: March 5, 1981

To: All Division Commanders

From: William N. Miller

Subject: Bee Reporter Dale Maharidge

Please advise all personnel under your command that effective immediately, if they are contacted by Dale Maharidge, reporter for the Sacramento Bee newspaper, that under no circumstances are they to answer any questions from him or engage in any conversation with him.

All inquiries from this individual are to be referred to the undersigned.

William N. Miller
Assistant to the Sheriff

~~~

REPORTING ON THE CITY COPS' homicide unit became a backburner project. Word had long since gotten back to Lieutenant Taylor about it. I was frozen out. At the same time, my colleague Hilary Abramson was working on a story involving the Ku Klux Klan and the appearance of right-wing hate groups. I'd told her about the Hitler poster on Taylor's door.

Hilary clicked record on my tape recorder and phoned Taylor on April 8, 1981.

"I'm from the *Sacramento Bee*. This may sound off the wall...I'm doing an article involving Hitler, and I heard you had a poster of him on your door. Is that accurate?"

"Who said that?"

"You hear these things. I heard it's no longer there. And I said this may sound weird, but I said I'm going to call and ask him."

"Who told you that? Maharidge told you that."

"Who?"

"Maharidge."

"You mean the guy who works here?"

"Yeah, yeah. It had to be him.... There was a joke one time—this is way back, six years ago. And somebody said, 'That's what we need here, a good fascist Hitler to run this police department.'"

"I had to ask you."

"You're doing a story on Hitler?"

"I'm doing a thing on ultra groups and followers in Sacramento…"

"I can't say I was a Hitler fan. You ought to do [a story] on Maharidge. That, that thing there is weird, I'll tell you. That little…! I'll tell you where he'd fit right in. Do you remember Hitler's Fifth Column? Overthrew Norway and Austria? Maharidge would have been an ace on his staff. That's all I can say. There's more similarity between Maharidge and Hitler than there is between Taylor and Hitler."

"Not that I was accusing you in any way. I just heard you had a picture on your door one time and wondered if you did. Thought I'd ask. And if you did, you were the one to ask."

"It was fun. Everybody was laughing. It was a joke."

"Well, part of my business is asking questions."

"I can understand. Mine is too. Most of my business is investigating. And old Maharidge is going to get investigated."

"What does that mean?"

"That's all I got to say."

"I really don't what you're talking about."

"Well, Maharidge is stirring a lot of crap up around here. In all the departments. Sheriff's office, the police department. When you throw a lot of crap, you're bound to get some on you."

~~~~~

AT THAT POINT, you couldn't be a reporter in California and avoid stories about the fallout of the war in Indochina. Of the estimated five hundred thousand Vietnamese who fled to America, two hundred thousand were in the state. Sacramento had a large concentration. The refugees came in waves: first the elite, then the Vietnamese soldiers, then the Laotians, who initially were held in overseas camps and began arriving in 1981.

Many Indochinese settled in South Sacramento and Rancho Cordova. On the second weekend in May 1981, several people went to these areas and plastered professionally made license-plate-size stickers on the doors and windows of businesses and apartment buildings:

Vietnamese,

You must get out of
California state capital...

KKK

"I came in Sunday morning and saw the sticker pasted to the window," I. T. Hatton, owner of the Tha Huong Market in Rancho Cordova, said. "It was spattered with red paint to make it look like blood." Hatton said he knew six families that fled to the Bay Area in the following days. School staffers said that many parents kept their children out of class that week. I phoned Harvey Hopkins, the local grand wizard of the Ku Klux Klan. He denied that his group had posted the stickers but said, "We don't believe they should be coming here and taking White men's jobs."

〜〜〜

POLICE CRIME INCIDENT REPORTS were called the "yellows," even though they hadn't been that color for years. What was made available was a photocopy—on white paper.

On June 3, 1981, I was leafing through these documents at a police department counter and came to a 261, the California Penal Code for rape. The report noted that the incident appeared to be part of a pattern in Midtown Sacramento. It was the third one in which the same perpetrator was suspected. The victim, a twenty-one-year-old woman, had been asleep. She awoke sometime after 3 a.m. to a man with a gun standing next to the bed. He had on a ball cap; his boxer shorts were tucked under the hat and covered his face. The man tied up the woman and raped her.

A two-inch brief ran on page B-2 of the *Bee*. The newspaper's policy was not to write about rapes except in the case of serial rapists, such as this one, as a warning to readers, excluding details that would identify the victims.

Three days later, on Friday, the phone at my desk rang.

"This is Gina." The voice was hesitant. She gave her last name. I recognized it from the 261. She asked to speak to the reporter who had written the story—the desk must have forwarded the call. I'd never before talked with someone who'd just been raped. I had a flash of worry that she was angry. She asked that I do a bigger story. I stammered, never expecting a call like this. I wasn't sure I wanted to do a bigger story. Gina insisted. She said she wanted "to help other victims. It's important." She pushed to meet. I agreed. We set a time for the following Thursday.

I had nearly a week to think about the meeting. I'd been writing about women dead from violent encounters with men, foremost among them Sabrina Gonsalves. She was in my nightmares. I couldn't talk with Sabrina. But I could have a conversation with Gina.

I was nervous on Thursday afternoon when I went to the escalator outside the newsroom and descended to the lobby. Gina had long dark hair and a wide smile. She brought a friend for moral support. We went to the employee cafeteria on the third floor, and she got an iced tea. We picked a table outside, overlooking Twenty-First Street and the crowns of carob trees. Gina was down for me taping the conversation, and I set the microcassette recorder between us. Twisting a napkin between her fingers ("Best for me to have something to do with my hands while we're talking," she said), Gina asked me a lot of questions over the course of the next hour—more questions than I asked her.

I was twenty-four, and Gina twenty-one. Just kids, really. I would spend the next two months meeting with Gina to understand the violence that she had experienced.

~~~~

By LIVING AT HOME with my parents while freelancing in Cleveland, I saved enough money for a down payment to purchase a home in California. The house, eleven miles from the office, was a ten-minute walk from the American River. I went to the river many evenings that summer to sit on the bank and think. Sometimes I'd pull off my shoes, roll up my pants, and place my feet and ankles in the cold water. This was not the lower American, where the body of a girl named Crystal would be found in just a few weeks. Downriver, as it nears the confluence with the Sacramento River, the American runs slow, deep, more like a waterway in Alabama or Mississippi.

The lower American is flanked by North Sacramento's poverty; to the south was the city's garbage dump. The American where I sat those evenings ran clear through a channel lined with cobblestones—mountain water fresh from the penstocks of Folsom and Nimbus dams. The river was flanked by parklands, and there was an illusion of wildness; one could imagine what it looked like in the time of Sutter. And one could do this safely on its bank as the sun vanished over the Mayacamas, because behind me were the suburban homes of the solid middle and upper-middle class, the secure world that I had moved into.

The immediate happiness that I'd imagined that refuge would bring was not happening, however. I was depressed from the unrelenting immersion in covering violence, cops investigating me, the newness of California, the feeling of being far from Ohio and everything I knew. I did not possess the level of maturity one would expect of someone with the title of "police reporter" at a major metropolitan newspaper, or with the word "homeowner" affixed to his name. I was in numerous ways a very young twenty-four. I had no sexual experience; I could be mistaken for a high school student; my entire adult life thus far had been focused on "making it" as a journalist.

Four years earlier, I had been riding the Yamaha to meetings all around Cleveland, dreaming of being able to understand the human condition, and write about it. And now with Gina I was presented with a story in this realm. Delmore Schwartz, a poet who was friends with the writer James Agee, titled one of his collections *In Dreams Begin Responsibilities*. I could write about the dead; that was comparatively easy. But to write about the pain of those surviving violence? Was I ready for this responsibility?

〜〜〜

Harvey William Hopkins Jr., the grand wizard of the Invisible Empire, Knights of the Ku Klux Klan, Order of the White Rose, was back in the news months after the anti-Asian stickers were plastered all around South Sacramento. At one in the morning on October 28, 1981, during a KKK party, Hopkins pointed a twelve-gauge shotgun at the chest of his wife, Pamela Hopkins, age twenty-seven, and pulled the trigger. Her corpse was found in the couple's bedroom in North Highlands after one in the morning; they had just moved there from Rio Linda. Pamela was pregnant.

On the booking sheet I saw later that day, Hopkins, age thirty-four, listed his occupation as "disabled—explosive personality." The couple had four children, all under age ten. They were raising the kids to be racist. Pamela had told Hilary Abramson, my colleague at the newspaper, for a story Hilary had published in June: "You should see them at cross-burning rallies. They leap in the air like there was a touchdown." Hilary had been leaving messages for Harvey, and she recalls that the first time he picked up the phone, he said, "Are you the Jew bitch who keeps calling me?" He told Hilary he'd kill one of his daughters if she were to marry a Black man. But he did not say "Black man." Hopkins denounced Black people living on welfare, yet for the previous four years he had survived on federal disability funds.

〜〜〜

The machines of war were located on the south side of the American River, not far from my suburban home.

The first one: Aerojet, a corporation that specialized in solid-fuel rocket engines, making them for the nuclear-tipped Minuteman ICBM missiles that were ready to be launched at the Soviet Union. When working in the backyard garden, I occasionally heard a sound that was startling, for it was unpredictable. The engineers would ignite one of their creations for a "static firing"—the rocket engine held in place for testing. The sudden roar even several miles away would cause one to freeze in fear for a moment; then the realization that this would be the *Dr. Strangelove* soundtrack for the day when scores of ICBMs burn into the heavens, with the equivalent "throw weight" from Russia soaring back at us through the atmosphere, and the ensuing mushroom clouds. Sometimes these test engines exploded, which is why the facility had been located on the wasteland of hundreds of acres of rocky tailings from the Gold Rush era.

The second: Mather Air Force Base, near Aerojet. Home to the Strategic Air Command's 4134th wing and its fleet of B-52 Stratofortresses carrying nuclear bombs, though the military would never confirm or deny this fact. Half of the planes maintained a constant state of readiness on fifteen-minute alert; B-52s were perpetually taking off and landing in what are called "touch and goes," the eight Pratt & Whitney turbofan engines on each aircraft spewing black smoke on ascent. This thunder was simply part of life in Sacramento, and it got so that one nearly no longer heard it, forgot its existence.

<center>~~~~~</center>

**Headline in the *Bee* on Sunday, August 8, 1982:
"First She Was Raped, Then Lost in a Shuffle."**

This story, by Hilary Abramson, ran at the top of the front page. It chronicled the rape of a woman who was kidnapped by three men in Yolo County and then driven across the Sacramento River and raped in Sacramento County. After she escaped, she found a Sacramento County sheriff's officer. In the next two and a half hours, there was confusion about which agency should handle the case—precious time that could have been used to search for the suspects was lost.

As Hilary later said to me, all rapes are brutal, "but some are more brutal than others." The story included details of the woman being pistol-whipped. There were bloody penises. The harrowing and horrible nature of the crime was vividly told. Readers "needed to understand every detail of what they did to her so that the reader could understand how brutal it was. Feeling what a victim feels and understanding how law enforcement supported by our tax dollars let the whole community down. I mean, not only didn't they catch them, but they let the whole community down by making light of it."

Editors, men, pushed Hilary to cut these details. Just say the woman was raped. Sanitize it. Hilary fought back. She described it as a battle. The editors said they'd excise the words. Hilary invoked a clause in our union contract: she'd take her byline off the story. The editors didn't want that—it would look bad for the paper to run such an explosive piece without the author's name. After much arguing, Hilary prevailed, because the story involved misfeasance by two law enforcement agencies.

Change would finally begin to happen in 1989. That year, Geneva Overholser, the top editor at the *Des Moines Register*, picked up the phone when a woman called, asking that the paper do a story on her rape. Reporter Jane Schorer Meisner was put on the story, which became a five-part series, and with the woman's consent, her name was published. When the project won a Pulitzer Prize, the judges wrote that it caused "widespread reconsideration of the traditional media practice of concealing the identity of rape victims." This is one way things are better than in the 1980s—though still difficult, a woman can tell her story of rape and sometimes bring her abuser to justice.

~~~~~~

EARLY IN 1982, Bob Forsyth had moved on to a different job. The city editor who replaced him was in charge when Hilary's rape story ran. A shitstorm came down from the publisher and others in lofty positions.

They were not ahead of their time. The new editor was made the fall guy and was booted down the hall.

That meant I had a third city editor since starting at the paper. This latest one eyed me in the same suspicious manner as Chief Clayton Crook and Lieutenant Hal Taylor had. He was old school, didn't like anyone who produced journalism beyond the "who, what, where, when, why." One day in the first week of his tenure, as I walked into the newsroom, this editor stopped me and asked, "Dale, do you consider yourself to be a writer? Or a reporter?"

"Both," I answered. "You can't be a great writer without great reporting."

This was his "gotcha" question. I was supposed to say "writer" to confirm that I was an inferior reporter. My answer flummoxed him. He said nothing but looked quite displeased.

The next day I was put on night cops for six months. Just a few months earlier, I'd finally gotten off the police beat to become general assignment, which meant covering a wide range of stories. Night cops was punishment—the hours were bad, and it entailed chasing things that came over the police scanner blaring in the newsroom. It was the shift given to beginners. Weeks later, I got my job performance review from this editor:

Inter-Office Correspondence
Subject: job performance review

Dale's strengths in reporting are initiative and creativity. Examples are his bum stories and hobo series…. His interests, however, appear to be too shallow. He should be gaining experience in other subject areas to round and to sharpen his newsgathering skills. He needs exposure to certain beats, such as court, urban, schools, etc., something with more structure than he now works with.

# Good Cop/Bad Cop

Sometime in the mid-1970s during my checkered days in college, when I started riding the Yamaha motorcycle to string for Sarah and Stephanie at the *Cleveland Press*, I came across a remaindered copy of the book *Stop the Presses, I Want to Get Off! Inside Stories of the News Business from the Pages of [MORE]*, edited by Richard Pollak. It was part of my self-education as a journalist. *[MORE]* magazine was launched in 1971 and had an eight-year run. It was decades ahead of the curve in press criticism. Its credo was that "objectivity" made it impossible to reveal truth. The book is a collection of stories from the magazine, by eighteen writers.

*Stop the Presses* came with me to California. It was stored with other important books in a half dozen boxes under a tarp in the Datsun's bed those three months I lived out of the pickup. I read it again during those early months on the police beat. I needed to reimmerse myself in the book, because I was questioning what I was doing and how I was doing it.

The opening chapter is a December 1973 article by Alexander Cockburn titled "Death Rampant! Readers Rejoice," a riff on disaster coverage by US newspapers, in the dark, satirical spirit of Ambrose Bierce's *The Devil's Dictionary*. In it, Cockburn addressed the relative news value of death. He noted that it would take three regular citizens dying for every famous person to merit a story. He also tallied the proportional quantities of deaths needed for an international story to make it into an American newspaper—if the disaster happened in Europe, it would take ten Europeans; if in Africa or China, there would need to be fifty to a hundred thousand dead.

I focused on a much smaller scale of death. From the time I started at the *Sacramento Bee* that November in 1980, through the last day of the year, there were nearly a dozen homicides in the city and county of Sacramento. Between New Year's Day and the end of 1981, there were eighty-eight. The most common method was by firearm—about half the cases. The next most preferred weapon: knives, used in a quarter of slayings. The rest were divided between beating and strangulation. In the unincorporated area of the county, under the sheriff's jurisdiction of Lieutenant Ray Biondi's unit, half the victims did not know their killers. This made sense, because that region had most of the serial killers, who for some reason preferred to operate in the suburbs. In Hal Taylor's bailiwick of the city cops, just one-third of the victims were strangers to their killers. Domestic fights were the cause of 20 percent of deaths in the city, 10 percent in the county. There were myriad other statistics. But there were no statistics for how we treated these deaths in the newspaper, or how seriously all of the murders were investigated by the two homicide units.

I quickly had a sense about the value of most human life in my world of the newsroom: zilch. I usually reported to one ACE—assistant city editor—each morning when returning from the two cop shops. This ACE loved the weird, the morbidly humorous. One morning, there was a report about a man who had body lice. It stated that he'd heard one could get rid of them by soaking the affected area in kerosene. The man lacked kerosene, but he had gasoline. He filled the bathtub with it and was about to jump in when fumes reached the pilot light of the water heater. The house exploded in flames, and neighbors reported that they saw the man running naked and screaming out the front door.

If there was a homicide, however, I'd give him details and he'd make a snap decision. Often before I finished, the ACE would decree: "Cheap." This meant for me to stop talking, that he wouldn't budget much, if any, space for a story. We had limited newsprint real estate amid the voluminous display ads for Weinstock's department store, one of our largest advertisers. The paper was packed with ads, with a relatively small news hole.

"Cheap." I had a lot of time in the first months of 1981 to digest the definition of this word as seen by the ACE. Poverty was the major metric, and one might think this would apply mostly to persons of color. Often it did. But Sacramento had a substantial population of low-income Whites, descendants of the 1930s Dust Bowl migrants who had not achieved a higher socioeconomic status. Many lived in Rio Linda, a census-designated place that Rush Limbaugh made fun of when his show debuted on KFBK a few years later, even though its residents were his most ardent listeners. He talked about it as a place with "cars jacked up on concrete blocks in the front yard" and dead refrigerators on porches.

One of Limbaugh's constant refrains when he was trying to make a point stupid-simple was, "For those of you in Rio Linda…" Many of the grandchildren of Tom Joad were cooking meth or selling it, or they were in biker gangs, and there was a lot of violence in these realms. Yet the vast majority of these descendants were living honest lives—driving trucks, working at the Campbell's Soup factory or at Aerojet or Mather Air Force Base; they were hardworking people enduring hardscrabble existences. No matter. If a killing happened in certain neighborhoods, the ACE often automatically proclaimed it "cheap." For Whites, this meant North Sacramento, West Sacramento, and Rio Linda; Blacks, Oak Park or Meadowview; Indochinese immigrants, Lemon Hill and Rancho Cordova; Latinos, most of South Sacramento. The area that most interested the ACE was east of downtown and north of the American River, stretching to the city of Folsom—an area dominated by the solid middle and upper class.

The ACE wasn't racist, but he was definitely classist—he judged by economic status. To get stories about the poor neighborhoods into the paper, there had to be something grabbing about the homicide—the victims very young or very old, a raging gun battle with police, or a suspect at large. Most of the forty-one murders in the city and county in the first half of 1981 received a two- or three-paragraph brief, or we simply did not write about them at all.

The city of Davis isn't cheap. Davis is eleven miles west of Sacramento via Interstate 80, and is surrounded by farm fields. It's home to a University of California campus that covers four thousand acres. In 1980, there were eighteen thousand students and ten thousand employees, over a thousand of them professors; the city had thirty miles of bike paths, and thirty thousand bicycles among the twenty-four thousand permanent residents and students. Davis was pro–passive solar energy, pro-bike, and anticar long before such eco-friendliness was popular. By one estimate, a quarter of all trips taken by citizens were made by bike—unheard of anywhere else in California. The city council mandated that homes be situated to take advantage of the low winter sun to cut down on heating energy use, with precisely designed overhangs to repel the summer sun, in developments such as the Village Homes, with streets named after locations in J. R. R. Tolkien's *Lord of the Rings*: Rivendell, Bree, Shire.

It was not a place where I expected to show up with a notebook in hand to cover crime. Many inhabitants were New Age, into things such as Reiki healing and crystals. The word "precious" defined much of the populace at the time; years later, they would be deemed "snowflakes."

I once dated a woman who lived in a tiny bungalow on one of the town's many quiet, shaded streets. On a hot summer day, she had parked her car at the curb in front of her house. A short time later, she was astonished when two fire trucks roared up, sirens blaring, along with a police cruiser. Authorities were focused on her car, and they surrounded it. A neighbor had noticed a puddle beneath the vehicle and assumed it was gasoline. Without checking, the woman had run inside her house and frantically punched in 9-1-1. It was not gasoline. The lawn sprinklers were on, and water had accumulated beneath the vehicle.

Following the murders of Sabrina Gonsalves and John Riggins in the fall of 1980, I reported hard starting Monday, the day the bodies were found, and in the ensuing days. The memorial service for the young couple was held the day after Christmas; it drew eight hundred people. I interviewed Sabrina's father by phone. He was in Hawaii, where the family had gone to bury their daughter. I interviewed the sister, friends, and many people in Davis. Ray Biondi and his detectives were stymied. It wasn't a robbery. They couldn't find evidence of sexual assault. Drugs weren't involved. Friends said the couple never drank alcohol.

Detectives believed the killer (or killers) was familiar with the area near Lake Natoma, about fifteen miles east of downtown Sacramento. As if the thick fog weren't enough, the dirt road leading into the grove of oaks was difficult to find even in daylight. I went to a nearby Rancho Cordova Fire District Station. Bill Wheat, a fireman, had been on duty that Saturday night of the killings, just one thousand feet from where the van was discovered, near a bar called Rudy's Hideaway.

"I feel there's a ninety-nine percent chance the killer knew the area," Wheat said. "I've fought fires back in that field, and I have trouble getting in there. If the killer had parked the van and walked back to the bar, no one would have noticed. You always see people walking up and down the road out there. And it was foggy. If I were going to murder someone, I would say this is an ideal place to get rid of the bodies and not be noticed."

Tips poured into the newsroom. Some said the murderers were followers of the Druids, pointing to ritual. The homicides happened on the night of the winter solstice, of significance to Druids, in an oak grove.

I didn't think of Alexander Cockburn's [MORE] article at all that week the Davis couple was slain, but I would very much do so in the coming months. Cockburn doesn't deal with American killers in his article. But as time went on, I thought a lot about the amount of coverage in the *Bee's* news hole based on where one resided. Cheap versus expensive. The Davis couple was at the pinnacle of expensive. It was the hottest murder story of the entire ensuing year. They were utterly innocent—pious churchgoers and polite. They were upper class and students at a highly ranked university. They were White. Beautiful. They had lived in Davis. Their value on a Cockburn-level scale was priceless. Their "worth" compared to that of other murder victims in the eyes of my assistant city editor? It would take about forty or fifty people like Mary London, that seventeen-year-old Black girl found stabbed to death in North Sacramento, or Deborah Leeders, the eighteen-year-old White girl shot dead in the driveway of her Elk Grove home by the jilted boyfriend, to equal one Sabrina Gonsalves or John Riggins.

As the months wore on, the murders of John and Sabrina remained unsolved.

Lieutenants Ray Biondi and Hal Taylor represented the extremes in my dealings with cops—the very best and very worst.

Biondi and I always got along. When Bill Miller—the sheriff's "flak," or public relations person—issued the directive forbidding anyone to talk with me, some captains and lieutenants froze me out. The first time I saw Biondi after that memo, he quipped, "Aren't I not supposed to be talking to you?" Then he laughed and gave me information. He always answered the phone or had me into his office to provide facts on any case.

Biondi never seemed like a cop. He was laid-back, with slicked jet-black hair and a dark mustache thick as the Bermuda grass that infests Sacramento County's suburban lawns. He had a sense of humor and the disarming manner of the character played by Peter Falk in *Columbo*, the television detective show that aired in the early 1970s. But Ray wasn't bumbling.

Being that this was California, there were a lot of mass murders, and after he joined the homicide unit in 1976, Biondi was soon immersed in some of those biggest cases. The "Sweethearts Killer," as the murderer of the Davis couple became known, was just the latest in a series. Before I showed up, there was the "Vampire Killer," the "Thrill Killer," the "Sex Slave" murders, the "Unabomber," and the "East Area Rapist," who'd killed two people. That one became very personal—a woman I was involved with a few years after I arrived in Sacramento believed she'd been raped by him. It would later be discovered that the EAR was the same man who became known as the "Golden State Killer."

46

Laid-back as he was, Biondi ran a tight ship. His detectives liked him, and he appeared by all measures to be dedicated to and quite adept at his job.

There was a critical difference between the two homicide departments, summed up in the final three paragraphs of a story I later published about the 1981 homicide statistics and clearance rates, which mean the murder was solved.

> Sheriff's detectives solved 78 percent of the homicides. City police solved 81 percent of their cases.
>
> Biondi said sheriff's detectives consider a case solved only when the district attorney's office decides to prosecute a suspect.
>
> City police consider a homicide solved when an arrest is made, and do not take into consideration whether the district attorney decides to prosecute, said police Sgt. Mike Roy.

Clearance rates mean everything to some cops. "Solving" a crime without regard to the strength of the evidence translates to a lot of bullshit cases, usually involving the arrest of people of color or the off-spring of Dust Bowl migrants. It's how innocent people end up in prison.

I'd been investigating Taylor's unit and learned many things. Some officers talked off the record, but defense attorneys were the best sources. One attorney representing a suspect in a murder over a meth deal gone sour told me his client had slapped a Led Zeppelin tape into a deck and hit record before the victim showed up at his house. There was an argument; gunshots were exchanged. Police confiscated the tape—it had run out and the machine had shut off. A detective in Hal Taylor's unit rewound it and started listening at the beginning, heard a few bars of a Zeppelin song, and turned it off. If the detective had let the tape play another two or so minutes, he would have heard the homicide. The attorney laughed as he told me the story. The tape would have convicted his client, a Hells Angel I knew from another story I'd worked on. The police gave the tape back to the lawyer.

Why was this attorney telling me this, even way off the record? It appears that this attorney so loathed Taylor that he was compelled to tell the story—that he hated what he saw as the ineptness of Taylor's unit, which worked against others of his clients, who were thrown in jail on thin evidence.

In the late winter and spring of 1980, my friends back in Ohio began getting strange phone calls asking about me. One day I was summoned to the office of the owner and publisher of the newspaper, C. K. McClatchy. He handed me a photocopy of a newspaper clipping that had been sent anonymously. It was an op-ed I'd published on February 20, 1980, in the *Cleveland Plain Dealer*.

### Worshipping a Flag is Dangerous

By Dale Maharidge

A Cleveland man was arrested recently because he burned an American flag in protest of resuming draft registration while attending a rally at Kent State University.

The story defended the man, who had burned a tiny flag; late that night, police tracked him down at his home in a distant Cleveland suburb and arrested him. (He would later be sentenced to thirty days in jail after being found guilty by a jury.) The morning the piece ran, my editor showed up for work and was nearly physically attacked by guys in the sports department. It was long before Twitter, but there was the equivalent storm of vitriol in the bundles of hate letters that arrived in care of the newspaper.

I studied the story that C. K. gave me. It had markings from the *Plain Dealer*'s library. Someone at the newspaper had given it to the sender. There's no proof that Taylor had mailed it, but he was the only one I knew who was trying to dig up "dirt" from my past. An unsigned note with the story suggested that C. K. should fire me.

"A little bit overwritten," C. K. said of the op-ed, with a smile. "But I absolutely agree with you."

In November 1983, a city police detective called me with a tip: Hal Taylor had been accused of theft and lying during an internal investigation. A member of the homicide unit had had an argument with Taylor. A few days later, when that detective left to go home, he

noticed that magnetic signs on his vehicle were missing; these advertised a side business he ran. Another officer who disliked Taylor saw
him at the truck and then watched him place the signs in the bed
of another nearby truck. At first, Taylor denied taking the signs. He
later confessed and was suspended for two days. The district attorney wanted to prosecute, but the detective whose signs were taken
declined to press charges.

I called Taylor for comment.

"Get lost, asshole," he said. Then he slammed down the phone.

I never completed the story on the homicide unit. One factor
was the time crush of other assignments, which left little room for
investigative reporting. Another was that in early 1982, I started riding
the rails with new hobos for my first book. And third was that I'd been
a reporter for only five years. I had yet to master the skill of creating
a database by filing a Freedom of Information Act demand for the
district attorney's case resolution files, which would have proven the
story that Taylor's unit was sloppy and interested only in clearance
rates, not prosecutions. It was a failure, but not my greatest one, on
the police beat.

The microrevenge in publishing the story on Taylor's swiping the
›write more about police misconduct. All journalists were hamstrung
in that era, however. Despite the many stories of abuse, there was no
video footage, no proof. Thus no story. Some cops acted with impunity because they knew they could get away with it. By default, the
system—city councils, the courts, and many in the media—trusted
them. "The police wouldn't lie," I repeatedly heard. I knew otherwise.
Officers told me that some carried "boot guns"—weapons that had
been illegally taken from crime scenes and would be at the ready for
an officer to throw onto the body of someone they had just wrong-
fully shot.

# The *Pogo* Factor

Decades before George Floyd and the emergence of Black Lives Matter, there were those trying to hold the police accountable. At least one politician and activists on the Sacramento City-County Human Rights Commission had attempted and failed to create a police review board in 1972. This board would have conducted independent investigations instead of relying on those done in-house by the cops, which were never made public. The commission returned in 1979 to try again, based on numerous charges of police brutality and harassment aimed at Latinos in South Sacramento. That effort also failed.

Those activists couldn't do anything more. But I could do this: I resurrected the issue in a story published in the early summer of 1981. The first sentence: "Who polices the Sacramento city police?"

The answer: nobody.

Stories then were measured in inches, not words. It wasn't just the mainframe computer's way of tabulation: for many stories an editor would say "Give me twelve inches." A major project on the other hand would have about eight feet of newspaper column space, or about four thousand words. With photographs, these pieces would run two or three full inside pages. More commonly, stories would be twenty to twenty-five inches, with as much as possible compressed into those two feet of type. The words were accurate. But how truthful they were is another matter.

I got forty-five inches for the review board story, but our subscribers didn't have to bother reading all those inches. One quote high in the story summed up the reality that existed in Sacramento and in other cities across America at the time, a reality that would remain unchallenged for the next forty years:

> "We [city council members] know much more about the Planning Department than the police," council member Thomas Hoeber said. He was the lone politician who pushed hard for the most recent proposal to create a review board. "But the political atmosphere is such that…nobody wants to appear to question the police for fear of being called anti-law and order. Politically, the Sacramento police are violently opposed to it and that means it probably never will go through."

Bill Miller, the spokesman for Sheriff Duane Lowe, had been wrong. I was in fact playing inspector general. No one else was holding law enforcement accountable.

The most important lesson about policing didn't come from my reporting on homicides, crime, or even the police. It came from observing my newsroom colleagues.

Bob Forsyth and a few other editors were voices for social justice in that newsroom. But others were opposed to Bob, and by extension, to me. There certainly was not universal support in the newsroom of my own supposedly liberal newspaper for doing journalism that questioned the power and actions of the police. I became aware of this when there was a hostile reaction in the newsroom to my story on police response time that ran four weeks after I was hired. And it accelerated with the story on the cops' using hollow-point bullets. Right after that story was published, Bob put me in the lead of his weekly photocopied memo on staff performance.

Monday Morning Quarterback

Jan. 12, 1981

It was a hustling week, particularly for Dale Maharidge, who managed to neatly balance breaking stories on homicides and wrap up the week with an excellent piece on bullets used by local cops.

But it was also a week in which we were sloppy....

√ We provided readers with a 91-word lead on a three-paragraph story announcing that a music concert was canceled.

√ We said that Sen. Alan "Robbins, a Jew, was circumcised at birth" without explaining what Robbins' religion had to do with circumcision.

√ We presented a three-column map that identified the Sacramento River as the American River and the American River as the Sacramento River....

Some colleagues and a number of editors didn't share Bob's opinion concerning my story. They appeared to be in favor of cops' using bullets banned in war that maim people if they survive. The first attack came from the chief of the copy desk. He appeared to be looking for any reason to trash it. His focus was on a sidebar, or a secondary story that runs alongside the main story. I replied to his charges:

Desk:

I take great exception to my "East vs. West" bullet sider being called "poor."

First, it passed the assistant city editor that night, and D— who is filling in for M—. On top of that I asked G— to read it to look for holes on Friday. So I don't understand when a copy editor says it is full of "glaring holes."

Just what is the job of the copy desk? To do major editing? Or look for minor errors?

I get the impression that C— wanted to trash the whole sidebar. Who is he to do that?

I established the East-West difference and then I wanted to establish the fact that more hollow point bullets are being sold nationally to police departments. The companies I talked to wouldn't or couldn't break down the regions they were selling more hp bullets to. But from my calls to big eastern cities, it was obvious the bullets weren't going to them, but to western cities such as Denver and Seattle that recently changed over.

My point in the sidebar was to compare big eastern cities with their western counterparts. Period. I wasn't worried about Peoria or any other tiny Midwest town; nor was I dealing with the South. Sacramento is a big western city. It would do no good to compare it to Meridian, Miss.

C— says he cut two "illogical" graphs and rewrote it, "salvaging" the page. I think he didn't improve anything. In fact, I think he may have made things worse.

Art Nauman, the newspaper's ombudsman, weighed in against me with a column about the bullet story. He wrote, "The effort drew a barrage of counterfire from readers who believe the news department had shown an anti-gun, anti-cop bias. Now, my own conclusion about this: Maharidge was dealing with a non-issue." He cited a response from Bob about guns being a hot current topic. "But the controversy involves guns in private hands, not guns in police hands. What kind of bullets used in those guns is irrelevant in the current public debate.... In my opinion Bee editors magnified the subject out of all sensible proportion.... I think it was an act of journalistic overkill."

Nauman had given me an advance copy of the column. I was prompted to write to him.

I take exception to your column, in which you call the bullet story a "non-issue."

...Journalistic overkill?

I don't think so. A .44 magnum a non-issue? How many people knew officers were using hollow-point bullets? Not many.

I've been accused of being anti-gun and anti-police. I don't think this is valid. My personal opinions are of no importance; I do consider myself politically oriented to the left...but I don't believe handguns should be abolished. Stories like this, no matter how much space you give to both sides, are controversial. The neo-fascists came out of the woodwork on this one, indulging in a feeding frenzy, like an army of garden slugs feeding on a rotten tomato. Your column is a rotten tomato that allows them to eat.

—dale maharidge 1/16/81

My tortured metaphor in the final lines notwithstanding, the copy chief's memo and the column are useful for absorbing the mindset in the newsroom of a large metropolitan daily newspaper in that era, which in turn reflected the attitudes of a large swath of the upper-class community.

The reality of the backlash against the bullet story and the other accountability stories—what one midlevel editor called my "poisoning our relations with the police"—had nothing to do with my being antipolice. It had everything to do with my supposedly being anti-community, and by "community" I mean the upper-middle class and borderline wealthy people who filled the newsroom, who resided in Land Park, River Park, and the unincorporated areas stretching along the north side of the American River: Campus Commons, the Estates at Wilhaggin, Carmichael, Fair Oaks. Or the city of Davis.

It must be remembered that Sacramento was and is a very suburban place, and the editors, copy editors, and ombudsman who disliked my efforts to examine law enforcement were the elite of these richest neighborhoods, who had no need to phone police to seek protection from acts of violence because they didn't have the economic stress of poverty to generate all the attendant ills. They didn't live where the "cheap" murders occurred. Neither they nor their children would ever take a hollow-point bullet to the body. Some editors were vehemently pro-cop no matter what the police did, due to either a conscious or subconscious desire to maintain order in their enclaves, while others may have simply been indifferent, though the end result was the same.

Nothing has changed about this attitude seen in the 1980s. One can go into the toniest of California suburbs today and see Black Lives Matter signs on lawns. But residents in these areas do everything to keep low-income people at a comfortable distance—the farther away the better. They live behind walls with gates and often guards. Their kids go to private schools.

Unlike in the 1980s, when it was easy for communities to blow off calls for affordable housing, the doom loop America of today has led to towns coming up with outlandish reasons to fight state mandates to create more housing. In 2022, after a California state law overruled local officials and allowed developers to build duplexes on single-family lots, officials in the wealthy Silicon Valley town of Woodside declared the entire city a mountain lion habitat. The given reason: they had to save the endangered cats. The real reason: they wanted to block the duplexes. The Woodside officials dropped the ruse only after the state threatened to sue.

And yet some residents from rich towns are repelled by the homeless they see on the streets when they leave their enclaves.

Today, as back in the 1980s, we are the real villains. To quote Walt Kelly, creator of the comic strip *Pogo*: "We have met the enemy and he is us."

# Gina

Gina twisted that napkin with both hands that first time we met when she came to the newsroom.

"I just want to—I want to know, what do you want?" she asked.

"I don't know."

I was not twisting a napkin, but my entire body was tense. We sat at a table outside the newspaper's cafeteria on the third floor of the building.

"You were talking about some of the reasons why you wanted to talk, and one was to make other people aware," I continued. "I think that's—that's basically it."

"Is that enough to give you a good story that you can write?"

"I think so."

*Two minutes in:*

"But I want to know if you want to go from a personal angle or from a general angle?"

"We'll just talk. There's no hurry."

*Six minutes in:*

"But I need to know if you want to know about me, or if you want to know about things in general."

"I mean, you can just talk."

*Seventeen minutes in:*

"I feel like we're not getting to the point, but I don't know what you need."

"We're getting there. In a roundabout way."

"I'm not used to talking about myself. I feel like I might be boring you."

"No! No, no—"

Long pause.

"The thing about reporting is—you know, if you just talk, you get there eventually. I think too many times in my professional life I hurry up interviews, and that's not good, because you miss a lot of things that way. Little things. They're important. As you say, it's a hell of a personal crime, and I want to talk generally and I want to talk personally."

*Twenty-seven minutes in:*

Gina went to the bathroom. The friend who didn't say much finally spoke.

"She's savvy."

"And brave. Gina is going to a place I'd never read about in any story about rape in a newspaper."

I used this as an opportunity to express why I was nervous.

"I've been in this business for almost five years now. A lot of it has been police reporting and related-type things. I've talked to grieving families. This is different. In a situation like this, what do you ask?"

Over forty years later, the ability to listen to this audio from a microcassette is a miracle.

Two microcassette deck players were in my storage unit, but they refused to function. To my surprise, one manufacturer still produced them. I bought one and then ran the microcassette contents into my Zoom H4n digital recorder. I reduced the noise and corrected the pace with an audio editing program, and I was transported back to that long-ago Thursday afternoon with Gina. But the technological wonder is the least of it. The miracle is hearing Gina's story unfold, and my interaction with her, realizing that my instinct had been to simply let Gina talk and tell her story. I also broke the fourth wall of journalism and let her in on the process.

I possess the tape, but I don't have a copy of the story that was killed. I'd placed a printout of it in a file cabinet next to my desk, which held research, mostly about the cops. A few years later, when a big new suspenders-wearing editor arrived, he wanted to "clean up" the newsroom. It was too cluttered. We had to get rid of all the file cabinets. After we reporters protested—the file cabinets contained vital documents related to ongoing stories—the editor compromised and had us put those steel cabinets in a chain-link fenced-off area in the vast basement of the building, with a promise that they would be safe. A few months later when I returned from an out-of-town assignment, I went to that caged room. All the locked file cabinets were empty. They'd been forced open with a crowbar, I would learn, and the contents thrown into a dumpster.

I'd used a bulky cassette recorder in my early days of reporting in Ohio, but it took four hours to transcribe each real-time hour, so I gave up on it in the crush of deadlines and relied on a notebook. In Sacramento, I seldom transcribed my microcassette recordings— I used them mostly to back up the veracity of my interactions with cops. But I cataloged the contents of each tape on a scrap of paper folded into the hard plastic sleeve. By the time I ceased recording in 1982, there were some forty hours of tape. These weren't stored in the file cabinet and lost in the basement purge. With Gina's interview from June 1981, possessing raw tape for my future self to listen to four decades later is an entirely different matter.

Gina was strong, ahead of her time. She was #MeToo before there was #MeToo. It would take decades for the rest of the nation to catch up with her, which is why I present her story here as she told it to me that day, only very slightly edited to eliminate "ums" and pauses. Gina mostly talked fast, as if there were no periods between the sentences. Her hands sliced the air as she spoke.

Gina went through the factual matters: Before she went to bed on the night of the rape, she closed the window. The lock was broken. After she fell asleep, something awakened her. A man stood over her, underwear over his head, pointing a gun. She screamed, loud. He ordered her to shut up. Later Gina would learn that the tenant upstairs heard but did nothing. The intruder wore gloves. He asked for money.

"I told him, 'I don't have money.' But I had ten bucks laying on my dresser, and I had $180 for the rent in my purse. He hadn't gone through my purse, didn't go through any of my things. He wanted me. He said, 'I won't shoot you if you just do everything I want.' I said, 'Okay.' So he asked me to pull back my covers. And I said, 'I really don't want to do that.' I was being real quiet because he told me not to scream again."

She complied, and he tied her up. He had difficulty with an erection. He got hard when he threatened her. There was something about the violent words that turned him on.

"He said, 'I know you like that now. I know this feels good. Move this way. You know I have the gun.' I thought, 'Man, I got to do what this guy wants.' Because I've had other bad sexual experiences in my life, I gave him the power he wanted. I called him sir. I didn't want to die for sex. At one point, my bed's this way; there's the window," she said, pointing in the air that afternoon, to where the window had been. "The man's pants were around his ankles; she got her hands so that she could unbind the ties. "I was thinking I could flip over and break that window with my feet and get out. But I was too afraid because of the gun." Gina focused on the window. "Right there was air and freedom. It was so close! So close."

But Gina didn't make the move. She just focused on that window while he finished. He wasn't getting off on the sex. In that time, Gina started singing something from 4-H Camp, sung by the kids before every meal. It was the "Johnny Appleseed Grace" song from the 1948 animated Disney film *Melody Time*. The song is about being carefree, singing with the birds and the bees, thanking God for all the good things in life.

Then he was done. The rapist told her not to call anyone or leave for five minutes, with the threat that he'd be outside and would shoot her. He slipped out.

"He must have known that the window didn't lock. He must have known my habits. So he's in the neighborhood, and I know he's been watching me. That's just not my paranoia. That's what they say at the crisis center. And that's what the detective says."

She thought: "Nobody will believe me." In those first moments, she decided not to even call the police. Instead she phoned a friend who lived across the alley. She told him she'd been raped, and he asked her to come over to him.

"I thought: 'That alley, it's like the Grand Canyon.' I thought: 'He's out there. He's got a gun.'"

Despite the rapist's warning, Gina went out into the alley, barefoot, wrapped in a sheet. She was terrified but did it anyway. Then she went back to her unit. The neighbor finally came over, said he was tired, and fell asleep. Then Gina phoned another friend, who came in a pickup. "For some crazy reason, we drove around in his truck with a baseball bat looking for the guy." Then they called the police, who came within minutes. She said the cops were great. When a detective later interviewed her, she learned that a rape had occurred in her apartment unit just two months before she moved in. Was it the same guy? And the detective said it was worse for that woman—the perpetrator had been more violent.

The eight-hundred-square-foot one-bedroom unit in the Victorian fourplex was Gina's first apartment. She'd just moved out of her parents' suburban home. She had taken what she'd thought were all the proper precautions before accepting the rental. It was in midtown Sacramento, and that worried her. So before signing the lease, she called the police, who told her not to put her full name on the mailbox, just her first initial and last name. The landlord told her the area wasn't dangerous, but she was lying. She didn't mention the rape that had occurred in the very unit Gina would be renting.

"She had my life in her hands. Just out of humanity, she could have warned me."

Gina wondered if she could sue the woman.

"If nothing comes of a lawsuit, I'm going to go up to that apartment whenever somebody moves in; I'm gonna tell them what happened. I'm gonna keep on doing that. I mean, this is the time to care about thy neighbor. That's why I'm coming to you. I feel personally responsible if anybody else got hurt or raped in that apartment. I'm being kind of upset here. Go ahead and tell me some things you'd like to know, and I'll go on from there. Sometimes it's hard for me to just—"

"Do you think it was an act of sex or an act of violence?" I asked.

Gina replied quickly.

"Violence. Power. Power. Not even violent power. It's an anger, a deep, deep anger in him. He was quietly furious. Quietly vicious. I knew he'd kill me. Instinctively, I knew that he would. You can feel death; you can smell death when it's going to happen. It's death, it's impending death. It's being finite and realizing it. He was being very mechanical and precise. He was having a hard time with his erection. So he talked and asked me questions. He said men don't have the power over women they used to have. He asked how I felt. He wasn't getting off on the sex. But he wanted me to. He told me to. So I pretended. I knew I had to act and give this guy what he wanted. He made no sound when he came. Then it was over and he was gone."

Gina now paused for a long time.

"When I was nine my step-grandfather tried to molest me. The same year, a man exposed himself to me. My grandfather molested me when I was eleven. It happened again two years later."

All that came flashing back—the fear that no one would take her seriously, the power dynamic. "Like when I was a child, instinctively I knew the power he wanted, and I gave it to him. I felt shame. I never got over those things. I never dealt with them until I was eighteen. Suddenly, I was alone and I flipped out. So I know I have to deal with this. And it's gonna take me a long time to get primed to stop running. I've been running from those things my whole life."

Gina was at death's precipice. She could've just as easily have ended up like the murdered women I wrote about on nearly a weekly basis.

"It becomes animal. Animal. It goes back to cavemen. Men can have a mentality over women, and they're angry. Angry. I can tell you about me. I'm strong. I'm a dancer. My legs are big, and I'm a strong person. I was the 'boy' in the family. I never thought of myself as a victim. Never. I was never afraid to do hard things or to be out. I never lived in fear."

Another long pause.

"And I know that was part of my stupidity. Naivete. I just didn't…I never thought people would hurt me. I feel responsible—"

She blamed herself. This time I cut in. I told her not to do that.

"You're right. It's not my fault. I shouldn't have to live a certain way."

The friend spoke: "You're showing your power by being in control."

"I seem like I'm in control, but I'm not, man. I'm fooling everybody. That's my power. I must be in control, but it feels like there's someone else at the steering wheel. Instinct takes over when there's too much pain. I know that. I've been in too much pain before. Gina moves around. Gina walks and talks. But she's not there. I can do all my stuff I have to do. But I can't…don't face anything. I couldn't sleep for four days. Right after, I got some Valium. Went to the hospital. Had the examination. All that stuff. Three hours later, Jack Daniel's and Quaaludes. I still didn't sleep. I got up that night and went out drinking, and the next day drinking and drugs. That Friday, I was supposed to be at my parents', and I hadn't told them. It was my little sister's high school graduation on my dad's birthday. My dad had driven by my apartment that day. No curtain. It was empty. No one knew where I was except for my sister…so when I got to the graduation that Friday, I just said I just decided to move out. Am I telling you too much?"

"No, no. Are you tapering off drugs?"

"Yeah, a little bit. It's all I want to do. I'm forcing myself to get out and do all these things. And the only way I can do that is doing a lot of drugs. I have not faced myself yet. I've gone back to work. I have shortened hours."

Her day job was an administrative assistant at a realty firm. By night she was a singer. She rattled off the places she'd performed at, including a club on Broadway that I often went to. She also performed at Rudy's Hideaway, where John Riggins's van had been found, not far from where he and Sabrina were killed.

"I sing blues. I haven't been able to sing since then. And every man I look at, I think, 'Hmmm, maybe you saw me onstage?' Before I sing, I'm just sitting in the bar. After that, I'm their outlet. I'm the one who's singing it. Singing what they're screaming inside, especially when you sing the blues, and that really makes you…just a target."

She was supposed to be onstage two days after the rape.

"I just couldn't. I tried. I kept driving past the place. I have to go in. But I just couldn't. I mean, my life has just turned around. It's just totally different because of one man."

Gina got paid for some gigs; other times, she sat in with local musical groups. About an hour after our conversation began, she said she realized maybe she could become a reporter. "I think now that I've talked to you…. I think I could do it because people talk to me."

It was a story. Or was it? I was terrified that I could do damage in writing about Gina, even just in talking with her, as I was doing on a patio of the newspaper's cafeteria. I wasn't a shrink, after all. I asked if she was sure she wanted to tell her story. She said a definitive yes. She wanted people to know what rape was really like.

"I'd like it to be a personal story," she said.

"Next to murder, it's the most personal crime really," I responded.

"But it's going to take me a while to tell you everything, and right now I'm really drained. I'd like to meet you again a different time, because I don't think I can do anymore today, to tell you the truth. Is that okay with you?"

"Yeah."

We walked down to the second floor, and I watched Gina and the friend descend to the lobby.

In the days following the meeting with Gina, I was busy. Among my assignments: a double-fatal car accident at Watt Avenue and Arden

Way. Dead were a mother and daughter: Kimiko, age fifty, and Sandra, nineteen. They were broadsided by a car that sped away. A Sacramento County sheriff's officer pursued the suspect, and after a high-speed chase, a twenty-five-year-old man was arrested and charged with felony drunk driving. Days later, there was a two-thousand-acre fire in the grasslands of the eastern part of the county. As cows mooed in the distance amid a charred landscape, farmer Dan Russell said he hadn't lost any cattle. Arson was suspected. When I finally found the time to again meet with Gina, nearly two weeks had passed. We met at the jazz-and-blues club on Broadway where Gina sometimes sang.

On the sound system was Mose Allison, playing a bluesy piece on piano.

"It got close, real close the other night," Gina announced of her mental precarity, which I interpreted as meaning she was suicidal. The previous weekend she had gone onstage to perform. One of the numbers was Bonnie Raitt's "Love Me Like a Man."

"It's a real burner," she said. "It's so sexual. It was a hard song to sing, because people there knew I was raped. I was halfway through and was going to quit. But I finished it. I feel like this gig…" Her voice trailed. "I've been doing a slow death trip all my life. He was my self-hatred personified," she said of the gunman. She now viewed the rape and facing death as a turning point.

"This is my warning. I have to start living now. This is my last chance. I'll be a better person after this—if not, fuck it. I'm real self-destructive. I don't think that I could put a gun to my head. But there are other things. My therapist says this is a classic sign of depression." She also was feeling anger. "I've had dreams. I wish I had a knife," she said, adding that she wished she could have hurt the man. "Nice long slashes. Someone with a gun and a problem came into my house and changed my life. I feel a deep sympathy for the child within me. The laughter of the gleeful child who ran and played and climbed trees, and who sings."

A lawyer she knew through work had seen that she was troubled and asked what was wrong. Over a lot of beer, she told all, showing him documents related to the apartment. She had noted on her lease that the lock on the window was broken. When she moved in, it had not been repaired. She said the landlord hadn't told her about the previous rape. The lawyer felt she had a winnable lawsuit—and she agreed to file a civil case.

When I expressed concern after she circled back to suicidal thoughts, Gina emphasized that she was trying to be positive. She wanted to get back to singing and was scheduled to perform at Tootsie's in Old Sacramento later in July—a few weeks away. I promised to come.

"Life is possible," Gina said, "if a song is possible."

In the ensuing weeks, Gina sometimes phoned, just to talk. But daily deadlines prevented me from finishing Gina's story as soon as I desired to.

Gina somehow got the phone number of the woman who'd been raped in her apartment. The woman told her that she'd resisted and that the attacker had hurt her, and that he'd put the barrel of the gun in her vagina and threatened to shoot. Gina also learned from the police that her attacker was suspected of three rapes.

She went to the neighborhood and put up signs, warning women about the rapist. Two landlords—both women—came behind her and tore down the posters, admonishing her that they wouldn't be able to rent their units with those signs up.

When the property management company that handled Gina's building insisted on the rent payment, Gina taped one penny to their demand, and then taped that paper to the door of their office.

When we met, I mostly listened. I observed her with friends, including a woman who was deeply suspicious of me. "All men are rapists," she announced. I left it for Gina to argue with the woman. Yet I wrote in my journal: "I felt guilty for being a male." I was trying to do justice to the story she entrusted to me. I wanted to tell it well. I spent hours crafting the story of Gina, working on it before and after nightly walks around my neighborhood.

When I finally turned it in to the desk, the editors—all men—immediately killed it. "We're *not* going to run a story about rape," one said.

# Shithole

Gerald Armond Gallego was born on July 17, 1946, in Sacramento. His father, Gerald Albert Gallego Sr., was in San Quentin State Prison serving time for an auto theft. When released, the elder Gallego went on to commit a string of crimes, including murdering two police officers in Mississippi. He was executed in that state's gas chamber in 1955, when his son was nine. By age seven, the boy had already been incarcerated by the California Youth Authority. His childhood crimes ranged from burglary to sex offenses.

By 1977, he had been arrested twenty-three times. That year, he was at the Bob-Les Club, a dive bar on Del Paso Boulevard in North Sacramento, where he met Charlene Williams, age twenty. He asked for her phone number, and the next day he had a dozen red roses sent to her. They were soon living together at Charlene's apartment. Their sex life was terrible. Gallego couldn't maintain an erection. In early 1978, he told Charlene about his fantasies involving young women, which he deemed "ripe for the picking." That July 17, he sodomized his fourteen-year-old daughter; he'd been sexually abusing her since the age of six. On September 11, when Charlene was two months pregnant, she had bad morning sickness. Gallego told her to get out of bed as he loaded a pistol.

Charlene ate breakfast as he outlined his plan to find a "sex slave." They then drove Charlene's 1973 Dodge van to the Country Club shopping center. Charlene went alone into the mall to look for girls. She spotted Rhonda Scheffler, age seventeen, and Kippi Vaught, sixteen. Charlene asked if they wanted to smoke weed, and she led them out to the van. Gerald aimed the pistol at the girls, forced them to lie down, and then bound their hands and feet with duct tape. He drove the van east, into the mountains, down a remote road, where he raped them. Gallego then drove them to a remote field southeast of Sacramento, where he beat them with a tire iron and shot them both in the head.

Two weeks later, the couple drove to Reno, Nevada, and were married. It was his sixth marriage, her second.

Over the next two years, Charlene helped her husband lure more young girls and women. In June 1979, they killed two teenagers and left their bodies in the Nevada desert. In 1980, the couple was busy: in April, they abducted two seventeen-year-old girls from another Sacramento mall and dumped their bodies in the Nevada desert; in June, a girl in Oregon; in July, a lone female bartender in West Sacramento.

The case vexed Lieutenant Ray Biondi, whose unit had been investigating what became known as the "Sex Slave Murders." A break came on November 2, when Gerald and his wife got sloppy. This time they abducted a couple—Mary Beth Sowers and Craig Miller, students at California State University—as they left a fraternity party at the Arden Fair Mall after one in the morning. They soon killed the couple. But a fraternity member had taken down the license plate as the vehicle drove away. It broke the case. Gerald and Charlene fled the state but were arrested in Nebraska later that month.

Within days of the discovery of the bodies of Sabrina Gonsalves and John Riggins, there was talk of it being a copycat murder. This was meant to help the Gallegos—the idea that there was another murderer, not them. This theory posited that Gallego had cronies do the killing, and that he would try to use this in court to prove his innocence. He later did try this, with no success. But at the time, sheriff's spokesman Bill Miller suggested there were similarities between how this couple had been slain and the Gallegos' case.

When I phoned Ray Biondi, he said he was not so certain. "Many points are different," he said. But he wouldn't elaborate. One similarity is that duct tape was used to bind the hands and feet of the victims.

In mid-1981, I was twenty-four. I had been at the newspaper six months. I was still proving myself—to myself, to my editors. In my mind, I was still hunched over the handlebars of a motorcycle going to meetings in Cleveland; I was the college dropout, the impostor. I was not long removed from living out of the pickup truck, as homeless as some of the people I was writing about. I feared ending up once again sleeping out of the Datsun, or slinking home to work in the factories of Cleveland. Journalism saved me from grinding steel.

Come fall I would get a step raise based on the contractually defined Newspaper Guild scale, and the weekly pay would exceed $500. I was about to buy the house along the American River, situated on nearly a half-acre, forested with trees—liquid amber, mulberry, a towering Himalayan cedar—and with a hedge of wild blackberry against the back fence.

As a journalist, I wanted to take on power structures, hold their feet to the fire. And on top of that I had to follow my hiring mandate of going for the "fucking throat." I had to make this gig work. There was no other option. These were my motives.

The motive for the cops who were my sources is clear. Every leak that came my way was driven by a desire for vengeance or some form of self-interest on the part of these officers. Malcontents found me; I didn't have to seek them. And so one day early that summer of 1981, a source made a proposition: would I like an unauthorized nighttime tour of the Sacramento County Jail?

This was a huge "get." The jail was beyond notorious. Long before I arrived, the newspaper had been asking for a tour and was always denied. The facility, built in 1906 and added on to in 1956, held 650 inmates, nearly two hundred over capacity. There were gang cells, called tanks, on each floor, designed for twelve men but containing seventeen—just over ten square feet of space per inmate. The jail teemed with cockroaches and mice. I'd heard about the "elevator ride," when deputies would beat men with rubber hoses while traveling between floors. A lawsuit had just been filed in US district court by the federal public defender against the county board of supervisors and Sheriff Duane Lowe about jail conditions. It was time to take a look.

The motive of the officer who was my source: conditions were so bad that sheriff's deputies who worked in the jail could not stand it. If it was that bad for them, what was it like for the inmates?

My motive: it would be a scoop. A story on a place that I would learn was literally a shithole would rock. This kind of story was exactly what Bob Forsyth wanted me to do.

Conditions were set. I'd have to wait a minimum of one month from the tour until the story ran, to put enough space between the visit and publication, to foil the memory of any officers who could rat us out. I'd have to dress in the "uniform" of an off-duty deputy: a baggy long-sleeve sweatshirt, blue jeans, tennis shoes. All the deputies looked like this when not on shift.

The night came. We began in the booking area. I was nervous as we entered the orange building at Sixth and H Streets, and hoped it didn't show. Newly arrested suspects waited while paperwork was completed. "I got drunk! I got drunk!" a man howled. In a corner, a young man swore bitterly at an officer, who ignored him. The officers on duty talked with my source. I nodded and smiled but said nothing as they chattered.

From the story I would later write:

Reverberating clangs from slamming doors echo down cavern-ous corridors littered with filth. An inmate screams. Then all is silent. There is the smell—a combination of booze, sweat and vomit. Antiseptic fails to mask the odors.

A heavy steel door ground open. On the other side were holding cells, each the size of an average living room, filled with hardened criminals and wide-eyed first timers, drunk drivers who appeared to be state workers. Men sat on a bench against a wall; even where there were empty spots, it appeared a shadow person was present, the wall imprinted with ghostlike human forms from countless dirty bodies. Nearby, for violent suspects, were three "scoobies," padded isolation cells with tiny windows. One window was filled by a hairy face pressed against the glass; drool dripped from distorted lips. Scrawled on a scrap of paper, taped above the window by a deputy, was the word "homo."

I entered an empty scoobie when left alone for a few minutes. The walls were covered with graffiti. I scrambled to write some of it in my notebook before my guide returned:

Heroin is my life...wife
Devil Worshipers
Keep faith in Jesus / He will set you free

When the officer came back, he flushed the scoobie's toilet. Septic water immediately rushed up through a floor drain, flooding the chamber. It smelled of shit.

We moved on to the control center, where a deputy counted a stack of $100 bills: $3,000 in bail for a suspected drug dealer. Jaws, the jail cat, slept nearby on a stack of forms. Then we got on the elevator. I asked my source about the beatings of inmates with rubber hoses.

"Sure, the guards will knock an inmate around," he said. "But that's only after he tries something with us." The elevator door opened to the top story of the jail, where the floors were crusted with filth: dirty underwear, used toilet paper, newspapers, dinner vegetables, and hardened bread. The debris was so thick our feet shuffled through it. The jail was understaffed, and there were few deputies on these top floors, my source said. Inmates could hear officers coming, so deputies often would sneak onto a floor; when they did, they often would find gang rapes in progress in the tanks crammed with seventeen men. My source said these tanks had been designed for minor criminals, but now that the jail was so overcrowded, homicide suspects ended up in them.

On the sixth floor, a deputy pointed to marks in the concrete. In 1975, an inmate named Edward Bareta had been stabbed to death there with a jail-made knife that was plunged nineteen times through his torso, so hard that it chipped the cement, and the damage still looked fresh six years later.

Each floor was the same—filthy, smelly, overcrowded. One man in a cell screamed at an officer standing outside the bars. The officer screamed back. It went on and on, and we ended up on the second floor, in front of a cell containing Gerald Gallego, thirty-five. Clean-shaven with a pudgy face, he lay on his cot, hands behind his head, feet pointing toward the bars. He stared hard at me. I stared hard back.

I believed that I was looking at the man who could be responsible for ordering the killing of Sabrina Gonsalves and John Riggins.

From my phone conversation with spokesman Miller on August 5, 1981:

"When did you go through the main jail?"

"I can't say when. I wanted to tell you and I wanted to talk—"

"Don't play games with me, Dale. If somebody violated the policies and took you in there secretly, then I'm gonna have to find out about it. We don't allow tours of our jail. If you've been through our main jail—and I guess I'm just gonna try to find out who took you through. I'm greatly offended that you would go through our jail in that manner. We've got nothing to hide…. I'm really, really upset. I think that's sneaky."

"Well, I think it was okay—"

"I'm going to start an investigation right now as to who took you to that jail, because it's directly against sheriff's policy."

The commanders at the Sacramento County Sheriff's Department investigated, and when they failed to identify my source, Lieutenant Robert Denham went on a public campaign to discredit my story. He compared me with Janet Cooke, the *Washington Post* reporter who had faked a story that won a Pulitzer Prize earlier in 1981—she had to give back the award. He wrote a five-page memo, which in part said that my article had "the same hollow ring of Cook's article. The article has the indications of being a fabrication gleaned from the federal lawsuit and conversations with inmates and officers assigned to the Main Jail."

Every time the cops came after me, their intent was to get me fired. I wrote a twelve-point rebuttal to Denham, including details about the graffiti in the scoobie, something possible only if in fact I had been inside that cell.

This kind of thing happened not only to me but to journalists at other newspapers. It was difficult to write about police officers who operated pretty much with impunity, and when one pursued stories like mine about the jail, they hit back hard. They seldom were held accountable for misfeasance or malfeasance. Then in 1991, a citizen videotaped Los Angeles police beating Rodney King. The thuggery of those cops was evident for the world to see. When a jury failed to convict the officers in 1992, riots erupted in Los Angeles.

Federal officials later won convictions against two of those officers in a civil rights case. The emergence of affordable video cameras, and later cell phones, has been instrumental in changing the attitude that police would never lie. This is one rare positive change from the 1980s. Some police officers who abuse power are now being held accountable for their actions.

But back then all I had was that little tape recorder. "Paranoia" isn't the word I'd use to describe my state of mind in the months between December 1980 and early 1982. I knew exactly who was after me. I was always on edge. Bob Forsyth cautioned using the CYA approach—he implored me to record each interaction with cops. This was mostly to arm me against internal newsroom enemies, to prove the accuracy of my work. That's the reason I recorded during those first few years—and why I had a recorder at the ready for the interview with Gina.

Phone tapes couldn't be used in court as defense in a libel case. California is one of eleven two-party-consent states. In other words, in order to legally record someone else over the phone, one must have the permission of the person on the other end. Yet many of my colleagues had a suction cup device attached to the earpiece of their handset, with a wire that ran into a tape deck.

These recordings were mostly for the sake of accuracy. The city hall reporter was selling a microcassette deck. I purchased it and a suction cup "bug" from Radio Shack. In the newsroom, I surreptitiously recorded; in person, I held the device in hand, openly taping, which is legal. If cornered with a lie by the cops, I could make the telephone tapes public. It would be unlikely that a cop or official would sue, and if they did, it would only draw attention to the story of whatever injustice I was writing about. These microcassettes were my "break glass in case of emergency" insurance.

# Crystal

battled the "cheap" designation. The desk continued to blow off numerous homicides in low-income neighborhoods. After I passed my six-month probationary period and gained more traction in the newsroom, I pushed hard to cover them, all the while loathing what it took to get those stories: the cold call. It meant going up to a door and knocking on the worst day of someone's life. You never got used to it. If it ever became normal, it meant there was something wrong with you.

It was vital to arrive before the television cameras. Once someone opened a door and faced a video camera lens and the question "How do you feel?" it was usually over for the next journalist who showed up. I'd rush to get there first and then slow way down near the door. My standard lines: "I don't want to be here. I'd rather not be here, and if you don't want to talk, I understand." Then I'd say something about wanting to know how their son/daughter/mother/friend had lived, not about how they had died. And I meant it. If someone declined, I'd turn and leave.

Once a man held a .45 caliber pistol on me; I got him to talk while standing in the threshold after he put down the gun. But the majority of the time, the door opened and I was invited inside. In all those years of reporting on homicides, I never once asked, "How do you feel?"

On Monday, October 5, 1981, Laura Synhorst at the Sacramento County Coroner's office told me they had a homicide victim, a teenage girl who'd been murdered on Sunday. Her body had been found that morning. Since I was being shut out by the city cops, the coroner's staff became my best friends, especially Laura. The girl's mostly nude body had been discovered by a fisherman on the bank of the American River. The autopsy would show she'd been raped. The girl hadn't yet been identified. I wrote a brief.

On Wednesday, when the identity was released, I pushed the ACE to cut me loose. The girl had lived in North Sacramento. I expected to hear "cheap." But he relented, perhaps because of the girl's age. I wanted to report and write this story for page one, not the inside section. The ACE was thinking short. I was thinking long.

I drove a company car and crossed the American River bridge, taking the Del Paso Boulevard exit for North Sacramento. The story was now "old," and I didn't think that television would be on it. There was no hurry. I passed Rev. Carl's Argonaut Club on the east side of the boulevard. This biker bar was neutral ground, where a mix of Hells Angels, Misfits, Grim Reapers, and Sundowners drank in rare peace. Reverend Carl Sandow, an ordained Universal Life minister, was the owner, and he brooked no bullshit. A cop told me that Carl had murdered his wife with a shotgun, but I never asked him about that.

Carl was a source I'd met early in the year, and I'd been to the bar several times. My previous visit had happened at three in the morning. Carl slept all day long and would awaken at five in the afternoon. Two or three a.m. is when I would interview Carl—after closing, the bar empty, just Carl and I in a small backroom office.

On that visit, Carl had been wearing a sleeveless black leather vest; a gold chain hung below his thin and scraggly beard. This was his uniform. He was balding. He told me in great detail how he'd helped some Hells Angels pay a visit to a man who'd ripped them off.

"You're here to break my legs, right?" Carl recalled the man saying upon opening his door. "Okay, let's get it over with." The man submitted to having them break his legs. More incriminating than this was detailed information about the big drug deal involved with that story. Carl was seated between me and the office door; the thought flashed that if Carl realized he was revealing things that could land him in prison for years, it might not be good for me. As he talked, I plotted how I'd rush past him if things went south. But Carl trusted me. When I walked out after four in the morning, he said he was eager for our next chat. It was a case of me being his free shrink.

Now, as I drove the company car farther up the boulevard, I turned right at the Bob-Les Club, that shabby bar where Gerald Gallego met Charlene, marking the start of the events leading to their kidnapping-and-killing spree. Seven blocks east was Empress Street and the home of Barbara Jones, mother of Crystal Dawn Reid, the sixteen-year-old girl who'd been raped and then beaten to death on the shore of the river. Two men had been booked on murder charges: Thomas C. Bolan, age twenty-five, and Roy Dean Daniel, eighteen.

I came to the address the coroner had given me. I parked and sat for a full minute. It sounds cliché, but I took a deep breath. This was a ritual before every cold call. I've always been shy, especially as a child. Not much had changed, but the spiral-bound reporter's notebook, thrust in my right rear pants pocket, was my talismanic power. When I emerged from the car and pulled that notebook to hold in my left hand, it transformed me: I was a journalist. I was on a mission. I could walk up to the home.

I faced a rusting screen door. Through it a woman was visible, seated at a dining table. She stared hard at its surface. I knocked on the wood frame. The woman slowly looked up. She had a face from a 1936 Dorothea Lange photograph for the US Farm Security Administration: round, framed by short-clipped hair, with eyes that had once been kind but were now hardened by too much life. I would learn she had been born in Van Buren, Arkansas—smack on the border of Oklahoma—in 1929 and lived through the Dust Bowl migration. I started my stock speech about not wanting to be there. Before I got halfway through, Barbara was already opening the rickety screen door. It slammed behind me.

We sat at the kitchen table. She'd seen the brief story in the newspaper about the body of a girl being found by a fisherman. She didn't want to believe it was Crystal.

"When I called the police, they said it wasn't her," Barbara said. "The police said forty other women called to ask if it was their daughter. There must be a lot of other girls like her out there."

Barbara looked over at a recent picture of her daughter. The girl had chestnut hair, falling to her shoulders. The face was long and narrow. She was smiling. She looked more like a child of twelve, not a blossoming young woman.

Without prompting, Barbara shared her motive for talking. "Crystal thought she could take care of herself. It's too late to help her. I just hope other kids realize it can happen. I'm all cried out. I don't understand the reason for this violence."

I didn't, either. How could one ever understand the actions of a Gallego or those two men accused of the rape and killing of Barbara's daughter? Had those men also thought that Crystal was "ripe for the picking?" I thought this but didn't ask many questions. As with Gina and others, I mostly listened.

Barbara told me about the final time she had seen Crystal.

"It was about noon Sunday. I asked her to go out with me to have breakfast with a friend. But she was doing her hair and said she couldn't go."

As Barbara continued talking about that last moment, the screen door opened and slammed with some neighborhood kids coming in. Barbara barely noticed as they ran into another room.

Despite what the homicide detective had told her, when Barbara learned that the only clothing on the body of the girl was a brown macramé top decorated with bear teeth and brass beads, she knew it was her daughter. She said it wasn't unusual for Crystal to leave home for a night or two.

"She wasn't any different than anyone else. Not that I didn't have a problem with her. She had been drinking and staying out all night, but she was starting to get it together." The girl, who'd dropped out of high school, had just bought books to study for the equivalency test. "It was starting to happen for her. And she was starting singing lessons. She had a beautiful voice."

When it came time to leave, Barbara remained seated at the kitchen table. The screen door slammed behind me. I looked back through the mesh. Barbara's gaze was fixed on her daughter's picture.

I then interviewed Crystal's friend Susan Foster, who lived in an apartment a few blocks from the Empress Street home. The police report said this was the last place Crystal had been seen alive.

"I knew her two years," Susan, age twenty, said. "She would always bring some kind of excitement to where she was at. She got away with a lot, because she was really pretty. She could talk herself out of anything."

Except this time, Susan added. She was reluctant to comment on the men who had gathered at her apartment that Sunday night with her and Crystal.

"We were just partying," is all she would say.

I wrote the story that afternoon and went long, some thirty-five inches. I took apart the crazy, added all the dimension possible to the story of Crystal's short life. The desk chopped it by more than half—made it fourteen inches. Yet it landed on page one. It wasn't above the fold; it was in a little box on the lower-right-hand corner. But it was page A-fucking-1. I had reported and written it so that Crystal could get there.

In the following weeks, Barbara mailed me poems about her daughter. She phoned a few times too. Even if I was on deadline, I made time to talk with her. Barbara said she was moving back to Arkansas. A few poems she mailed me were postmarked from there. They were from the heart, real, which made them powerful. I kept those poems. But they were also lost to the destruction of our files by the big new editor.

# El Camino High School

When I was in ninth grade, my parents got me a single-shot twenty-gauge shotgun. No one in our family hunted. But friends did, and I joined them in the fall and winter, going after rabbit and pheasant, sometimes deer. It was part of Ohio culture. I never hit any creature. Along the way, I acquired a few other firearms. I'd lost interest in hunting by the time I moved to California, yet several guns came with me.

Guns made me feel increasingly uneasy as I covered violent crime in the 1980s. Yet I held on to my small collection, stored unloaded in the back of a closet during that era. Though I wasn't antigun, after a steady diet of murder on the police beat, I began to question the ready availability of weapons, believing stricter rules were needed. The term "doom loop" didn't yet exist, but there was strong evidence that gun laws were going to be rolled back, and this didn't seem like a good idea. The National Rifle Association was in ascent and aggressively pushing to loosen regulations. Thus when I saw a flier for a gun show at a local high school tacked to a telephone pole near my house, I paid a visit.

The Sixteenth Battalion of the California Cadet Corps was established at El Camino High School in the Arden-Arcade neighborhood of suburban Sacramento, with the goal of instilling "leadership, citizenship, patriotism, academic excellence, [and] basic military knowledge" in students. In early March 1982, I showed up at this school, with its low warehouse-style buildings and part of the San Juan Unified School District, and paid a one-dollar admission fee to attend a fundraising event by the cadets.

A Nazi flag for sale formed a backdrop for the auditorium, which was filled with folding tables, on whose tops were an array of firearms—pistols, rifles, shotguns. Books for sale described how to blow up bridges, and there was a small cannon.

"This baby is sweet," said the seller. "You haven't lived until you've fired a cannon."

One man marched around in a Confederate uniform.

The thirteen- to eighteen-year-old students held one of these gun shows every two months in order to raise money to send cadets to rifle meets. Students would check in people's guns at the door, collect money from vendors, and do everything else necessary to make the show work.

I bought a .22 caliber Ruger Single-Six revolver. If I were to have obtained that weapon at a licensed dealer, I would have had to wait fifteen days for a background check. My transaction took less than one minute, and no questions were asked. I hung around and witnessed other cash-and-carry deals.

The students weren't breaking the law because they weren't actually selling guns, a cadet named Mark, age sixteen, said. "We just provide the time and place," he said.

One of the group's most profitable shows had been the previous December. It grossed $6,000 and netted $3,800, according to another cadet, Kristina, eighteen.

"This show is different than other shows," Colonel Thomas Armstrong, who headed the cadet program at the school, said. "It's a benefit. The crowd that comes here comes to talk about guns."

When I contacted the San Juan Unified School District for comment, there was a long delay in their response. I was eventually told the district had checked with the state attorney general in the interim. The answer wasn't that guns should not be sold in a high school. That was fine, according to Bartley Lagomarsino, assistant superintendent of secondary education. "We're going to copy sections of the penal code that govern the exchange of handguns and distribute them at the show," he said. "If we're in a position to observe anyone not complying, we'll report them to authorities."

My purchase of the Ruger was part of a project for the newspaper on how easy it was to buy guns and explosives. Before I started, the editors asked someone from the California attorney general's office to come to the newsroom. That official told us that I wouldn't be prosecuted because his office recognized intent—my goal was not to engage in an unlawful activity but to expose it. With that blessing, I set forth on my mission. Over a period of several weeks, I bought chemical precursors for making bombs, and guns. For $500, I assembled a small arsenal and enough explosive materials to do serious damage if my intent were nefarious.

As for the apparent violation of the law, Bill Miller told me that the Sacramento County Sheriff's Department didn't have the resources to police the shows. Only one federal agency was charged with enforcing gun laws: the US Treasury Department's Bureau of Alcohol, Tobacco, and Firearms. My source there, Special Agent William Bertaloni, was frustrated. After Ronald Reagan was elected president in 1980, a directive was handed down from Washington that the ATF should not mess with gun shows. Bertaloni suspected that pressure for this edict came from the National Rifle Association.

"We have laws to work with," he said. "But the position of the bureau is, we don't engage in that activity. The NRA has just about beaten us to death."

I phoned NRA spokesman John Adkins. "Basically, it's a matter of harassment. We see nothing wrong with gun shows and the legitimate sale of firearms. At one point, the ATF was saying the gun shows were a source [for] a lot of criminals, but they later said they couldn't substantiate this."

There was evidence against this assertion, published a few months earlier in Patty Hearst's book *Every Secret Thing*, about her time with the Symbionese Liberation Army. The SLA had hidden out for a while in Sacramento, in a house near downtown. Among the string of crimes committed by the SLA was the robbery of the Crocker National Bank in suburban Carmichael on April 21, 1975. Hearst and five other SLA members pulled off the heist, during which the shotgun held by SLA member Emily Harris went off, killing Myrna Lee Opsahl, the mother of four children. That was the bank I used—it was a five-minute drive or a seventeen-minute walk from the house I'd bought in 1981.

Hearst wrote that the SLA had found it easy to purchase weapons at a Sacramento gun show. Bill "General Teko" Harris and Jim Kilgore bought two Colt revolvers, two Smith & Wesson .38s, and a .357 Magnum revolver.

"Teko and Jim Kilgore returned from the outing with wild stories of 'right wingers and Nazis' selling guns, Iron Crosses, and Nazi mementos to anyone," Hearst writes in the book. "Teko thought it was a fine way for revolutionaries to arm themselves—buying their weapons from right wingers."

# Free Men

You felt the emerging doom loop if you were in a newsroom in the 1980s, if you worked the street—if you listened to farmers in Iowa, jobless industrial workers in the Great Lakes region, former coal miners in Appalachia. White people mostly. You could feel a gathering gyre of discontent. I heard it in September 1984, in Cedar Rapids, Iowa, when we covered a campaign speech by President Ronald Reagan. The coverage was part of "The Pulse of America," a two-month-long coast-to-coast road trip in which I reported from a company SUV that election year, done with photographer Michael S. Williamson.

We arrived early at the airport to observe. Bleachers had been set up next to the tarmac. In front of the stands were some one hundred supporters, who wore Reagan-Bush hats and carried small American flags on sticks. They had arrived several hours before the event to rehearse spontaneous cheers. After their practice, we had to wait for the president. I talked with some of the supporters and discovered a collective sense of aggrievement, of loss, of longing for a great leader. When *Air Force One* eventually landed, the "elite" of the national press corps bailed out and were escorted to the bleachers, where there was a wide platform at the top.

Only once the television cameras were set up did Reagan walk over to meet the very White crowd, stationed between the lenses and the president, to make the best image of Iowa love for the evening broadcast news. The assembled supporters performed the practiced cheers and waved their flags. What was going on with White anger? We decided to further explore this. From there we drove on to Peoria, Illinois. We literally went to Main Street, where in front of the courthouse a White woman told us what was playing in Peoria: "The whole city is broke. I can go look for a job five days a week and still there's nothing."

She had worked in a small mom-and-pop store that went bankrupt after being robbed at gunpoint three times and being stiffed by customers passing bad checks. She was at the courthouse for a case regarding the latter. We moved on to Flint, Michigan, and heard this from an auto worker: "Technology? It will lead us down the road to starvation. What have we accomplished if we can build cars with one-third the men?" And from another: "You can't fight automation. It's like trying to fight going bald."

Next was Youngstown, Ohio, and its fifty thousand lost jobs from the shutdown of the steel mills: "You get crazy mad here," a former steel worker told me. Steel companies weren't investing in technology to make the plants competitive, and foreign nations were "dumping" steel in the US market below the cost of making it—and both neoliberal Democrats and Republicans were in thrall with the idea of the "free market." This anger among Whites witnessed in the center of the country was the audience that Rush Limbaugh understood back in Sacramento—he would ride their anger to conservative fame. That future wasn't known in 1984, but what I did know was that the rage in these dying industrial cities would not have a good end.

I wrote stories on a Radio Shack TRS-80 Model 100 computer, which had debuted in 1983. It cost $1,099 and had a tiny screen that displayed eight lines of text, or forty characters. Memory: thirty-two kilobytes, about the length of one long story, two short ones. The screen was difficult to see—it was a liquid crystal display, not backlit. As crude as it sounds years later, this device was state of the art at the time. Small crowds sometimes gathered to gawk and ask questions when I sent a story using a public phone, using suction cups affixed to both the ear and mouthpiece; the device made loud screeching sounds as it connected. The file would be uploaded to the newspaper's mainframe.

We affectionately called them "Trash '80s" in the newsroom. I often composed stories on this computer while Michael drove.

By the time we reached the East Coast, we'd documented a stream of anxiety, anger, and fear in the center of a nation that had fundamentally changed. We had the sense that many of those we interviewed desired a decisive president—someone tough who would roll back the clock to some era of glory. Some who planned to vote for Reagan were doing so reluctantly—he wasn't far enough to the right. Many didn't see that they were being played by the Republicans, who distracted them from their financial precarity by focusing on racial division and gay marriage, all the while pushing to kill labor unions and lower taxes for the rich. This use of bogeyman social issues would continue; the current attacks on trans people and "wokeness" is a descendent of this strategy.

The White people we interviewed, however, actually wanted more than Reagan was giving. No one used the word "autocrat." By many measures, Reagan did not embody this word, yet he appealed to a base using code language that fed their desire for this kind of president. What I witnessed across the nation felt dangerous, and I wanted to contextualize that sense with history. So when we arrived in New York City, I interviewed a Holocaust survivor. She showed us the number the Nazis had tattooed on her arm in a work camp. I asked why she didn't have it removed. Her reply: not only did she never want to forget, but she kept it as evidence against Holocaust deniers, and to show children. She wanted Michael to photograph her arm.

"I'm afraid of what's going on in this country. It could happen here." She saw the US heading toward electing an autocrat—if not Reagan, then someone worse someday. I wrote a sidebar on this woman to go with our main filing out of New York. The big new editor spiked the story. He announced that he would not allow *my paper* to describe the Republican Party as having the potential to lurch toward fascism.

I couldn't let go what I had experienced in our twelve-thousand-mile journey around America, as well as what I'd found in my other reporting. Then, in December 1984, news broke of a siege by the FBI on Whidbey Island in Washington state. Agents had surrounded the home of Robert Jay Mathews, the leader of The Order, a white supremacy group that funded its separatism efforts by counterfeiting money, burglarizing, and robbing. The Order had assassinated Jewish radio talk-show host Alan Berg in Denver, in June of that year. In July, a dozen armed members in paramilitary uniforms had pulled off a $3.6 million robbery of a Brinks truck in Northern California. During the Whidbey Island standoff, Mathews blasted some one thousand rounds at FBI agents. It ended with his fiery death in the house.

Mathews was an offshoot of a chain of white supremacists. In 1964, Reverend William Potter Gale founded the Ministry of Christ Church in the Sierra foothills town of Mariposa, California, near Yosemite National Park, and started the Identity Movement. Identity teaches that Jews are the children of Satan. (Ironically, Gale's father was Jewish.) Tied in with Gale was Richard Butler, who moved from California to Idaho, where in 1973 he began the Aryan Nations, which in turn begot Mathews and The Order.

Gale and others created yet another group on July 4, 1984, when they met in Mariposa to form The Committee of the States. They took the name from the Articles of Confederation, which called for a committee of states to run the nation when Congress is in recess. The group interpreted the language of the statute to allow them to indict and outlaw the US Congress, the California legislature, the Federal Reserve, and the courts. They mailed letters calling for officials to resign and be placed on trial by the committee; anyone who challenged the authority of the committee would be punished by death.

Among the forty-four signers of the document they created, called the Committee of the States Compact, that Independence Day in 1984 were Richard Butler and Arthur Stigall, who a few months later published a pamphlet titled "How to Form a Common Law Grand Jury: The Way to Regain a Self Governing Republic." It was a detailed explanation for creating a "citizen grand jury" composed of twenty-four residents in each county, and how they would notify the county sheriff and district attorney of the "intention to perform an investigation as a grand jury." Under the heading "Jurisdiction," Stigall writes that "the people's" authority included:

> The power of arrest, law, and jurisdiction of courts rest with the citizens both *directly* and *indirectly* through his lawful 'representatives.' The *de facto government* called the federal government has no authority other than that voluntarily submitted to by the citizens of *the United States*...

Fifteen White men were gathered in the dark living room of a modest North Sacramento home in July 1985. They stared at an image on a screen from an overhead projector of the kind used in classrooms during that era. It was stifling, and there was no air conditioning. Several fans blew hot air that did little to cool the room—sweat dripped down all faces. Speaking in a low voice over the noisy fans and the faint barking of neighborhood dogs was Stigall, a former mathematics teacher. He read what was on the screen—he'd copied his recently completed citizen grand jury pamphlet. The United States must be overthrown, Stigall announced, and the power put back in the hands of the people.

"Is there a war going on?" Stigall, age forty-three, asked. Fifteen hands shot up, and there was a chorus of "yes, yes, yes, yes." Stigall told the men that the leaders of the United States had become traitors whose "satanic" actions had turned the nation into a "mystery Babylon."

For two months, I'd been coming at 7 p.m. most Wednesdays for a meeting of committee members at Stigall's home on Albatross Way. The gathering often continued until two in the morning. The men present had turned in their driver's licenses and removed the plates from their cars—a rejection of state authority over their lives. They often talked about the only law being that of Yahweh, the Old Testament name for God. Some Wednesdays only five members showed up. Others, as many as twenty. Stigall welcomed me when I got in touch with him, and he invited me to sit in on sessions with the condition that with the exception of Stigall, I would use no real names.

Was a show being put on just for me? That's why I kept returning, sitting quietly in the back of the room in the hope that the longer I was around, the more these men would reveal themselves.

I invested in those Wednesday evenings because of what I'd digested from my recent reporting around America. The energy was not coming from the far left; by the mid-1980s, the call for revolution had shifted from the left to the right. It seemed more than plausible that the level of violence would escalate in the coming years. I wanted to understand the right side of the mirror.

What I heard all those nights is distilled in these sentiments that were repeated over and over: individuals are king. Man has become a slave to the federal government and international bankers in a Jewish-inspired Communist takeover. Congress has shirked its duties. Ronald Reagan is a conspirator. The courts are conspirators. Courts are functioning under martial law, an "admiralty jurisdiction," with laws geared to favor merchants and the banks. The highest legal authority should lie with the counties and citizen grand juries—the *posse comitatus*. The federal income tax should be abolished. There should be no federal regulations. The Bible is above any of man's laws. Abortion for any reason should not be allowed.

Despite the nights I spent in that living room and elsewhere with some of these men, there was the feeling of a stage set. What were they really doing? Was it more serious than what they allowed me to see?

At the start of each meeting, Stigall stood next to the overhead projector. He lifted the cover. The blinding white light blasted his face, bright on the shock of gray above his tall forehead.

"Is anyone here an informant?" he asked at the beginning of each session, studying the room. "Or ever been an informant? Or trying to entrap us with firearms sales?"

The men always shared suspicious stares. Stigall, face bright in the projector's spotlight, would slowly look into all eyes—the way Jack Benny used to work a room, with his head rotating like a gun turret. Stigall told me in private that he believed there was an informant. I had confirmation of this from a federal law enforcement agent. Two weeks before that hot July night, some of these committee members had gone to Gale's Ministry of Christ Church in Mariposa to watch a film of machine guns fired upon a car. It was some kind of training. How else would the federal agent know this? This source said that the North Sacramento chapter was the largest of the committees in the country, with twenty-five members.

I was pretty certain who the mole was. Most often, some of the men who were around seventy years old fell asleep by midnight, snoring, as Stigall droned on about *posse comitatus* theory. But men never fell asleep when Dastardly came to a meeting.

That summer, I was with Dastardly driving west on Interstate 80. His beard was ragged, and he was a bit overweight. He was probably in his late thirties, but he looked at least fifty from a grunge life. He pulled a Russian-made Tokarev pistol from his jacket and began waving it around.

"I'm weird!" he exclaimed. He wouldn't put the pistol down. I feared our being stopped if a CHP unit drove past. But Dastardly was flooring it, going at least eighty or more, so we'd pass any cop. I was with him on the way to a gun show in Vallejo where he wanted to buy weapons. But he just window-shopped that afternoon, talking with one seller about how to file down the pin on a semiautomatic rifle to make it "rock-and-roll."

"Dastardly" was his self-appointed nickname. All he ever did was talk about guns, and the more he tried to show me how real he was, the more I suspected he was an informant. I had plenty of evidence to believe so. I had his real name and knew a lot about him. He had once been a federal undercover operative—a fact confirmed by my colleague Paul Avery, who had covered that story. But when I confronted Dastardly, he insisted that he was not undercover, that in fact the feds were pissed and on a mission to send him to prison. He also worried about the men his testimony had put behind bars. He feared retribution, one reason he always packed. He made a living by selling guns and teaching survival training.

He vowed that he stayed on this side of the law with his weapons sales, but after one meeting at Stigall's house, I heard him talking to some men: "Wanna buy a belt-fed sixty-caliber for twenty-eight hundred dollars? An AK-47? Wanna thirty-eight-caliber? Cheap. Grenades? Only sixty dollars each."

He stunk of informant. But who knew? Perhaps he was too obvious to have been the mole. Only one thing was certain—the hypercharged anger in that living room.

One young man who rode a motorcycle to the meetings said he didn't want to wage war. He just desired to be free. The first thing to become free: "You begin by rescinding your birth certificate. That's like the trunk of the tree—by rescinding that, you break the first contract with the state." The man had turned in his driver's license, marriage certificate, social security card, and many other documents. He now felt that the state no longer owned him.

Stigall seemed to be edging closer to some dark place. He told me that it was his God-given right to travel without government control. Two times he had been cited for expired license plates. He spent nine days in jail, because he would not sign any of the release forms when he was arrested. He was appealing that case and was driving around without a license or plates. The previous September, Stigall had been in Sacramento municipal court when he advanced toward the judge to serve him with a notice demanding the resignation of every elected official in California within thirty days. Stigall was restrained by a bailiff and arrested. The judge offered to suspend four days of a five-day sentence if Stigall promised not to cause any more disturbances in any court. Stigall refused. He served all five days.

Each encounter with authority simply hardened his determination to fight.

"They're going to wipe out the United States, and I don't know if we can stop it or not," Stigall said with urgency one night. "We have to step up to a level of higher performance. We'll be getting close this year to the point where we're running the country. Our goal is to put the United States back in the hands of the people."

I asked what kind of government he envisioned.

"A benevolent dictatorship is best. Jesus Christ would have one if he comes back. Democracy is anarchy. Mob rule."

The rebellion of angry White men began long before the 1980s. Richard Butler was the OG white supremacist. In the 1930s, he belonged to the Silver Shirts, an American group with as many as fifteen thousand members that emulated the Nazi Brown Shirts in Germany and found inspiration in Adolf Hitler. A significant number of Americans embraced fascism during the Great Depression. In the early 1960s, Butler, Gale, and another man created the California Committee to Combat Communism. In 1964, these three men formed the Christian Defense League. Butler went on to found the Aryan Nations in Idaho.

For years, these guys were outliers. But something had changed by the time I sat all those Wednesday nights in that living room on Albatross Way in North Sacramento, something that the Holocaust survivor in New York City had sensed was coming, and that I'd felt talking with people in depressed cities in the middle of the country and even in California. It's as if Butler and others had camped out underground for decades, waiting for the next era of economic despair among working-class White people to once again try to seize their moment. It wasn't just what I was hearing in that living room. One solid piece of evidence that more men felt the same way came when I telephoned Erwin Cooper, a spokesman for the California Department of Motor Vehicles. "They seem to have some kind of network," Cooper said, adding that for a while, the DMV had been receiving about two cancellations of driver's licenses per week from men declaring themselves free of the state.

This expanding network was of concern to two agents from different federal law enforcement agencies, who didn't want their names used in my story published that July 1985. One suggested I telephone Larry Broadbent, the undersheriff of Kootenai County in Idaho, where the Aryan Nations was located. Broadbent was more than happy to have his name associated with his concerns. He'd been studying hate groups in America since 1972. I told him about what I was seeing during the meetings at Stigall's house—the mix of mind-numbing boring speeches, members who wanted to merely serve papers on officials versus others who saw violence as necessary.

"That's how our group here more or less began," Broadbent said. "There were the moderates, the pacifists, and those more extreme. One side wanted to take more action, and they did."

Broadbent said the lack of success was making some on the right frustrated. He said the longer they went without seeing political change, the more likely they would resort to terrorist actions.

"It's only a matter of time," he said.

In 1995, Timothy McVeigh parked a Ryder rental truck filled with over two tons of explosives in front of the Alfred P. Murrah Federal Building in Oklahoma City. When the truck detonated, 168 people were killed and nearly 700 wounded.

In 2015, neo-Nazi Dylan Roof shot nine Black parishioners to death during a Bible study program at the Emanuel African Methodist Episcopal Church in Charleston, South Carolina.

In 2018, Robert Gregory Bowers opened fire inside the Tree of Life synagogue in Pittsburgh during a morning Shabbat service. Eleven people were killed and six wounded; the victims included a few Holocaust survivors. It was the deadliest attack on Jewish people in US history.

In 2019, Patrick Crusius, a white nationalist, went on a shooting spree at a Walmart in El Paso, Texas—he targeted Latinos. He left twenty-three dead and an equal number wounded. It was the biggest attack on Latinos in US history.

Then on January 6, 2020, groups such as the Oath Keepers stormed the US Capitol; all of them had roots essentially or actually tied to the 1980s.

Even without knowing any specifics of the mass killings to come, I knew bad things were undoubtedly in store by the final meeting I attended at Stigall's house in 1985.

That night, an older man with a peppery beard talked with another member about his private conversations with Yahweh. That other member was happy that abortion clinics were being bombed.

"That guy is a member of the Army of God," Dastardly whispered to me, referring to a violent antiabortion group. "These people are upset. There's going to be a war. That guy over there has a Mini-Fourteen automatic assault rifle." Dastardly got up and went to that man, discussing the merits of the Mini-14.

Most committee members left early that breezeless night. It was too hot for a full meeting. At one point, just four guys remained: Dastardly, Stigall, a man named Tim, and another man. Stigall, perhaps for my benefit, countered the gun talk by saying they could not initiate violence, only respond to what came their way. "We can't break the law," he said. "Running around with machine guns and bazookas is suicide. We won't need it if we succeed legally."

"That's a gamble," Tim said.

"Life's a gamble," Stigall said.

Dastardly said he was tired of the meetings, which were dragging on with no apparent victory in sight.

Stigall agreed. "I'd just as soon the ones who aren't serious get out." He twisted a pencil. "Put up or shut up. We have to get more serious about what we're doing, or time will pass us by." He said they needed to take more action in the courts, and send more notices out that politicians were illegally holding office.

"It won't happen in the courts!" Dastardly exclaimed. "The courts aren't going to listen to us. We're going to have to quit playing games. People should be willing to die for life and liberty. You have to have that mental attitude. There are people out there with guns doing things. Not just talking."

# Kent State

Another autumn had come to Kent State University. Students strolling across campus shielded books from a misting rain. Oddly, the cold wind smelled like hickory nuts. Colorful leaves blew across a grassy knoll at Taylor Hill. It was Wednesday, October 3, 1984, and it was quiet. It doesn't seem possible that on May 4, 1970, thirteen seconds of gunfire came from the top of this hill, when National Guardsmen killed four students and wounded nine others protesting an expansion of the Vietnam War into Cambodia.

"Four dead in Ohio." This sentence became a mantra, lyrics in a Crosby, Stills, Nash & Young song. For some in my generation, the words and the date would be forever etched in memory, as Pearl Harbor Day was to our parents.

Not much was left to remind anyone of the events that had occurred fourteen years earlier when I showed up with Michael Williamson on our cross-nation election project. But one could find evidence: An M1 bullet hole remained in a steel sculpture. Trees whose trunks had been splintered by some of the sixty-seven bullets fired that day were healed; these spots were marked by black scabs of bark.

As I leaned down and felt the bark of one tree, two people climbed Taylor Hill. They sat beneath a pagoda at the top of the knoll to escape the rain. This is where a cluster of guardsmen had stood when they opened fire. When I greeted them, Cheri, a freshman from Pennsylvania, told me she was giving her visiting brother, Brian, a tour of the campus. She pointed.

"From what I hear, the students were down there," she said. "They were mad. I don't know what they were protesting. Before I came here, I never heard about this. I was four years old when it happened. I don't know what to think about it."

Brian, twenty-three, knew it had something to do with the Vietnam War. But not much more. I offered a few details. Student unrest began on the campus after President Richard Nixon announced the expansion of the Vietnam War into Cambodia. There were two tense days of protests. On May 4, 1970, guardsmen ordered students to disperse from a noon rally. Some students threw rocks. Guardsmen climbed the hill and, for no apparent reason, opened fire. They said later that they had feared being injured. The nearest student had been two hundred feet away. Eight guardsmen were indicted by a federal grand jury. All were acquitted.

"The war was over a long time before I had to sign a draft card," Brian continued. "That's all I care. It doesn't mean a lot to me."

The topic switched to present-day politics. Brian said he liked President Reagan's stand on reducing taxes. He felt that if Walter Mondale were to win the election the next month, it would be a disaster.

"To me, the biggest problem in my life is economics. I just got a job. For the first time in my life, I'm getting a paycheck. I've got to cut it up like a piece of meat. I'm like every person. I don't like taxes. I'd like to keep as much of it as I can. I've weighed the issues and chosen to be a Republican."

They walked off.

I strolled down Taylor Hill to where Curt, eighteen, and Tony, nineteen, had stopped to study a granite marker where the students had fallen. It read:

In Living Memory of
Allison Krause
Jeffrey Miller
Sandra Scheuer
William Schroeder

May 4, 1970

"We come by it every day," Curt said. "I never really stopped to look at it. Last night in the dorm, they showed a movie about Kent State. It made us curious. So we stopped to look."

Tony was a member of the Reserve Officers' Training Corps, a program that prepares students to enter the military as officers. ROTC had been a target for students who opposed the draft and the Vietnam War. The ROTC building had been burned to the ground before the shootings. Tony felt that what the National Guard troops had done was wrong. "How could they shoot unarmed people?" But he said the Vietnam War had been a just cause.

"Things are different now," Tony said. "It won't happen again. But we've got to have a strong military. You just can't trust the Russians."

Curt agreed, saying Reagan would emphasize military strength.

"Yeah," Curt said. "Reagan's going to get us back up there. He doesn't take any bullshit from anyone."

Enrollment in ROTC at Kent State reflected the attitude of Curt and Tony. I'd already interviewed Captain Bob Skebo of Air Force ROTC. He said there had been a dramatic increase in the number of students enrolling in ROTC the previous few years.

"Like John Wayne said, 'America right or wrong,'" said Tony, misquoting and misattributing words actually uttered by US senator Carl Schurz, who opposed US imperialism and the Spanish-American War. The full and correct quote is, "My country, right or wrong; if right, to be kept right; and if wrong, to be set right." But I didn't correct Tony, who went on: "When you're a fighter pilot, what else do you do? I'd go to Central America."

"I know a lot of people who want to go," added Curt. "I know guys who were in Grenada. You've got to die sometime. It doesn't scare me."

Tony was certain how the election would turn out—he'd placed a fifty-dollar bet on Reagan's victory.

"Our professor in government class is anti-Reagan. He makes me sick," said Tony. He vowed to someday tell off that professor. "He was a draft card burner!"

"I don't get along with people who burned their draft card," said Curt. "You should feel obliged to go."

Murray Fishel is the professor whom they disliked so much. I found him in his office after talking with Curt and Tony.

Fishel had been eating in the cafeteria on May 4, 1970, when he heard the shots. When we got around to the current politics of the campus, he let out a long sigh.

"It's different," he said. "Most of the students today are like the adults who were against the students then. I'm not sure what it all means. If you use labels, you'd say the students are more conservative. But that doesn't describe it. They may be in favor of Reagan, but not in favor of Reaganism. You'd find they generally disagree with the Republican platform. They're conservative on economics. But most are for the Equal Rights Amendment and are very progressive about the quality of life. They're opposed to toxic waste and nuclear power. Symbolically they understand Reagan. He has a magnetism that could be likened to Michael Jackson."

Fishel opened a file drawer and pulled out student essays that had been written in the days after the four were shot dead at Taylor Hill. One student wrote that he was preparing for years of revolution, which Fishel said seemed a likely prospect.

"It makes little difference to die here or in Asia," one student wrote.

But some writers said they wished more students had been shot, and that the dead and wounded deserved what they got. I wasn't surprised. The Kent State campus had always reflected the values of the types of families that a majority of students came from—working class and White. Growing up not that far away, knowing a lot of people who went to Kent State, I understood the culture: most of the kids were fundamentally conservative. They were clones of their parents.

"I have trouble every time I read them," Fishel said.

After I left his office, the rain was still falling. I returned to the pagoda. No one was there. A nearby church's bells rung, playing a rendition of "God Bless America."

Down in the parking lot, student newspaper editor Jim Shimko was searching for something in the wet blacktop. He said small peace symbols had been painted where each of the four bodies fell.

"They're gone. That's really wild," he said. "The school has tried to forget for years. There's never been a real memorial built. They put a gymnasium over part of the site. Planted trees in the firing line. No one wants to talk about it. No one seems to care."

If you were a child of the 1960s, hearing the cynical conservativism of Brian and Tony and Curt was shocking in 1984—that and the fact that those students knew little, if anything, about a violent and shape-shifting event that had happened on their campus. During a lunchtime conversation I had in Chicago with author Studs Terkel in the 1980s, he lamented that we were a "country with no memory." But more than this, in 1984, any sense of the commonweal was evaporating by the day. It was all about money. All about "me." That afternoon at Kent State was a microcosm of what would be seen in the coming years. For the children of the 1960s, especially their offspring and grandchildren, the focus became identity politics. Instead of organizing collectively as was seen in the 1930s, the left counterparts of this era focus on various silos of identity, and many shun politics. While the Proud Boys are running for local offices, left activists prefer to remain out in the street shouting through a bullhorn. As was famously written by my colleague, the late Todd Gitlin, "While the right has been busy taking the White House, the left has been marching on the English department." The observation appeared in his 1995 book appropriately named *The Twilight of Common Dreams*.

And "all about me" for some of those who eschew identity, their mission is money. "Greed is good" is the famous line from Oliver Stone's 1987 film *Wall Street*. The movie was made, Stone said, "as a morality tale." The villain was named Gordon Gekko, after an Asian lizard, and was played by Michael Douglas. But instead of being repelled by Gekko's greed, corruption, and avarice, a legion of young people saw Douglas's oily character as heroic and were drawn to work on Wall Street.

Gekko was America's future. In an interview, Stone said he was inspired to create Gekko based on a composite of several power-hungry people, among them Ivan Boesky, Carl Icahn, and—in unwitting prescience—Donald Trump.

# PART THREE

## War and Poverty

# Escape from El Salvador

On the mornings of January 30 and 31, 1986, Francisco Nieto-Nunez and his wife, Sandra Huezo Velasquez de Calderon, entered the United States district court building on West Congress Street in Tucson, Arizona. They'd been arrested in 1985 on charges of illegal immigration by federal agents in New Jersey. The agents had been watching them since their arrival in the United States the prior year after fleeing death squads in El Salvador. That surveillance was part of a much broader investigation into the Sanctuary movement, a loose-knit coalition of 150 American churches of all denominations that publicly declared they would smuggle and house high-risk refugees.

In the wake of the civil war in El Salvador that began in 1979, over forty thousand noncombatants were killed, many by right-wing death squads made up of police and government soldiers. The Sanctuary movement was cofounded in 1981 by Jim Corbett, a Quaker, and Presbyterian minister John Fife. In December 1983, the US Immigration and Naturalization Service and the FBI began a joint investigation called Operation Sojourner. It lasted until the following October, and it resulted in the indictments of Sanctuary movement leaders. Eleven of them were now on trial, with sixty-seven felony counts against them; they faced years in prison.

The movement had smuggled Francisco and Sandra, both thirty-two and the parents of three children. Now they were hostile witnesses, compelled to testify. Francisco took the stand the first day. But he wouldn't be able to talk about how he had been brutally tortured. At the start of the trial, United States district judge Earl H. Carroll ruled favorably on motions by US attorney Donald M. Reno to prohibit testimony about torture suffered by those smuggled by the defendants. Nor could they cite international law and the US Refugee Act of 1980, which the defendants said made their actions legal.

Francisco was a medical student, and he had been treating old women and children in refugee camps; in the eyes of the government, this made him a leftist, thus he was sent to prison and repeatedly subjected to torture. When Reno examined Francisco on the stand in court, he asked about the journey north with Sandra and their children. The basis for the questioning was rooted in knowledge from earlier depositions. (Those depositions remain sealed over three decades later, so we can't know exactly the genesis of the information that was used by both sides.)

Francisco told the court how the family had been flown from El Salvador to Mexico City. There he met Jim Corbett and two other men, Americans, both twenty-seven. The family was then flown to Ciudad Obregón, where they once again met those two men and another Sanctuary volunteer. Reno knew exactly what had happened in Mexico because, as Corbett would later learn, the volunteer was an undercover US agent. Not spoken in court: this volunteer was supposed to be the smuggler. Corbett wasn't present—he was back in Tucson.

This volunteer suddenly became "incapable," and the two young Americans took over and smuggled the family north through roadless desert. Those young men couldn't be indicted for what happened in Mexico—the US Justice Department didn't have jurisdiction there. Thus Reno didn't bother to focus on that, though he knew exactly the actions of those men.

Reno grilled Francisco about the border crossing. One defendant, Peggy Hutchinson, a lay Methodist, had met the family at a safe house in Agua Prieta, Mexico; she and another woman and one of the young smugglers brought the family across the frontier in July 1984.

The next day, Friday, Sandra was put on the stand. She also was examined about those two twenty-seven-year-old smugglers. Not spoken in court: she liked the men. They'd discovered a route around a dangerous roadblock. Salvadoran refugees, if caught at roadblocks, suffered gravely. All women were raped. Men had electric cattle prods taken to their testicles.

In his cross-examination, the defense attorney asked Sandra about the journey north, in particular when she and the others entered the United States.

"Was Peggy Hutchinson with you at the moment that you crossed the fence?"

"I went together with the reporter. He helped me to cross over."

"Yes. And tell the jury actually who held up the hole in the fence when you went through."

"The reporter."

Gasps came from members of the press seated in the courtroom. That's because those two twenty-seven-year-old smugglers happened to be me and Michael Williamson. I wasn't in the courtroom but learned about the gasps because, while taking time off from the newspaper and working in Alabama on a book about former sharecroppers, I checked my voicemail and found two messages, one from the Associated Press and the other from the *Arizona Daily Star*. I phoned both back. The reporters wanted me to comment on Sandra's testimony. Had I lifted the barbed wire fence when her shirt got stuck on it?

"It wasn't me," I told them. The reporter Sandra had referred to in court was Michael; I hadn't been present for the crossing. The family, Michael, Peggy Hutchinson, and another woman had gone separately from me. I'd been dropped off at the Border Patrol station because of the fear that too many people walking in the desert would increase the risk.

The AP man asked, "Did Michael then say, as Francisco testified on Thursday, 'Welcome to American democracy?'" I had no idea what Michael might have said, and Michael was unavailable. He was out of the country, on contract for *US News & World Report*, to cover the Philippine election in one week, on February 7.

My alleged criminal activity didn't happen in America, so the United States Department of Justice in theory couldn't do anything to me. Michael's alleged crime happened in the United States. In essence—or actuality—his lifting that strand of barbed wire made Michael an unindicted coconspirator.

On May 4, 1981, Jim Dudley stopped to pick up a hitchhiker in Arizona. En route to Tucson on Interstate 19, fifteen miles north of the border, there was a roadblock set up by the US Border Patrol. Agents arrested the hitchhiker, a Salvadoran man who had just entered the country illegally. Dudley, who had nearly been arrested himself, was shaken by the incident.

That evening, Dudley went to the modest home of two fellow Quakers, Jim and Pat Corbett, who lived in north-central Tucson. He shared what had happened, and this led Jim to try to locate where the Salvadoran man was being detained. When he found him, Jim rushed to fill out federal form G-28, which would guarantee the detainee a hearing before a judge. But the US Immigration and Naturalization Service was faster—they had already expedited that man's deportation by the time Jim came back with the form.

Jim discovered that four-hundred-square-foot cells at the INS detention center were holding as many as forty men each. Refugees told him stories about what had happened to them in El Salvador, of torture and rape, and about their perilous journey north. Jim and Pat took a loan out on a trailer they owned and posted bail for some refugees. Jim had never before thought much about Central America or the migrants who were crossing the border. Now he was deeply troubled. On May 12, 1981, he penned a letter to his Quaker community about the need for active resistance. In part, it said:

Speaking only for myself, I can see that if Central American refugees' rights to political asylum are decisively rejected by the U.S. government or if the U.S. legal system insists on ransom that exceeds our ability to pay, active resistance will be the only alternative to abandoning the refugees to their fate. The creation of a network of actively concerned, mutually supportive people in the U.S. and Mexico may be the best preparation for an adequate response. A network? Quakers will know what I mean.

That hint at history dates to the eighteenth and nineteenth centuries. Quakers had long opposed slavery, and members were involved in the underground railroad, smuggling slaves north via a series of safe houses. A network. Jim soon visited priests in Mexico to establish safe houses, and he began pioneering ways to get refugees across the border. He studied topographic maps to figure ways to outmaneuver the US Border Patrol. He became a pro bono coyote, guiding refugees to holes in the fence. He traveled deeper into Mexico, to the southern state of Chiapas, to explore routes.

His backstory made him both likely and unlikely for this dangerous undertaking. Jim was born in Wyoming in 1933. He had a mix of European and Native American heritage—he was part Blackfoot. His parents were professionals, but he spent a lot of his youth on a ranch, as long as six months at a time, herding sheep. He went to college, and then he was awarded a scholarship to study philosophy at Harvard; he graduated with a master's degree in 1955. He was a librarian at Chico State University, and he was a teacher. But he returned to his passion for a rural existence. He raised livestock near Tucson. He studied bees and goats. He called himself a "pagan redneck."

He wasn't religious until the early 1960s, when he became a Quaker. Yet he didn't consider himself political. He had to retire early because of worsening rheumatoid arthritis. His feet became twisted, and his toes splayed sideways; he had to cut holes in tennis shoes to make them fit. Despite the crippling effects of the disease, he herded goats. In the 1970s, he became involved in a goat-milking cooperative. He was a fluent Spanish speaker, and he undertook a three-year exchange program with seminomadic goat herders in the Mexican state of Baja California Sur. From this experience, in 1979, he wrote a two-part article about the region's goat cheese economy for *The Dairy Goat Journal.*

His fingers were also afflicted, which made it difficult for him to type; he did so very deliberately. In one passage, he writes:

> There is another kind of economic development that is an aspect of community growth rather than political subjugation or techno-cratic alienation. Most of the time, most of us love life; we want to meet and know others—other people, animals, plants, lands—and, regardless of mixed motives, we care about those we come to know. Meeting, knowing, and caring, we cultivate symbiotic bonds that enhance the harmony, diversity, and beauty of life on earth.

This story is not about the civil war in El Salvador. Michael and I documented it for two weeks, traveling all over the country. We were in some tough situations, but there's no need to focus on those details. One learns rapidly after covering one war that by the time one has witnessed the second, all wars are the same—and one imagines this is true at any point in history. The weapons and uniforms change, but that's about it.

This story begins after those weeks, in the middle of a bridge over the Rio Suchiate, which marks the border between Mexico and Gua-temala. The newspaper's booking agent at Weinstock's World Travel Bureau thought it was a joke when I said that we only needed one-way airline tickets to El Salvador, because we were going to walk, bus, boat, and drive back home. She was still laughing when I hung up the phone.

I now recalled her laughter. We were off to an ominous start of the journey north once we reached the Mexican border. What would happen in the coming week in Mexico, where there was in theory no war, was far more terrifying in numerous ways than anything we expe-rienced in El Salvador.

After we get off the bus that had taken us north from Guatemala City that morning, the border agents on the bridge, both exiting Guatemala and entering Mexico, act oddly as they check our identification. When the Mexican authorities stamp our passports, the stamp says Chiapas, not Mexico. Chiapas, while a state of Mexico, operates as if it's a separate Central American nation.

We rent a hotel room in Ciudad Hidalgo, where we are scheduled to meet Jim Corbett, who was flying into the nearby city of Tapachula the next day. Michael wants pictures of the coyotes ferrying Salvadorans across the river on rafts, so after renting a car, we drive back to the bridge and park nearby. We walk a half-mile to the Guatemalan checkpoint, where we're told we need a new visa to enter the country. We reenter Mexico and go to a station in Ciudad Hidalgo that issues visas. This outpost has a roof but no walls. Chickens run in and out as the official, seated at a worn desk beneath a slow-moving ceiling fan, uses a Royal typewriter to create new visas.

Then we once again go through the Mexican checkpoint—the border agent laughs. When we get to the Guatemalan border booth, the guard tells us the new visa is no good and we cannot reenter; we have to wait three days. Something about a law to prevent drug running. We turn back. Midway, Michael takes pictures of smugglers, who give us the finger and yell that we can go *chinga* ourselves and our mothers in various ways. At the Mexican checkpoint, the man who had laughed at us earlier now also tells us we have to wait three days to reenter Mexico. "*¿Dormir aquí?*" I ask incredulously in my halting Spanish, meaning, "Sleep here [on the bridge]?"

"*Sí,*" the man says. He is no longer smiling.

"*¿Hay algo que pueda hacer?*" I say. ("Is there anything I can do?") This is the polite way one suggests *mordida*, "the bite"—a payoff—to have an official such as a cop or border agent ignore the rules. The answer is a firm no, which is when we realize that something much bigger is going on, and that we are in trouble.

Because I'm marginally better at Spanish, I am the one who asks to speak to the *jefe* in the office. The boss smiles oddly as he tells me there is nothing he can do. Despite this being my first international reporting assignment, some instinct kicks in. After I call myself "*estúpido, estúpido*" for not knowing the law about how to get us freed, the *jefe* for some reason brings up the US State Department. I don't fully understand why—the Spanish is too fast—but I latch on to this. With total bluster and bluff, I tell him that US officials are expecting a call from us. In terrible Spanish, I say, "*¿Por favor, puedo usar el teléfono?*" I want to call the U.S embassy. But no call will be necessary. The border official suddenly relents and allows us to pass back into Mexico.

The next morning, we are still asleep when Jim knocks on the door of our $9.07-a-night room at the Hotel San Francisco in Tapachula. He informs us that a few weeks earlier, Mexican immigration officials shot a Salvadoran refugee dead in a volley of gunfire. That refugee had been circumventing the Huixtla roadblock using a jungle trail Jim had pioneered. Jim has returned to explore a new route around that roadblock, just north of us. That is our mission for today. We tell him about our evening being stuck on the bridge over the Rio Suchiate, and I relate my part in getting us out of the jam.

Jim suggests an early lunch. We go to a nearby restaurant and pick an outside table not visible from the street, far from other diners. We order chicken soup. Jim also orders a large plate of cut papaya, which promptly arrives at the table. When the soups show up, I get a leg in my bowl. Jim has two wings. Michael's bowl has solely two skin-and-bone chicken feet; claws emerge from the broth. Michael picks up one of the claws and stares at it.

Jim believes the border guards knew about us in advance. Our presence—and his—are known. There is a secret death warrant on him, issued by the governor of Chiapas. On his last visit to Tapachula, a priest told Jim the police acting on those orders had a plan to kill him. He fled. This is his first time back in one year.

I ask: "Is this not dangerous?" Meaning for him and, by extension, us.

"Yes," Jim says.

He has many approaches to remaining safe. "You never stay more than a few days. You leave before they see a pattern. You leave before they put together what is going on. You never sleep in the same place twice. He says they probably will not shoot us. They can't explain that away. Our car will be forced off the road, the vehicle flying over a cliff or submerged in a river. Shit happens.

"This is a hard place to document things. You start digging and you blow it; you'll have an 'accident.' You want to ask the heavy questions about two hours before your plane leaves." Jim plays two cards. Here in Tapachula, where tourists never visit, when he's questioned, he points to his deformed feet. Citing health reasons, he says he comes for the weather; it is cheaper to stay here.

"You've got to be exposed to do a job like this. I play the retired arthritic to the hilt." The other card: Americans are in essence modern-day Romans. Being White and American in class-oriented Mexico means you must be someone of status. And in Chiapas, perhaps you're a CIA agent. As in the time of the Romans, who were given passage based on fear and class privilege, it allows for a certain freedom in mobility. Jim doesn't like this cultural imperialism, but it's a reality that he takes advantage of.

Being Romans, he says, probably worked for us on the bridge. We are reassured by his confidence. Then Jim says: "Let's hope we don't get caught."

We travel northwest toward the sea, on roads bisecting savannas for grazing cattle and past occasional banana plantations. We are in the lowlands, a region known as Soconusco, a narrow band of coastal plain between the Pacific and the Sierra Madre de Chiapas. I drive, keeping an eye on the rearview mirror; the road remains empty. Jim relates the slim details about what happened a few weeks earlier at the Huixtla roadblock. He says twelve Salvadorans were walking through the jungle when police or soldiers opened fire, killing one and wounding an unknown number of the others.

"It looks like they wanted to send a message. There was a panic reaction in the system not to send people through." Jim heard about the shooting from one of the Salvadorans who made it to the United States. Other details came from a member of the underground railroad in Chiapas.

We are now in a jungle and reach a dead end. There's a dock and the dark, still waters of a mangrove swamp. A boatman is waiting. We get in the motorboat with two locals who sit in front, a middle-aged indigenous couple who lean on a stack of dozens of flattened brand-new cardboard boxes that appear destined to be filled with fruit grown on their remote farm. As soon as we board, the man at the engine's throttle wends the boat through the mangrove-flanked channel, which is barely wider than the craft. The helmsman wears a gleaming white shirt and cream-colored cowboy hat. The boat is smaller than the one Humphrey Bogart pilots in *The African Queen*, but equally shaky and ancient. Tropical birds scream from the tangle of mangrove branches just feet from our faces, and there's a roar of insects. The shaded water appears nearly black. Jim, seated in the center, doesn't speak. His limp hands are crossed on his lap.

We motor for hours as the channel widens to a broad estuary. There are a few houses on stilts where the boat gets docked. A short walk brings us to a white beach that vanishes into the northern distance. It's pristine wilderness. Jim walks to the edge of the heavy surf, the wind blowing his slightly graying hair. He likes what he sees. Refugees can walk the beach to a place where there's a road. It's dozens of miles out of the way, but a safe route to give wide berth to Huixtla and the town of Escuintla. The boat costs four dollars for a full day's rental.

We sleep in a different hotel each night we are on the Soconusco plain. The bill for the first hotel is three dollars total for all three of us. The tiny beds smell of mold, and mosquitoes invade en masse through poorly screened windows. We have nets to cover us but fear dengue fever carried by the insects.

The next day, Michael drives us north. Jim urges caution with the big rigs that pass us at high speed on the narrow, winding roads. In the previous year, five nuns and a priest who were helping refugees were killed in "accidents," their cars run off the road by big trucks. No investigations were conducted. We are not exactly incognito: three White guys, and Jim has a distinctive gray goatee and thick eyeglasses, the face of a weathered rancher.

We come to a place where Jim wants to investigate a trail through the jungle—another alternate way around the Huixtla roadblock. Even with deformed feet, he walks faster than we can keep up. How can Jim not be in pain? Many weeks earlier, when we were getting to know him and his wife, Pat, in Tucson, there was a dinner party; a friend of his confided in a whisper that Jim was in constant pain but somehow rose above it. Jim is fifty but moves like a man half his age.

We end the evening pulling into the village of Puerto Madero, thirty kilometers north of the Guatemalan frontier. The main business of the town has long been shark fishing: men venture out to sea in twenty-seven-foot skiffs to hunt the creatures. The work is dangerous and the pay low. We are looking for two or three brothels that Jim saw one year earlier. There are not enough men in town to patronize them, and Jim has suspicions that he wants to investigate. But the establishments are gone. We are told that the *zona de tolerancia*, the red-light district, has been moved. Jim is aghast when we find the new *zona*: it's at the edge of town, and it has increased nearly sixfold, to about one dozen brothels. "This is something you would find in Tijuana," he says as we exit the car just outside the district. "How can this area support this?" The answer, as we will find out, is that it cannot.

We walk to the *zona* as oncoming headlights blind us on the dusty streets. Residents seated in doorways study us with suspicious eyes. "*Nunca vemos gabachos por aquí*, a woman says icily, and without prompt. ("We never see White Americans around here.")

We enter one of the brothels.

Donna Summer's "Bad Girls," her song about the world's oldest profession, blasts from a jukebox: "You ask yourself who they are." We didn't have to ask. Most of the women are distinctly *Salvadoreñas*; the others look Guatemalan, though the women of Chiapas have the same indigenous features. No men are present. The women bump and grind on the dirt floor. The irony of the song is lost on them. None speak English.

The women are curious about us. We don't fit in. When we ask them who they are and where they are from, they retreat. We order half-size Coronas. We squeeze lime wedges into the necks. Mosquitoes swarm through doorless entryways. The air is thick and tropical. Hands are kept busy murdering mosquitoes. We drink many pony Coronas, sweating them out fast as we consume them.

Finally, one woman approaches. She's nervous. "*Los hombres siempre vienen buscandos hermanas,*" she says. ("Men always come through looking for their sisters.") By this she means Salvadoran men, seeking their vanished *hermanas*. There's a world of pain and terror in that single sentence: I imagine men trying to save a woman like Elisia, whom we met in El Salvador, but I put Elisia out of my mind to focus on what the woman is telling us. She is tense. She talks in a low voice and says some of the women are sent here by *la migra*, Mexican immigration. She's revealed enough. Too much. She falls silent.

When she drifts away, Jim tells us that there were no brothels here before 1980. "They started the brothels when most of the refugees started moving north." He says we are in one of a series of holding sites for women "owned" by Mexican mob bosses—*migra* officials sell captured *Salvadoreñas* to them. Jim believes they are being kept here until they're shipped north to other states of Mexico. Some, if not all, of the women we are looking at are slaves. He's heard this from several women helped by Sanctuary.

The story of one: she was captured by *migra* agents at a bus station. They told her she was valuable—a brothel owner would pay them $100 for her. The agents were smug, bragging about this fact to her because they operate with impunity. (Every woman I interviewed who had been captured by agents said they were raped.) Jim says the woman pleaded with the agents to let her go to the bathroom. Inside, she cut her hair short, changed clothes, and applied makeup. She walked out past the *migra* officers, who didn't recognize her.

Local papers recently ran a story about a gun battle between a federal official and local police at a brothel in the nearby city of Cacahuatan, not far from Tapachula, in an apparent fight over control of the Central American sex worker slave trade.

We return to the *zona de tolerancia* in the following days, and after visiting most of the dozen brothels, we never see more than twenty men total. There is one brothel we have not stepped foot in. We save that place, where we plan to ask the toughest questions, for the final afternoon in Chiapas, hours before we are to board a jetliner in Tapachula to fly to the Distrito Federal, or D. F. (pronounced "dey eff-ay")—Mexico City. There is a holding camp for women at the end of a road that we have avoided because it is the biggest. It must be run by someone powerful. An armed guard is at the entrance. As we get out of the car, parked outside of the gate, I ask: "Isn't this dangerous?"

"Yes," Jim says.

But we are Romans. Or CIA. *Act like we own the place.* We walk into the camp, past the guard, who doesn't know what to make of us. We don't look back. Naked *Salvadoreñas* who have just showered stand in doorways. Other women, topless, wash clothes in a big zinc tub set on the muddy ground. There is a bar at the far end; the owners of the camp make what money they can on these women while they hold them for transport north, Jim surmises.

We enter the capacious bar, with over a dozen widely spaced tables. We are the sole patrons. Beatriz, an attractive woman probably no more than twenty-three, takes our order—half-size Coronas. She assumes we are here for something else. We drink three rounds. After bringing a fourth order, Beatriz, with a shock of dark black hair falling over her brows, looks at me with her huge dark eyes and coos, "*Muy guapo. Muy guapo.*" ("Very handsome.") She touches my arm, then hugs me. We inform her that we are here for other reasons. Her wide eyes narrow.

She tells us she is Guatemalan and was a nurse before she tried to go north to the United States. Her dream is to eventually get to *el norte*. But she is suspicious and won't reveal how she ended up stuck here. She won't talk about the owner of this camp. She admits she is not like some of the Salvadorans—she has more agency. At the same time, she contradicts herself and says the women are not allowed to leave the boundaries of the camp, or they will be immediately arrested by local police or federal *migra*. She is nervous and sad.

Jim pulls a sheet of paper. In Spanish it tells about the Sanctuary movement and the underground railroad. She studies it. She is clearly smart, and she reads fast. Jim says he can help her escape. Now she is especially wary. Nothing can be good about our presence; I see it in her eyes.

"You can leave," Jim tells Beatriz. "I'll help you." She gets up and exits the bar. I stand to watch her go to a bamboo hut that must be her quarters. A lot of eyes outside the bar are on the door and me standing in it. I'm a bit drunk but sober enough to feel the bad vibes. Jim and Michael have come to the same conclusion. We have remained too long. As we walk out of the camp, past Beatriz's hut with its closed door, Jim says, "She's wondering what the angle is. She doesn't trust me. In her world, nobody helps you for nothing."

We stride past the guard. As we drive off, Jim is despondent: "I wish I could help them."

I had the window seat. As the Aeromexico jetliner arced on ascent over the Pacific Ocean, I looked straight down at the mangrove-flanked lagoon and the desolate beach where we'd stood days earlier. From some six or eight thousand feet, I had a view north up that empty coast. Then we were in clouds. I looked over at Michael and Jim. Their eyes were closed. I couldn't close mine. D. F. scared me. Something very bad had occurred to Elisia in D. F. about ten days earlier. I'd heard about it in a phone call to Sacramento when Michael and I were in Guatemala City. I told myself this: Elisia was going to do what she was going to do regardless of our presence. But I also told myself that if I had not gone to El Salvador to meet her, I would be ignorant of her suffering and fate—ergo, in theory, a happier man.

We must return to motive. One learns to discern motive early in a journalism career, as I did on the police beat, if one is to be successful. By definition, being a journalist means being a student of motive. Every subject has a reason for talking; otherwise they avoid the journalist. The most common motive is vanity or narcissism. Other reasons: they can't afford a shrink, and we are a free substitute; they are lonely, and we listen; they want revenge on a boss or an institution, and we are the conduit for payback; they might get better treatment from the health care or legal system if we are documenting their case, because of the presence of our pens, recorders, and cameras; we can help them find a missing something or someone; they want to use us to advance their political, business, or artistic career. The reasons are many. The journalist identifies motive and plays into it. It's a subconscious and instinctual reality of what we do. It's not transactional. It's life.

While we become adept at identifying motive in others, it's much more difficult to look in the mirror to determine our own. I'd thought a lot about my motive for pursuing this story during those nights in the cheap, mosquito-infested hotels of the Soconusco plain. I wasn't certain of my motive for flying one-way to El Salvador, and this could be for two reasons: one, I was deep in the middle of the story, and the middle of anything is never a good place to figure something out; and two, I was young. Only six years had passed since I was shooting high school sports and developing Kodak Tri-X 400 ASA film on Friday nights at the newspaper in Medina, Ohio.

*I could still be doing that,* I thought. I would be safe. I would not have the weight of knowing the terrible stories I was hearing. I wouldn't know about Elisia. But that sheltered life would be a soul-crushing death. Did I want my journalism to have an impact and change the world? Yes. Would I have liked to win a Pulitzer Prize? Yes. Did I desire to move up to a larger newspaper? Yes. Was I keenly interested in the social justice aspects and the geopolitics of the United States' long intervention in Central America, the legacy of Winfield Scott, the conquest of Aztlán, the fact that 46,041 noncombatants had been killed in El Salvador since 1979, many of them by death squad members who by day were soldiers and officers in a government that the US gave half a billion dollars annually to prop up? *Yes. Yes. Yes.*

But none of these reasons even in combination truly explains my motive for this and other stories that I pursued in these years. The path to understanding didn't begin until the mid-aughts, when I dated a poet. I told her about what Tom Wolfe called his "theory of everything," his belief that people are motivated by status. This affected his approach to his books. I told the poet that my theory was based on class. And she quickly responded, "No. Your theory of everything has to do with dislocation." It was the common thread in my work, she said.

She was correct. But that wasn't quite it. I can see the answer only now, decades later. A driving force in my work is my father's damage from a traumatic brain injury in war, and the resulting impact his rage had on me and the rest of us in the family. It wasn't apparent at the time I was living it. I was in the middle of the story. It wasn't clear until my parents were both gone. In documenting the pain of others, I was dealing with my own. It could be as "simple" as this.

I cannot speak for Michael and what his motives were, but based on what I know about his past, I suspect it's the same for him—and it's probably why we kept teaming up on these kinds of assignments. We were drawn to the same place in the inferno. As for Jim, I know only of his physical pain, which he never complained about, and his abiding Quaker faith.

Back in 1984, I was certain of only one person's motive: that of the new top editor, who had arrived that spring. The newspaper was becoming increasingly corporate, and he'd been brought on as a catalyst for this transformation. It must be remembered that newspapers in this era typically had 30 percent profit margins; our small chain had "only" about 20 percent. For comparison, grocery stores were pleased with 3 percent net.

All of the top editors at the *Bee* suddenly became "executives" after 1984. The most senior of them were men, and all but one of them began wearing suspenders, which were favored by the big new editor. There was potential for more profit, and it was rooted in a new mindset at the paper, which instituted "management by objective." These executives lunched apart from us in a new executive dining room.

One sure sign of success for the new editor would be for the newsroom to quickly win a Pulitzer Prize on his watch. Or two or three. The last time the paper had won one was in 1935. He made no secret about this desire. In fact, he called Michael into his office, and as Michael recalls it, the editor said, "As you may or may not know,

I've dug through the clips, and I know who's who in this newsroom. I want to win a Pulitzer, and I want to win one soon as possible"—the implication being that Michael could be a vehicle to achieve this goal.

Michael and I were savvy enough about newsroom politics to exploit the new editor's desire. We were hungry, much hungrier than a decisive majority of the staff, many of whom resented us for wanting more than they had with their careers, writing or editing inverted pyramid stories that wrapped in all five Ws by five or six o'clock each day, printing their photos and attaching cutlines by the same deadline. There was plenty of room for all of us—those who wanted to lead normal lives, and those of us who desired more. I was friends with some of those "normal" people. I respected their work. Most Sacramento residents are content to sit back and watch their children, lawns, and home equity grow. It was and is not a place one goes to remain very long if they aspire to bigger things—unless they are politicians. We were not judgmental of those colleagues, but we were judged. A lot of animosity was aimed at us from certain quarters. No matter. Michael and I saw an opening to engage in the kind of work that we'd always wanted to do. We were the flavor of the moment, and we had to act on it. After a bit of research, we proposed the El Salvador story, and the new editor instantly greenlit it. We wouldn't have been sent to Central America before his arrival, and maybe we wouldn't get to do this kind of story in two years—a fear that proved all too prescient.

I began researching the El Salvador project within days of the new editor showing up, connecting with Georgia Lyga, director of the social justice ministry for the Sacramento Catholic Diocese and a member of an interdenominational coalition of religious people helping immigrants in Sacramento. We talked for the first time in a church office.

Georgia was a former Maryknoll Sister who'd spent her youth in Chile and then worked to support Cesar Chavez's United Farm Workers in the Central Valley in the 1970s. Her church was helping a Salvadoran family—Oscar and Teresa Martinez, who'd come to the United States in 1982. Georgia's coalition of church workers had brought the family to Sacramento that March 1984. The couple lived in a rented house with their five children, along with Oscar's brother and his six kids.

We soon met. Oscar and Teresa recounted many horrors in their village, which soldiers called "Little Cuba." Oscar had been assisting a priest in building homes; death squads threatened him, and the priest fled. The couple's daughter, now thirteen, had witnessed her teacher being raped and killed because of supposedly being a communist. Teresa told me that her best friend from childhood, Elisia, was in hiding from the death squads that were hunting for her. Elisia was saving money and preparing to come north with Teresa's nephews, Carlos and Juan. She was going to leave El Salvador whether or not we interviewed and photographed her. We weren't going to influence the story. Or would we?

By the journalists' code of objectivity, we weren't supposed to get involved. Sure, we could document the stories of her and the nephews and then wish them luck as we waved goodbye, using them for what we needed to make our story and leaving them to fate. But objectivity, when someone could die? This wasn't just about journalistic ethics; there was a question of morality.

To stay on this side of both the ethical and moral lines would mean remaining north of the border, meeting refugees after they arrived. But that journalism would be missing veracity. This wasn't our first lesson in the messiness of this kind of documentary journalism—but it was certainly the biggest to date. We couldn't talk with our editors about any of this, because we couldn't trust their facile answers. They weren't living it. So Michael and I made an executive decision: if possible, we had to at least try to connect Elisia and the nephews with some resources.

We prepared as much as possible. We soon traveled to Tucson, spent a few weeks hanging with Jim Corbett and John Fife, the pastor of Southside Presbyterian Church, and others. We went on one smuggling run in northern Mexico, and amid this, we told Sanctuary members about Elisia; if we did end up meeting with her, the underground would smuggle her through Mexico. Besides getting to know key people in Tucson, we visited a refugee help center, the Casa Oscar

Romero, in Texas. The center was named after Salvadoran Catholic Bishop Oscar Romero, who was shot dead by right-wing assassins in 1980 in the middle of his officiating a mass.

By the time we flew to San Salvador, we'd been given some one dozen contacts for movement members. But we were met with extreme reticence. One by one, they fell through. These contacts were being watched. "I don't smuggle anyone," one person told us. "We just counsel them." In one meeting, a Lutheran churchwoman noticed a man sitting in a chair watching us, hand on his chin. We shook him, and once out of his sight, the woman began sobbing. It was always like this, she said—she was always being observed in this manner. All church workers had memories of the four US Catholic missionaries who were raped and killed in 1980 by members of the National Guard of El Salvador; three of them were Maryknoll Sisters.

Salvadoran government agents also repeatedly let us know we were being watched. One incident: we'd talked with our editor the night before we were to go to another part of the country. Minutes later the phone rang. It was the front desk. "So you will be checking out in the morning. Do you want to take care of your bill tonight?"

Amid this justifiable paranoia and rejection, we came to the last name on our list, a Mennonite in his early twenties. We met him at a Bonanza steakhouse. Several high-ranking Salvadoran military officers were also dining there, and a phalanx of men with raised guns stopped anyone who tried to enter the restroom. It wasn't the most conducive place for clandestine discussion. My contact whispered, "We've had people killed down here. It's too risky at this point." His answer: "No. I can't help." We left, dejected.

The next morning the Mennonite called our hotel room; after a night of sleep, he had changed his mind. When he met up with us, he told us: "That's why I am here. Of course I will help." The young bearded man, who looked like what years later would be called a hipster, drove us in his beat-up Volkswagen to the city of Santa Ana. The meeting had been arranged to take place in a crowded public plaza; we'd use a code word that we'd set up with the Martinezes in Sacramento. We were the only White guys in sight. A man approached.

He whispered: "Sacramento?" It was Carlos, one of the nephews. Moments later, Elisia walked up, riven with fear, trembling. Carlos told us it was too dangerous to talk there. We arranged a meeting in another public place. But when we went there, Elisia's fear morphed into sheer terror. She blurted that she had never heard of the village the government called Little Cuba. She ran off into the crowd.

Elisia, Carlos, and Juan came north on their own. Over a week later, in a phone call to the Martinez family from Guatemala City, I heard what had happened. The trio had wanted to avoid the dangerous land journey, so they took a TACA airlines flight to D. F. They had tourist visas, but Mexican immigration authorities were suspicious. Elisia had only one tiny bag. If they were tourists, why didn't they have luggage? They were imprisoned. Elisia was raped and beaten so viciously that she couldn't walk. Carlos and Juan were also beaten. All three were bused to the Guatemalan border. The nephews left Elisia there; they were now traveling north without her. After one phone call from the nephews, the Martinezes had not heard from any of them in days. This is what I knew as the jetliner began its descent for landing at the Aeropuerto Internacional de la Ciudad de México.

It's just after midnight. We leave the Hotel Edison to walk to Jim's favorite greasy spoon restaurant when he's in D. F. Jim is like us—he relishes the night hours. He tells us his contacts here have grown more cautious in the past few weeks. "The Mexican government is really cracking down," he says. There is new pressure at the airport—Elisia and the nephews were victims of this pressure. Church leaders fear arrest and that the Quaker-run safe houses will be closed down. For security reasons, even Jim doesn't know the location of these safe houses.

Jim points out something very odd. The closer the Salvadoran refugees get to the US border, the more Mexican officials now try to stop them. Logic would dictate that they would be happy that the Salvadorans were exiting their nation. What was the motive for not letting them enter the United States? Jim says the US State Department has ordered the Mexican government to halt the flow. (Weeks later I call the State Department, and I am told they will neither confirm nor deny this.)

When we return to the Hotel Edison, two men stand in an open doorway at the far end of an exterior walkway, about twenty-five feet from our rooms. Their arms are crossed, and they give us the stink eye. They smell of cop. Jim says it's always like this. Federal agents watch him each time he visits. There's nothing secret about it. Those two cops will tail Jim in the coming days; he has to lose them each time.

The days in D. F. are like living in a spy novel. Jim starts each morning by calling a number and leaving a message. Another man calls back and tells Jim to meet at Matthew's, Luke's, or Mark's—code names for restaurants. Jim must carry that day's copy of the newspaper *Unomásuno* under his right arm. The contact wears a Band-Aid over his left eye. They exchange code words. It gets complicated, Jim tells Michael and me one night over a plate of sliced papaya, as we drink beer. Often he forgets his own codes.

We are waiting for a high-risk family to smuggle. Their exit is being arranged in San Salvador. There are several afternoons when nothing happens. Michael and I visit a museum housing murals and paintings by José Clemente Orozco, depicting suffering and a dark view of the Mexican Revolution. One evening when Jim is out meeting contacts, I am on the bed in our room at the Hotel Edison, on the phone talking to Catherine in Sacramento. The bed begins violently rocking—an earthquake. It's no exaggeration to say it was like being on a small boat on a wavy lake. The earthquake lasts sixty seconds—an eternity. The walls ripple as if made of rubber, and the building creaks and makes strange grinding sounds. There is no fleeing, because there is no standing or walking. Finally the quake ceases.

One afternoon, we take part in the spy novel: We lose the two federal agents in a crowd and then go by taxi with Jim to meet Francisco Nieto-Nunez at a secret location—with Jim keeping an eye out the rear window to ensure we're not being followed. We hear Francisco's story of torture and horror at the hands of the death squads after he was arrested, including having his hands tied to his feet behind his back and then being hoisted with a rope. This was called the "little airplane"; sometimes a man stood on his back, and this man was called a "pilot." They threatened to kill their baby in front of him, and Sandra was raped by soldiers. Finally Sandra sold their house and bribed a judge, and the couple was given a deadline to leave the country, after which Francisco would be killed.

Jim gives Francisco instructions for the next part of the operation. He and Sandra, their two children (one a two-year-old toddler), and Francisco's brother will fly north to Ciudad Obregón, closer to the border, and Jim, Michael, and I will be waiting at the gate to greet them. We will act like we are old friends, and we will hug; with three White Americans joyously welcoming the family, *migra* won't question them.

We end up at the greasy spoon late that night. We eat papaya and drink many beers. We ask Jim how he copes with repeated stories of rape and torture; we are having emotional trouble with them. Jim does no better. He says he's heard stories like those Francisco told us that afternoon a hundred times. Each one is equally disturbing—he never grows used to them. We tell of our meeting in El Salvador with Carmen Campos, who, after protesting her husband's disappearance, had her right breast hacked off in front of her neighbors.

"There's a thread to the reign of terror," Jim says. "Perverse sexuality is a necessary theme. They use violence to keep people in line. By slowly murdering a man in front of a dozen friends, the government can control them better than if they are robots. You dominate a population psychologically. You don't need an army to subdue them. Something bad has happened to our society. I think Americans know enough now to know we're the torturers in this hemisphere. If you would transfer that knowledge to the 1940s, it would have brought about revulsion. Today, it prompts acceptance. People say it's dirty, but it's got to be done."

We flew from D. F. to Tucson. Jim had business come up there and had to remain in Arizona. Michael and I immediately drove south in a 1964 red panel wagon to Ciudad Obregón, some four hundred kilometers south of the border. We were with "George," who had never made a run with refugees through Mexico as a lead smuggler. Just north of Ciudad Obregón, we discovered a brand-new roadblock set up by federal Mexican authorities. It appeared to be part of the recent crackdown Jim had told us about.

It looked hairy, but we couldn't tell much in the dark. It wasn't like the smaller checkpoint at a place called Benjamin Hill, just north of Nogales, close to the border; Sanctuary smugglers often drove refugees through there without a problem. This new roadblock threw a major wrinkle into our plans. We went into a nearby restaurant, and George began falling apart; he was suddenly reticent, which freaked us out. It meant the lives of the family coming tomorrow—including the toddler—were in our hands. We had to take over.

None of the primal terror I felt in that moment and in the next two days would end up in the story I wrote for the newspaper. There was no room in standard journalism for what faced us. I had just read, for the first time, *Let Us Now Praise Famous Men*, written by James Agee and with photos by Walker Evans. Agee's words about lying being necessary for journalism were in my head:

> Journalism can within its own limits be "good" or "bad," "true" or "false," but it is not in the nature of journalism even to approach any less relative degree of truth. Again, journalism is not to be blamed for this, no more than a cow is to be blamed for not being a horse. The difference is…that few cows can have the delusion or even the desire to be horses…. The very blood and semen of journalism, on the contrary, is a broad and successful form of lying. Remove that form of lying and you no longer have journalism.

Michael and I went to the basement of the restaurant, where there was a pay phone across the hall from the men's bathroom. I called the big new editor to ask for guidance.

"Figure it out," he told me when I got through to the line in his glass office. "Don't call me with this shit." Then he hung up. I relayed the conversation to Michael and we ducked into the bathroom.

"What should we do?" Michael asked. "Take them through the new roadblock and hope for the best?" I argued against this. We began yelling; things got hotter. At the exact same moment, we went to kick each other. Our right feet hit midair. It hurt like hell. We jumped around the bathroom on our left legs, each of us rubbing our throbbing right foot.

This sobered us. We stopped arguing and made a plan. Michael wanted to go look at the roadblock in the morning, to see how bad it was, before the family flew in from D. F. He thought it might be like Benjamin Hill: when we'd gone through it on the first smuggling run weeks earlier, we all wore goofy sombreros like *turistas*; the two sentries didn't even look up as we drove through. The dudes we'd seen in the dark at this new checkpoint looked different. To humor Michael, I agreed to check it out in the morning.

But I was still doubtful, so I devised an alternate plan. That night in the hotel, I spread a map of northern Mexico on the bed and charted a route on dirt roads that went east and then north along the base of the Sierra Madre Occidental. Those dotted routes on the map would lead to a place beyond the roadblock. Sure, we didn't know how good or bad those dirt roads were. But there would be no federal *migra*.

In the morning, we left George behind and drove the panel wagon to see the roadblock in daylight. It was far worse than we'd expected: it was manned with federal soldiers toting automatic weapons. They looked scary. We couldn't make a U-turn—that surely would be suspicious—so we went up to the lowered wooden arm and played *estúpido gabachos*, pretending we couldn't speak Spanish.

"*Donde ES el* AIR-port?" Michael said loudly, like a typical American tourist. Two soldiers, with total bitch-face and clearly annoyed by us, pointed to where we had come from. We drove to the airport.

We got to the gate and waited. Francisco, Sandra, the brother, and the children emerged. There was another woman, Silvia, who had been added to this run. We hugged all of them and smiled and laughed, following the plan Jim had outlined. We spoke English to the family, things like: "It's been a long time! So good to see you!" The *migra* agents paid us no mind—we breezed right past all those guys with guns.

I told the family of the plan to drive into the desert to avoid the roadblock. Their trust in us was total. I projected confidence but was terrified. I looked at the toddler, then at the wide eyes of Sandra. We put the family into the old panel wagon. I drove, found the dirt road. It ran along a dry riverbed. It was pretty good as dirt roads go, but it began getting rougher the closer we got to the Sierra Madre. Soon there was no road; I was driving the panel wagon up the dry creek channel. The map lied—it showed roads that might never have existed.

When we reached the base of the mountains, I turned left, driving up out of the channel. I piloted the panel wagon across the trackless Sonoran Desert, around cacti, ocotillos, and other flora, using the sun and the position of the mountains as my guide. We went cross-country for miles, at a grinding pace not much faster than a walk.

Maybe two hours had passed when we came to a hacienda where the occupants used horses and didn't have any vehicles. When we all emerged from the panel wagon, the family that lived there invited us inside; a woman who appeared to be indigenous was cooking for the children—tortillas and eggs, with milk. When we offered her money for the food, the woman pounded her chest and said something like this in Spanish, "No! Help comes from the heart."

One of the cowboys pointed us northwest on horse trails and gave us instructions. The woman told the family accompanying us, "Good luck on your journey and your new life." We came out on a paved road some thirty miles north of the military roadblock. Twelve hours after we'd begun in Ciudad Obregón, we arrived at a safe house in the Mexican town of Nogales, run by a church. My tension melted. We knew this place, because we'd slept here on the first smuggling run weeks earlier.

The next morning, two Sanctuary members from Tucson appeared. They argued with Michael and me, saying that press wasn't allowed on crossings. It's one of the few times I've seen Michael get angry with sources. He said, "Look, lady, we just smuggled this family through Mexico. One of us is going."

We struck a compromise: Michael would go with the family, and I'd walk through an official checkpoint solo. A woman drove away in the panel wagon with the toddler and the other kid from the family, pretending they were her children to get through the border crossing. After they entered the United States, the vehicle immediately broke down. The engine was blown beyond repair.

The next day, the family, Silvia, the two new Sanctuary workers, and Michael walked some sixteen miles through the desert in 110-degree heat. They ran out of water—the Sanctuary workers hadn't brought enough. One of the women started having convulsions. They didn't think they were going to make it.

When they crossed, several "bird-watchers" were waiting to spirit them to Tucson.

We are back in Sacramento. We visit Oscar and Teresa Martinez. Carlos and Juan, whom we met on the plaza in Santa Ana, are there. They arrived in Sacramento only days earlier. It took them weeks to get from the Rio Suchiate to Mexicali, Mexico. They paid a coyote $700, sent by the Martinezes, to bring them across the border. Both Carlos and Juan are about to seek work in farm labor camps in the Central Valley to repay the money.

When I ask about Elisia, Carlos grows sad. No one has heard from her since they parted.

In the coming weeks and months, no one will hear from Elisia. The family will assume she is dead. I begin to have nightmares. My screams sometimes awaken me. I cannot sleep overnight with a woman; I fear scaring her. There are cumulative origins for these nightmares: in 1982, when Michael and I became hobos to document the new jobless, we spent a few years riding around America with other hobos. "No Thumbs," an old hobo who taught me about riding trains, was murdered in his camp, just a few weeks after we'd last seen him.

There are other bad things, many of them, but in the early months and then the spring and summer of 1985, my night specters center on Elisia. Surely there was more I could have done. Why didn't I get her to overcome her fear and accept help?

I visit Georgia Lyga at her church office, and she admonishes me sternly: "Not everyone makes it. That's just the way it is. You're going to have to get over it."

In late 1985, I cover the start of the Sanctuary trial. A scrum of journalists mob Sanctuary leaders. Jim Corbett says, "This reminds me of opening day of baseball season." John Fife, standing nearby, mulls over the ruling by the judge, who had just decreed that none of the eleven defense attorneys could mention politics or religious motives. John asks: "If we're not doing it for profit, what is the reason they are going to tell the jurors?"

Thirty-six years later, I'm back in Tucson. I'm seated in John's office at Southside Presbyterian.

He grins when he talks about how they beat the rap. He'd fully expected to go to prison. "I thought, 'Yeah, I'm gonna spend some time as the guest of the federal government.'"

We share "war stories" from the past. But that's not the reason for this journey to Tucson, which is to plumb meaning from what Sanctuary did in the 1980s and if there are lessons for today, with the US-Mexican border dominating the news. John jumps on the question. He points to the now-militarized border, the only place on Earth where an allegedly first-world nation abuts the third world—a tangible edge of the American empire. Conservatives have called for a wall along the entire frontier to stem the increasing flow of migrants from Latin America, but that isn't the answer, John says. The solution is so much bigger.

"I don't think people give up wealth and power because it's the right thing to do. They don't. Never. Now, I have a theory. We're going to have to share it because of climate change. We can't dominate it anymore like we used to. Climate change is the issue that's going to make us have to sit down at the table and come up with more equitable economic sharing with the rest of the world. We can't do it in a battle. We've got to do it at a table. But we don't have that table. We've got to create it. And then we've got to sit down at it. The climate crisis is going to push us to do that. People are not going to sit in poverty and violence. They're going to move. We don't know how to stop that. So they have to go to that table and do something about migration. And that's going to mean the move toward more global economic equity. People won't leave if they have health care, if they have education, and they have a way of making a living."

# Empire: The Philippines

In January 1966, I was nine years old, in fourth grade. My mother's job was raising me and my two siblings. My father earned $5,998.93 that year in his job as a steel worker. There wasn't much money, so we made things last. The AM radio, purchased after my parents married in 1950, was a black Bakelite RCA Victor, about the size of a contemporary microwave. It was set on a gray Formica counter just off the kitchen. I'd climb a stool and stare through the ventilation slats at the inner workings of glowing vacuum tubes. If my older sister turned it on, the dial was tuned to WIXY-1260. That station played The Beatles. She'd seen them perform at Cleveland Stadium in 1964. Mom's station was WJW-850. That winter, "The Ballad of the Green Berets," sung by US Army staff sergeant Barry Sadler, played often on one or both of those stations. The lyrics glorified the US Army Special Forces in Vietnam, who wore green berets and were bravely fighting for America.

At the end of January, Sadler appeared in black and white on *The Ed Sullivan Show*, which we always watched. Sadler, chisel-faced, was in uniform, wearing a beret. He stood at attention, belting out the song. It was a chart-topping hit that sold nine million records. Sadler was called a hero.

About this time, I learned a new word from the news that was on our television each evening: "guerrilla." My mother deflected my question about its meaning, but I soon figured it out. The Vietnam War was a constant background soundtrack—the wails of a teacher at our school after she was told her fiancé had been killed in action, and the announcements of rising body counts of American soldiers on the evening news.

American history schoolbooks told us about Manifest Destiny; General Winfield Scott; the sinking of the battleship USS *Maine*, which spurred the Spanish-American War in 1898. The US gave Cuba independence but kept other Spanish colonies, appropriating Puerto Rico and Guam as territories, and declaring sovereignty over the Philippines. In World War I, we saved Europe. Then Japan attacked us for no reason; we again saved Europe. Korea was a necessary police action. We had to stop communism. Fear the Russians.

Precisely at noon each day, our town's air raid siren atop city hall would go off, a test for the day when "The Bomb" would drop. The newspapers carried graphics showing the blast zone for a warhead destined to hit Cleveland; our village was in the death ring. We sometimes drove past the Nike Hercules antiballistic missile site at 11000 York Road in Parma, meant to protect us. East Germany was bad. North Korea was worse. North Vietnam—even worse.

In 1968, John Wayne starred in *The Green Berets*, featuring a cover of Sergeant Sadler's song. "The Duke" told us that we were winning. The Tet Offensive that year countered his assessment. Democrats held their convention in Chicago, and the police rioted against antiwar protesters. Bobby Kennedy and Martin Luther King Jr. were assassinated.

In early 1970, I had to make the choice of moving on to the Catholic high school or going to the heathen public one. Kids were political at the public high school. All the boys I hung out with talked about Vietnam. Would we go? Lloyd, with a buzz cut, was certain he would. Geoff, a long-haired hippie, planned to move to Canada. I had no idea what I'd decide—I was simply scared. One afternoon, my friend Tom and I went to another friend's house on Royalton Road. Inside their barn was the plywood box his brother's body had been sent home in from Vietnam. It was a very blue-collar thing to do. You didn't throw anything away.

I took an English class from a teacher who had just graduated from Kent State. He had been standing next to Sandra Scheuer on May 4 earlier that year during the campus protest. Her blood had sprayed all over him when she was shot by the Ohio National Guard. She fell dead, along with three others. That teacher spent two class days telling us what had really happened, not the version that President Richard Nixon and Republican governor James Rhodes wanted us to believe. That teacher's contract was not renewed the next year.

In other classes, I read Abbie Hoffman, Dick Gregory, Malcolm X. Our chemistry teacher had a twenty-five-pound drum of highly volatile potassium chlorate in the lab's storeroom—enough to demolish half of the school. That teacher might have belonged to Students for a Democratic Society, a precursor/adjunct to the militant organization the Weather Underground. He taught us how to make bombs, "in theory." In actuality, I dabbled with explosives in my home chemistry lab. I detonated my creations in the woods. It was a good skill to acquire, given what was going on in the country, even though I had no desire to engage in violence. By the time I graduated in 1974, the Vietnam War was winding down. I never had to face conscription. I never had to blow anything up. I went on to become a journalist, doing battle with words and not by fulminating mercury in a test tube with regent-grade nitric acid.

I grew up with the mythology of America. John Wayne fighting Indians. Cowboys good; Indians bad. Heroes at the Battles of San Juan Hill, Samar, Khe Sanh. Heroes among the scientists and military leaders protecting us. At a young age, however, I began to be disabused of this fiction, albeit slowly. It took time to understand that the stories of heroes almost never hold up. These things were learned:

Wounded Knee was not a battle. It was a massacre.

The USS *Maine* was not sunk by Spain—the boiler accidentally exploded.

All those atom bomb tests out in the Nevada desert sent radioactive clouds across America. That fallout came down in rain and was ingested by cows. We drank the milk. Radioactive strontium is in our bones from those tests. We bombed ourselves.

In 1978, Barry Sadler shot a love rival dead, placing a bullet between his eyes. The Green Beret served only twenty-two days in prison. He moved to Guatemala City, where he spent a lot of money on prostitutes and partying. Then a few years later, Sadler himself was shot in the head. Friends initially said the wound was self-inflicted; later the story changed to an attack by a gunman. Sadler barely survived, his chiseled head missing a piece, cratered from the blast, and he was left in a vegetative state. He died a year later in Cleveland.

By 1985, I was exploring the American empire in a distinctly first-hand manner, doing something I never thought I'd do, had never wanted to do—ending up in a jungle in Asia, surrounded by soldiers with belt-fed .50 caliber machine guns and grenade launchers. I was in the Philippines, on the island of Mindanao, just a few hundred miles north of the Equator, with Michael Williamson, on assignment for the newspaper. We'd embedded with twenty-one members of the Philippine Third Marine Brigade, at the start of a multiday patrol through the jungle, in territory controlled by the New People's Army.

It was a hot war. Some five thousand died that year, six hundred on Mindanao alone. Three Philippine Marines in an adjoining unit we met up with would die two days later, killed by a booby trap. The guerrillas were ostensibly fighting dictator Ferdinand Marcos, but in reality they were combating the United States, which had long supported Marcos. The reason: after the United States lost its bases at Cam Ranh Bay in Vietnam and in Iran after the fall of the Shah, the ones on the South China Sea in the Philippines grew more important.

The naval base at Subic Bay and Clark Air Base on the main island of Luzon were considered the biggest, best, and most strategic outposts of the American empire. The arc of history is an inconvenient reality for nationalists at any point in time, in any country on earth. Nationalists never want to look back. But it's equally true that they don't look forward. Actions spur reactions. Blowback. Commodore Matthew Perry steamed into Tokyo Bay with US Navy warships in

1853. That would ultimately lead to the militarization of Japan and Pearl Harbor. The US regained this piece of empire but was now about to again lose it.

Embedded with the Philippine soldiers, Michael and I stood on the banks of the rain-swollen Davao River, running hard alongside whitewater rapids. Across the river was a cliff topped by thick jungle. The soldiers were being ferried to the other side in a dugout canoe, four at a time. It was a perfect place to be ambushed, and that was precisely the point, Lieutenant Venerando Vargas told us. The Philippine Marines hoped NPA soldiers hiding in the forest would open fire, and then the Marines would return heavier fire. It was the only way to engage the enemy in combat, Lieutenant Vargas said, and to kill a few of them at a time.

"This is very dangerous here," because the unit would be "divided on both sides of the river," Lieutenant Vargas said, eyes on the top of the cliff. Once we all got across, we'd march for eighteen kilometers, bushwhacking into the town of Dominga. This was a strategic supply route for the rebels. The previous week, the NPA had used the same canoe to cross at this very spot, informants had told the Marines.

Lieutenant Vargas was pumped up, or putting on a show for us— or both. "We will fight the NPA," he said. "Anytime. If we are lucky, we will get one today. They usually fire their guns one or two times, hit somebody, and withdraw. They don't face us. Scared? No! I'm not scared of the sons of bitches. We're winning."

We made the crossing. The skinny, shirtless local man somehow paddled the dugout canoe hard enough to power us through the rapids. Hard rain began falling, the drops so heavy they hurt our bare heads—like being pelted with small ice cubes, only they were hot. It would rain like this for the next ten or so hours of our march. We were quickly soaked to our underwear.

At first, we walked up the middle of an ankle-deep river populated with leeches. Then we used trails to ascend and descend through the jungle; in places there were meadows of sawgrass that sliced skin as cleanly as steel razors. Birds, coucals, made haunting cries of "Oooh! Oooh! Oooh! Oooh!" The soldiers told us that the NPA soldiers would imitate this call to communicate with each other. Were the cries we heard birds or snipers?

We climbed slopes as steep as cliffs that were slick with mud, and we hung on to roots to prevent backsliding down several hundred feet. We passed coconut plantations and carabao, a kind of water buffalo. A boombox strapped to a Marine's backpack was tuned to some distant station in Davao City that faded in and out depending on our elevation. It blasted The Beatles' "Let It Be." The station was lost before the song ended, and the unit sang in unison to finish: "Let it be, let it be."

We were exhausted when we made camp amid the still-pounding rain in the dark. There we met First Lieutenant Henry B. Moral, trained at West Point. He wore a "We Are the World" T-shirt and invited us into a hut with a palm-frond-thatched roof. He immediately had his men kill a goat to cook for us, and bring two cases of beer. The three of us were to consume it all. As we drank, he related his philosophy of life.

"You smoke, you die," he said as he puffed away on a Camel cigarette. There was the sound of rain hammering the woven palm fronds over our heads. The air smelled of distant cooking goat. Then, exhaling, he said: "You don't smoke, you die."

The ballroom at the Manila Hotel was packed. We were waiting for Imelda Marcos to ascend a stage. Red carpets and garlands had been put out for her. Her husband, Ferdinand, had called a snap election to reassert his power as dictator. His chief political rival, Benigno Aquino Jr., had been executed on the tarmac of the Manila airport two years earlier, having just gotten off a plane after returning home from exile in America to campaign against Marcos. Cory Aquino, Benigno's widow, was running against Ferdinand Marcos in the coming election.

The Marcoses had pillaged the Philippines while being propped up by the US. A few examples: Imelda had purchased a seventy-carat blue-tinted diamond worth $5.5 million. The couple had funneled state funds to purchase dozens of luxury homes, and had decorated them with the artwork of Cézanne, Monet, Picasso, and Van Gogh.

Most estimates of how much money the couple ripped off range between $5 and $10 billion. Some estimate even more. Guinness World Records once had Ferdinand listed as the record holder for the "greatest robbery of a government." His official annual salary was $13,500.

The Western press filled a back corner of the ballroom that day. Many of our fellow journalists were staying at this five-star hotel. We couldn't afford the rate, over $100 per night. The entire budget for Michael and me, for over a month on the islands, was $2,250 each—including the flights. We'd gotten a deal through a friend to rent the top floor of an apartment building for a weekly rate of $120. Oddly, only women lived on the other eight floors. Loud and obnoxious Australian men kept coming and going at all hours, sometimes knocking on our door. It took six days for us to realize we were renting in a brothel, and that we had to move to a real hotel on Roxas Boulevard.

Imelda loved the Manila Hotel. By order of her husband, the government had appropriated and upgraded it. It was the "in" place to be seen during their family's reign in the years of martial law. In her speech that day, Imelda talked about beauty and her love of the Filipino people. I didn't pay much attention. We weren't covering the day-by-day events of the campaign. I was there to observe other details, among them the garbage produced by the hotel, before visiting the site where that garbage was taken.

To say the hotel was opulent is to understate. The lobby, over one hundred feet long, had gleaming white Doric columns. Philippine marble, mahogany, and red velvet abounded. When I went to the restroom, the attendant insisted on preflushing the urinal. A second attendant, despite my protest, flushed it when I was done. A third attendant turned on the faucet for me to rinse my hands, and insisted I take perfume and a comb.

The hotel was a result of President William McKinley's plan to Americanize the Philippines after the islands were seized from Spain. The US government had commissioned architect Daniel Hudson Burnham to showcase the waterfront of Manila Bay. Burnham was chosen because he had built Union Station and the Postal Square

Building in Washington, DC. He envisioned a grand boulevard along the bay and an impressive hotel designed in the California Mission style. What emerged was more like a palace, with 550 rooms.

It opened on July 4, 1912. The choice of American Independence Day was no coincidence. Between 1935 and 1941, the penthouse was the residence of General Douglas MacArthur, when he was the military adviser to the Philippine Commonwealth. When the Japanese landed, he fled the hotel, retreating with American soldiers to the Malinta Tunnel on the island of Corregidor, at the entrance to Manila Bay. MacArthur later stole away on a PT boat in the dead of night. The remaining American soldiers wound up in the Bataan Death March. Until MacArthur returned when US troops landed on the Philippine island of Leyte in 1944, the rising-sun flag flew over the hotel.

Not long after Imelda's event, we were in a taxi heading to the place where the garbage trucks went from the hotel, five kilometers to the north. Hundreds of trucks brought loads of trash to that site each day, and many were laden solely with human shit. People called it Smoky Mountain, because it was shrouded in smoke from burning trash fires. And on top of this growing hill of shit and refuse were four thousand people who called the dump home. Those who knew about Smoky Mountain implored us to purchase knee-high rubber boots for our visit. And advised us that once we left, we should kick off those boots without touching them and throw them away. They warned us that the smell would stay on us for days no matter how much we showered.

We wrapped rags around our faces to repel the stench. Billowing smoke as thick as tule fog blasted down from the top of the mountain. We walked past rows of hundreds of tightly packed shanties, assembled from rusting bedsprings, cardboard, splintered boards. These crude hovels sheltered between nine and a dozen people each. Small children emerged and ran up to us, not to beg but simply to touch these strange White visitors. When we reached the top of the mountain, we came upon swarms of residents waiting for garbage trucks to offload. They would comb through the waste for metal, plastic, and bone. The average resident, after a twelve-hour day of scavenging, made between $1 and $1.50 from their finds, which they would sell to scrap dealers.

Observations: A truck far below churned up the dirt road, kicking up clouds of dust that mixed with the smoke. A radio someone had found amid the trash played George Harrison's "My Sweet Lord." As the truck neared, clouds of fleeing flies erupted from the ground, pelting faces like hard drops of black rain. Dozens of people ran behind the truck. The wheels spun, spraying them with human shit. The strongest men scaled the sides of the truck and pitched down metal cans and bones to friends, who scrambled to stow these items in large wicker baskets; these people stood amid rotting melon rinds, chunks of foam, maggots, Marlboro boxes. The truck's bed tilted; the men at the top of the load rode it down as the contents thundered out. Those at the base, some barefoot, were buried to their waists, but they paid no mind as they frantically dug for any scrap worth pennies.

A very tall man emerged, like an apparition, out of the smoke—an American with disheveled hair and a sweaty face. He didn't look at us. The man opened a Bible. His lips twitched for a long few seconds before he began reading to children digging through the freshly dumped garbage.

"Psalm 51:5 says, 'Surely I was sinful at birth, sinful from the time my mother conceived me. Yet you desired faithfulness even in the womb; you taught me wisdom in that secret place. Cleanse me with hyssop, and I will be clean; wash me, and I will be whiter than snow...'"

The man read on through the chapters to the youthful diggers, who ignored him. He eventually turned to us and announced that these children were sinners. He was on a mission to save them. He called them "little ones for Jesus." He informed us that there were 2,500 children among the 4,000 residents of Smoky Mountain. He introduced himself as Eugene Schwebler. We didn't shake hands. He was clutching the Bible tightly. He was forty-four. "I was a sheet metal worker, and the Lord called me here." He'd quit his job in Milwaukee and come to live at the dump a few months earlier. It was the first time that he'd ever traveled outside the United States.

"There's a lot of disease, mostly among the children," he said. "Cholera. A whole lot of tuberculosis. Lots of eye and ear infections. And respiratory problems from the smoke." Eugene wiped sweat from his eyes. He then abruptly turned and walked off, Bible cradled in his hands, reading more passages to no one. He spoke only to the smoke.

Two boys made a discovery—an aerosol can. One of the kids, about fourteen, used a sharp object to puncture it. He wrapped it in a rag, and another boy began fighting him for it. They both inhaled the fumes. One fell over and smiled. In perfect English he announced, "Good high." He giggled.

On the walk off the mountain, we met Elizabeth Melendrez. She was twenty-three but looked fifty. I asked if the government gave them any help. She laughed. "No!" she said, as if it was the dumbest question she'd ever heard.

"There are no jobs. I was born here, but I moved away. My husband lost his job, so we had to move back. We do not make much. There is no water here, so we have to buy it for two pesos per bucket. Some people do make more money. They hold up [rob] people at night. Or, if you are lucky, you sometimes find a gold ring."

I'd covered poverty in America. Nothing had prepared me for the Philippines, however. It went beyond Smoky Mountain. There were legless beggars who used skateboards to propel themselves around Manila. On the island of Negros, people were so poor their clothes were, without hyperbole, rotting off their backs. Everywhere on the islands, desperate women propositioned us to marry them. When we were at dinner in Tagum, near Davao City on Mindanao, six women slipped us notes with phone numbers and addresses as they asked us to take them to the US. People on the southern islands knew little English, but they knew this much: "Hey, Joe! Hey, Joe! Marry me!" Americans were called "Joe," as in G.I. Joe. In some places, we were the first Americans that residents had seen since the end of World War II. (On one island, a very old man came running up to me and grasped my shoulders to thank me for kicking out the Japanese, muttering, "Thank you, Joe! Thank you, Joe!")

Some journalists took advantage. One reporter for a major organization had a wife in Bangkok, and when he came to the Philippines, which was often, he slept with an endless succession of beautiful Filipinas, each one hoping that he would spirit her away to the riches of America. He told us about this matter-of-factly and was befuddled to learn that we had not and would not have sex with any of these women.

We are at the Subic Bay naval base on the Bataan peninsula, next to the City of Olongapo, the main supply center for the Seventh Fleet, which patrols US interests in the South China Sea, west of the Indian Ocean. Subic is a tropical and small-scale version of the San Francisco Bay. At the peak of the Vietnam War, as many as seventy ships would be anchored in the harbor. Now the Soviets have built up Cam Ranh Bay in Vietnam, an hour's fighter-jet flight away across the South China Sea. Without the US presence, common perception goes, that sea is a "Russian lake."

We're being given a carefully orchestrated tour by US Navy brass. We're escorted through the vast machine works, and employees are told to talk with us while the officers stand a few feet away. The workers are some of the twenty-eight thousand Filipinos at the base. The men are nervous as they recite how much they love their jobs. Later, I'm able to steal away and speak on the side, one-on-one, with a drill press operator.

"We were told not to talk with you," he says. I promise not to use his name. He says he'd be happy to see the US leave when the lease for the base ends in 1991. He'd use the free training from the Americans to get a job in Saudi Arabia that pays a lot more than the $1.25 per hour he makes from the US Navy. Low wages embolden thieves. A US Senate report estimates that $1 million worth of goods, including firearms, is stolen annually at Clark Airfield. There is no report on Subic, but we hear a joke: everything has been stolen but it hasn't yet been taken out the gate.

We board a destroyer. We make our way to a control room. A giant electronic board, a map of the western Pacific, dominates. There are dozens of blinking lights evenly spaced between Japan, down through the South China Sea, and all the way to the Middle East. A high-ranking officer asks, "Do you want to know why we are here?" He doesn't mean on this battleship at this very moment. He means the entire Seventh Fleet out in the Pacific at this juncture in the late twentieth century. He points to the blinking lights. Each one is an oil tanker. One line of these glowing dots is steaming west, empty; the other line steaming east, full of crude oil from Saudi Arabia.

"You're talking a one-way stream of oil tankers running for ten thousand miles direct to Japan, and each ship is no more than sixty miles apart," he informs us.

"Oil," the officer concludes. "That's why we are here."

For as long as anyone alive can remember, sugarcane has grown tall and sweet at the base of Canlaon, an eight-thousand-foot smoking volcano that rises above the cane fields on the Philippine island of Negros. For decades, men have harvested the crop with thin steel cane knives; those knives make a ringing sound as they strike plant flesh, the cadence resembling that of wind chimes. It's a kind of music—a lonely dirge. Until the 1970s, the two million people who live on Negros made their living off sugar—they grew, harvested, and processed most of the sugarcane in the Philippines, and much of that product went straight to the United States, into cans of Coke and Pepsi.

But in the early 1980s, the market collapsed. Part of the reason is that the major buyers—the Coca-Cola Company and PepsiCo, Inc.—switched from cane sugar to American-grown sugar beets or corn syrup to sweeten their products. American growers pressured the government to enact an import quota on cane sugar. That quota was two million tons in 1974; by 1985, it was 235,000 tons; the 1986 quota was 165,000 tons and promised to fall further. In this diminished market, those Filipinos who were able to land work earned fifteen pesos for each ton of raw sugarcane they harvested. A good worker could cut maybe one and a half tons, two tons tops—more than the weight of a Toyota Camry—per day. For two tons, the worker earned US $1.50. That's less than one cent per hundred pounds.

Negros was beset by starvation. The only thing of value that could be produced on the five-thousand-square-mile island, the fourth largest in the Philippine archipelago, was sugarcane. In the first half of 1985, the Corazon Locsin Montelibano Memorial Regional Hospital in the city of Bacolod reported that 370 children died from hunger. The government said that two-thirds of the children on the island suffered from malnutrition, and the Catholic church in Bacolod said that twenty thousand children were in danger of dying of a lack of food. Negros was called the "Ethiopia of Asia," after the mass starvation in that African nation.

We had so much to cover in so little time, and I wasn't sure we were going to be able to make it to Negros. Then one day in Manila we interviewed a leader for the outlawed National Democratic Front. (We'd made this connection through sources we'd met with in the San Francisco Bay Area.) The NDF was the governing body that directed the two wings of the revolt against the Marcos dictatorship: the armed New People's Army and unarmed political groups staging street protests.

Government troops would kill demonstrators almost every time there was a mass action. A few months earlier, in September, twenty-one unarmed people had been shot dead by soldiers in the city of Escalante, on the eastern shore of Negros. They had been protesting the thirteenth anniversary of the imposition of martial law by Ferdinand Marcos. The biggest demonstration ever on the island—in the city of Bacolod—was about to happen in a few days, with thousands promising to fill the streets.

The NDF leader begged us to fly to Bacolod. "If the Western press is present, the soldiers will not kill anyone," he told us. Most of the Western press wasn't leaving Manila or Luzon. Everyone was covering Marcos and Aquino—the horse race. As far as the leader knew, no one else in the international press was going to Negros. The Marcos government was quite aware of the bad optics created by the killing of defenseless protesters captured by American cameras.

"If you go, people—a lot of people—will not die," the NDF leader insisted.

We booked a flight on a Philippine Airlines "puddle jumper" to Bacolod. In the meantime, we covered another campaign event by Ferdinand Marcos at the Manila Hotel. We joined the press in back. There was an Italian photographer whose name I forget. Frustrated by something Marcos's press people were doing, he roared, "Jeeeessuusssss fuckkkkking Chrrrrrrist!" in Italian-accented English. It was the dozenth or so time I'd heard this eruption from him in a few weeks.

Marcos gave a forgettable speech filled with platitudes and untruths. He ended with this: "*Mabuhay ang ating kilusang bagong lipunan! Mabuhay ang sambahyang Pilipino!*" ("Long live our new society movement! Long live the Filipino people!") He was eminently unquotable.

The scrum of three hundred journalists represented locations all over the world. We hung around those who were doing street reporting, among them Willie Vicoy, a photographer who worked for Reuters and who had shot for United Press International during the war in Vietnam. We'd had several dinners with him over the previous few weeks. He was kind and generous with advice. Willie always wore a Mao cap with a red star on it. (He would be dead four months later, accidentally killed by an NPA rocket-launched grenade in an ambush while embedded with the Philippine military in northern Luzon.)

There was Gregg Jones, an American freelancer, a friend I'd met in the US; and Ray Bonner, who would become a friend. And Susan Meiselas, the Magnum photographer whose work Michael and I both admired. Susan was freshly arrived in Manila. She had documented the civil war in El Salvador and the revolution in Nicaragua. I don't know what happened, but she was instantly deeply suspicious of us, and that first meeting was beyond awkward.

After the event, we raced to the airport to make the flight to Bacolod. Once we'd settled in our seats, just before the door closed, Susan rushed onto the jetliner. She gave us a withering look as she stuffed her camera bag in an overhead bin. When the plane landed, she quickly vanished. We jumped into a taxi and went to a hotel in downtown Bacolod; Susan was at the front desk checking in. We talked, and whatever misunderstanding had existed was extinguished.

She then realized we were the authors of the just-published book *Journey to Nowhere*, which she'd read.

With peace made, the three of us went to dinner. A culinary craze had recently swept the islands—*inihaw na manok*, barbecued chicken—and near the hotel was a sprawling outdoor waterfront restaurant that served it. We ordered and sat at a picnic table—Michael and I on one side; Susan, the other. We were besieged by an endless stream of child beggars.

Oddly, there were numerous German men. We'd seen them at the hotel and on the street. We knew their nationality from overheard conversations. Halfway through the meal, Susan's eyes fixated on something.

"Don't look now," she said, "but there is a German man kissing a small boy behind you." Of course our heads snapped. A bearded German, in his forties or fifties, was kissing a Filipino boy no older than about twelve, two picnic tables away. He noticed us watching and kissed the boy more deeply in defiance. He then paraded the boy around the tables, fondling him as they walked. We would learn that Negros was a destination for European pedophile tourism. Mostly it was Germans who came on junkets in chartered planes. Parents, desperate not to see their children die of hunger because of the crashed sugar market, would sell their sons twelve and younger to men for about ten pesos a day, or US fifty cents.

I interview Stuart Ross, a Pepsi spokesperson. Ross blames sugar beet growers for the quotas that led Pepsi to switch to corn syrup a few years ago, around 1981. In the US, cane sugar costs twenty-five cents per pound; corn sweetener, twenty cents. I then interview Mark Preisinger, a spokesperson for Coca-Cola in Atlanta. Preisinger lauded the switch to corn syrup as a boon for American farmers.

"We're a business," Preisinger says. "Our business is to offer people who own stock in our company the highest return possible. Corn sweetener is substantially cheaper."

The Sugar Information Bureau in Washington tells me that one hundred thousand US jobs are directly related to sugar, and that without the quotas, eighteen thousand US family farmers would be harmed.

Coca-Cola sold in the Philippines lists real cane sugar in its ingredients. A bottle costs a dime US—three to five cents more than the price of a coconut sold in roadside stalls. Sellers hack the coconut with a machete, exposing the white interior flesh, and stick in a straw. It's a satisfying—and safe—way to hydrate in the many places where bottled water is unavailable. In a country where coconuts grow by the millions on trees, the fact that soda is not much more expensive is an impressive lesson in capitalism.

The Reverend Ireneo Gordoncillo, a Catholic priest, is trying to help the sugar workers. He is angry and frustrated by the starvation that has befallen the people of Negros. He tells us, "The United States came here at the beginning of the century and said this would be a good source of sugar. They developed the feudal structure of this society." And then, "overnight," they cut Negros off without a second thought. "As the hunger increases, so do the protests. I don't see a peaceful solution. The options are being made by reality. Violence is a last resort, I agree, but don't call it violence. Call it armed struggle. When you are pushed against the wall, what do you do?"

I stare, frozen in a long moment, at three-month-old twins who could be dead within the day, two at most, we are told. The infants are in tiny hospital beds. The face of Raymond, the boy on the left, is one of pain. His eyes are closed, his mouth downturned. This face looks like that of an old man. He does not cry; what emerges is a whimper. Tubes run into his head and abdomen. René, the boy on the right, has his mouth open as if in a howl, but no sound comes out. Tubes also enter his body. The right hand of Nida Castillo, his mother, is on his chest. The other grips the iron bed frame. I notice that the frame is smooth and shiny, worn from the grasp of her hands and those of others—other mothers who watched their babies die. Her head is down, and she weeps. Her arms are like sticks, all bone. She has not eaten well in months.

The nurse at Corazon Montelibano hospital tells us the twins are suffering from third-degree malnutrition. This is the final stage before death. Nida kisses René's ulcerated face. The nurse says Nida's government allotment of a few dollars for antibiotics has run out. There is no way for her to get additional medicine, the nurse says, and this is why the boys will die. Nida tells us her husband cuts cane and earns some $1.50 per day for chopping four thousand pounds, if he can get work.

We give Nida money for antibiotics. We return later with food for her. René has stopped breathing, and we watch as the nurse struggles with a respirator to revive him. We come back a few days later, and the two babies are still alive—barely. We give Nida more money to buy medicine.

At least ten thousand people—likely a lot more—filled the streets of Bacolod the day of the demonstration against Marcos and against the misery that had befallen the island of Negros. We started out as three—me, Michael, and Susan Meiselas. We found a group of men seated inside a small bamboo-walled store. They were talking about Coca-Cola and Pepsi.

"After the revolution," one man said as he took a big swig of Coca-Cola, "there will be no more Coca-Cola." The man told us he supported the New People's Army and that despite drinking Coke, he hated it for what it represented—the American system and capitalist exploitation.

Susan told the men that she'd heard the same thing in Nicaragua before the 1979 revolution that deposed dictator Anastasio Somoza. But as soon as the Sandinistas won, the first thing people demanded was Coke, she said. The revolutionary government was forced to import it.

"You cannot get rid of it," Susan said.

"The best thing we can use it for is to make Molotov cocktails," the man countered, holding up the now-empty glass Coke bottle. "I don't think we would be very unhappy without Coke. We are in more need of food."

"You'll see," Susan said as the three of us split up and wandered off in different directions.

I became lost in the throng of chanting protesters with their anti-Marcos signs. It was a mass of humanity so vast, I had no idea where to begin interviewing. Susan reappeared and pointed to a short, thin man with a 1964 Beatles-style haircut.

"You need to go talk to him." I went over to the man, who began reciting lines of Tolstoy. There was shouting all around us, and I didn't know which Tolstoy work he was quoting from, and there was no time to ask amid the crush of the crowd. I forgot about the literary reference in the events that ensued in the coming days.

The following dialogue is from the 1982 film *The Year of Living Dangerously*, with Mel Gibson playing journalist Guy Hamilton and Linda Hunt as cameraman Billy Kwan, who is quoting Tolstoy.

> *Billy:* The people asked and he said, "What shall we do then?" From Luke, chapter three, verse ten. What then must we do? Tolstoy asked the same question. He wrote a book with that title. He got so upset about the poverty in Moscow, that he went one night into the poorest section and just gave away all his money. You could do that now. Five American dollars would be a fortune to one of these people.

> *Guy:* Wouldn't do any good. Just be a drop in the ocean.

> *Billy:* Ah, that's the same conclusion Tolstoy came to. I disagree.

> *Guy:* Now what's your solution?

> *Billy:* Well, I support the view that you just don't think about the major issues. You do whatever you can about the misery that's in front of you. Add your light to the sum of light. You think that's naive don't you?

> *Guy:* Yep.

*Billy:* That's all right, most journalists do.

*Guy:* We can't afford to get involved.

*Billy:* Typical journalist mindset.

I didn't watch the film for the first time until after the Philippines, in April 1988, with a group in Cambridge, Massachusetts. We'd gotten a videotape of the movie in preparation for spending the next afternoon in conversation with Linda Hunt, who'd won an Oscar for Best Supporting Actress, playing a dwarf man who was Guy Hamilton's photographer and fixer.

Our discussion with Linda continued past the allotted time, well into the evening when most of the group filtered away and just a few of us were left with her, as day became night. I was keen on hearing about her take on Manila, where most of the filming was done, even though it depicted events surrounding the 1965 overthrow of Sukarno, president of Indonesia. (The Indonesian government wouldn't allow the film's director, Peter Weir, to film there.) During the moment in the movie just before Kwan implores the journalist to understand the value of five dollars as they walk past desperately poor people, when Kwan brings up Tolstoy, I recalled that day in Bacolod city and recognized the words of Tolstoy that the man had quoted during the protest. I was excited for the memory, to finally learn exactly which work the passage was from, and to meet someone in the United States who understood that level of despair and my reaction to it; no one in my circle outside of Michael got it. It was just too overwhelming to discuss, and no amount of description would translate what we'd seen. The few times I'd attempted to talk about it with friends, I'd been reduced to babble.

Linda got it. We focused on a line of narration she delivers early in the film, describing the arrival of the naive journalist for his assignment covering a revolution: "Most of us become children again when we enter the slums of Asia." This line came from screenwriters David Williamson and Peter Weir, in an adaptation of the eponymous novel by C. J. Koch that the film is based on. What did it mean to become a child? For me, it was seeing poverty with an entirely different set of eyes; it also meant understanding the impact of the American empire and questioning the arc of history.

What if Commodore Perry hadn't forced free trade—would Japan have remained isolationist and not militarized? What if we had not gone to war with Spain in 1898? Maybe Japan's nationalists would not have been emboldened, Japan would have not bombed Pearl Harbor, and my father would not have had brain damage from blast concussions that night on the Orote Peninsula during the Battle of Guam, or when a tomb filled with munitions blew up on Okinawa. What if Coca-Cola and Pepsi had not switched formulas? Perhaps then the scene of Raymond and René, the babies dying in the hospital cribs, might not have existed for Michael and me to witness. Yet the fact is we did invade. First with military might. Second with its capitalist equivalent. "The military and the monetary," as encapsulated by poet and songwriter Gil Scott-Heron. The logical conclusion, it seems reasonable to expect, is that we as a nation bear some responsibility. But accountability was shirked—by our support of Marcos as he stole from the citizens of his country.

And now, decades later, I see how I was a child in other ways. During the pandemic in 2020, I recalled the Philippines: "Most of us become children again when we enter the slums of America." I had PTSD when I walked into the homeless camps in the forests and meadows along the rivers in Sacramento, where my own Billy Kwan—an outreach worker for a local nonprofit—gave me a tour of the vast encampments.

When I'd been a reporter in Sacramento, the homeless in the woods numbered in the dozens. Joe Smith estimated, based on the food his nonprofit distributed, that there were as many as ten thousand people dwelling in tents and shanties along the waterways and in other secret places around downtown. They were living much like the poorest Filipinos. I had been a child because I was naïve enough in the mid-1980s to believe that we would never have the kind of poverty one finds in Asia on our own shores, on such a scale, because we would never allow it to happen.

Meanwhile, the markets were roaring, hitting record highs.

But all of this—my seeing the film, Linda, and the homeless encampments in Sacramento—is in the unimaginable future. We are still in 1985, in the Philippines, on the island of Negros.

The mouse, loudly squeaking, was stuck to a large, flat paper glue trap set on the floor. Rain thundered against the metal roof. As the mouse continued its struggles, I couldn't sleep. But I couldn't intervene to save the creature. I was a guest. It was sometime after midnight, and I was on a cot near the room being slept in by the owner of the hacienda—the man who had quoted Tolstoy to me in Bacolod. His name was Emilio Y. Montalvo, and as the demonstration wound down, we'd gotten in his vehicle after learning he'd turned what had been his 247-acre sugar farm, founded by his grandfather, entirely over to his one hundred former workers.

The drive took us past cane fields, rice paddies, and the foot of the smoking Canlaon volcano, threatening to spew lava. It was the most active volcano in the Philippines and had erupted thirty times in the previous two centuries. Emilio didn't seem concerned about the potential for lava and mudslides. A bigger crisis faced the people of Negros. Emilio told us that landowners end up looking like the bad guys.

"But the system has fallen apart. We're all finished. The old way will never return. It's dead. Now I want to do what is proper. I made a promise to my people. I will not eat if you do not eat. Ten years ago, I would not have walked barefoot. Now, each day, I walk my land barefoot. We are in the throes of a revolution."

I thought of smoking Canlaon towering out there in the night as the mouse grew quieter, weakened by its writhing. This house was twenty-four kilometers south of the volcano, fifty from Bacolod.

Everyone we met in our days on Negros used the term "feudal" to describe the societal structure of the island. This system dated to the Spanish. For two centuries, landowners had cared for their workers. It was virtual slavery, though we always heard it described as "patriarchal." Whatever one wanted to call it, that ethos collapsed when the American soda companies stopped using cane sugar. Landowners abandoned farms or planted less labor-intensive crops. Wealthy people from Manila bought small farms on the cheap. Farmers who were in debt had to sell because the interest rate on money they could borrow to save their farms had reached 40 percent. Emilio was not crushed by debt, and he had the liberty to let his workers raise food for themselves—chickens, rice, potatoes. A priest would tell us that Emilio had provided them with fertilizer and tools.

In the morning, Emilio gave us a tour of the haciendas around Isabela. He was missing a front tooth, but he wasn't self-conscious about it. He often smiled. He wore a faded T-shirt and shorts, along with tinted aviator glasses. The glasses were the only thing visible about his person that separated him in terms of class position from the people we met all morning and afternoon. He was barefoot. We passed endless huts, surrounded by hundreds of idle people. Men squatted on their haunches, spitting sugarcane pulp to the muddy ground. They first stripped bark off with their teeth, or with a knife if they didn't have teeth, exposing the white core. Everywhere people were chewing cane. It's how they alleviated hunger. I'd tried it a few weeks earlier on Luzon. It tasted like a mix of weak table sugar and sawdust. One chews until all the sugar has been extracted, then spits out the fiber. Most children had distended bellies from the early stages of malnutrition. Many had sores all over their bodies.

Emilio felt compelled to tell us he had once worked on a campaign for Ferdinand Marcos. He now loathed him. His brother, the mayor of Bacolod, still belonged to Marcos's political party, the Kilusang Bagong Lipunan.

"We do not talk much anymore," he said of his brother as he drove us down a rutted dirt lane. It was flanked by sickly sugarcane belonging to growers struggling to hang on. Emilio said the farmers couldn't afford fertilizer. There was almost no market for cane. "They think I am crazy," he said of his brother and some of his neighbors. "They call me a Communist. I am not a Communist. I am a landowner. I stand to lose if the Communists win. I do what I do for the people."

We stopped. The sound of distant gunfire from a battle on the flanks of Canlaon drifted down from the north. Emilio pointed to a spot where a unit of the New People's Army had recently jumped out from a thicket of sugarcane and ambushed a bus carrying government soldiers. A civilian woman had mistakenly been killed. Emilio sprinted across a field to talk with men chopping cane; his long black hair, straight as a horse's mane, bounced wildly. It was hard to keep up with him. He seemed younger than his fifty years. One worker told us the owner of this farm was so greedy that if it were possible, he'd plant cane beneath their houses. The clothes worn by these men were threadbare, some shirts more hole than shirt. How did they pull on the rotting pants without tearing them apart?

We resumed the tour. At another stop, we entered a hut made of bamboo and thatch, raised on poles about ten feet off the ground. It was no larger than an average-size living room in a small American home. The woman who was present said that she, her husband, and their three children slept on the slatted floor. The room had a table, two chairs, four cots, a metal cooking pot, a houseplant in a tin can, a hairbrush, a cracked mirror, a picture of the Virgin Mary, and next to it, a picture of a bare-breasted White woman cut from *Playboy*; and absolutely nothing else.

We headed back to Emilio's farm. On the way, we pulled up next to two wizened women who were on the road with a four-year-old girl. They chewed on stalks of sugarcane. Either woman could have been the child's grandmother by their wizened faces. It was a shock to learn they were in their early thirties—but we shouldn't have been surprised. Over and over, the people we met on the island were far younger than they appeared.

"We are walking into town," one of the women said. They had no money. "We will try to borrow some rice for dinner. If there is no food at dinner, we will just chew cane tonight." We came to a hacienda where another landowner allowed his workers to grow food. An old man struggled to cultivate shriveled stalks of corn. The workers lacked insecticides, fertilizer, carabao for plowing.

"Their corn grows, and the insects come and eat it," Emilio said. "These people are completely lost. These people are like children. They cannot come up to your level. You have to go down to their level. That doesn't mean you demean them. But that is the only way you can understand them."

In the late afternoon, we walked Emilio's land. We followed him along a muddy dike separating two rice paddies. My hiking boots were caked in muck. Emilio delighted in watching the dark goop squish through his bare toes. He waded into the water where two women were planting bunches of rice plant starts. As he talked to the women, I stared at the volcano. Canlaon was bathed in bright orange light; the sun was low enough to bounce off clouds, amplifying the glow. Smoke from the summit merged with the clouds.

Emilio rejoined us on the muddy dike. We talked about how the rich lived behind ever-higher walls in San Salvador. Emilio jumped in, saying he'd read about those walls in a book—I wondered, Joan Didion? Her book *Salvador* had come out two years earlier. But I didn't ask, because he was excited and I didn't want to interrupt; he said he'd brought up the topic of those walls in a recent conversation with some friends in Isabela, who feared the NPA and the poor. Those friends told him they were going to build a walled compound and arm themselves. It would make them feel safer.

"We cannot live behind walls with guns!" Emilio insisted. "That is no way to live. We have to change! We cannot be free otherwise. The only way you can truly be free is to be free from fear."

Rain blasts down beyond the porch overhang. It's night and 95 degrees Fahrenheit, with at least 95 percent humidity. It's as if the heat is evaporating the entire Sulu and South China Seas into the heavens and blasting that water right back at the island. Father Rodolfo Pacheco has invited us for beers on the porch of his church in Isabela. We are with Emilio and some other men at a long table. It would be just guys tipping a few, but we are Americans, and the men with the priest almost never get to talk with Americans.

Zeusian lightning over Canlaon flashes on the faces of the men; during one of the multiple strobes as we seat ourselves, Father Pacheco announces, "I want to share my feelings with you—it may help you understand how we feel." He's an expressive man, and his hands wave as he talks. "I was born in 1939. I remember a few things about the war. Americans died for us. When I was growing up, being grateful to the Americans was part of our heritage."

"I look on you as gods, liberators," Emilio says. Japanese soldiers killed both of his parents; he witnessed Japanese troops throwing babies into the air and spearing them on their bayoneted rifles as they came down.

The positive feelings toward Americans, however, began fading for both Emilio and Father Pacheco starting in the 1960s. "In 1963, when I was a new priest," Father Pacheco continues, "they assassinated Diem in Vietnam." By "they," he means the US government under the administration of President John F. Kennedy. South Vietnam president Ngo Dinh Diem was unpopular, but the coup simply led to even more inept leadership. "My bishop at that time said Kennedy was not a good Christian. They killed the only honest man in Vietnam. Then I began reading about America. I was waking up. America was killing children in Vietnam. I realized these people I always thought were heroes had become villains. Now we are being exploited by the very people who once helped us. The next generation will forget what the Americans did."

We are now on our second and third beers. For the first time in our days spent with Emilio, we hear anger in his voice. "Do you know when we were in school, we were not allowed to study Philippine history? They taught us American history. They put down our language. They took away our culture. They never asked us, 'What do you want?' They said, 'This is what you should do.' When I met with [US embassy chargé d'affaires] Philip Kaplan last month, I told him I am not anti-American. I love Americans. I am anti–American foreign policy. The trouble with American policy is they never learn. They always support dictators, and when things go bad, they disassociate themselves after it is too late. People say the US didn't impose martial law. But the US backed Marcos up."

An older man who has remained silent at the far end of the table suddenly slams down his beer. It froths and splashes all over. He is old enough to have fought against the Japanese in World War II. "You can speak the truth here!" He says there is freedom of speech in the Philippines. The men, he says, are being too hard on the United States. He plans to emigrate to America. "It is not as bad as you say! I am not afraid to talk! As long as you tell the truth, you are safe. It worked for Jesus."

"Yeah, but look what happened to him," says Emilio.

The men shout down the pro–United States World War II fighter. He sulks and drinks more beer, remaining silent for the rest of the evening.

"They treat us like we are fifty cents and they are one dollar," says Jose M. Pacheco, an attorney and the brother of the priest. "If they want to change things, they must treat us like family, not vassals or a colony. They have no business discussing our fate. US ambassador Stephen Bosworth talks as if he is the president of the Philippines." The attorney says the US bought Philippine sugar when it was convenient. He says the US only cares about protecting the military bases. "What do they need the bases for? To protect their oil lanes."

Americans, he continues, could have done more to improve the Philippines after the war. America helped Japan become an industrial power. "In the war, Manila was leveled to the ground. It was the city worst hit, after Warsaw. How much help did the Americans give us? Why didn't they do the same thing for us? They don't want us to industrialize, because we'll compete with them, just like the Japanese. Long before we were conquered by the Spaniards, we had a culture of our own. And when we were about to liberate ourselves, the Americans came in!"

"We need to be like Costa Rica," Emilio says, meaning independent and neutral.

We turn away from politics. I ask, "Why do people keep having large families in the face of so much hunger?"

"They are rich," Father Pacheco says. "They are rich in children."

We debate this. The priest sees beauty in the large families, a form of wealth. I see bringing innocent lives into the world to suffer and die. I also see a planet that cannot sustain an ever-expanding human population, but of course it is a futile first-world argument. I let it go. Instead I talk about how scary it is to drive in the Philippines. Children and carabao will just suddenly dart into the road.

"We expect that," Father Pacheco says. "We see the child on the porch, we know that child will run into the street. We are ready for that. The problem with Americans? They don't expect the child to run into the street."

We are back in Manila, leaving the Philippines tomorrow. It is cheaper and easier to get a flight on Christmas Day than on Christmas Eve. I find it odd when Michael vanishes, without warning, early in the evening from our Roxas Boulevard hotel. He's gone for hours. I worry. It's after midnight when he returns. He is reluctant to say where he has been. Troubled, he finally confesses.

There is a backstory: Earlier that year, our newspaper proposed new work rules that could lead to the weakening of union and eventually its demise. Many of us would be classified as senior writers, exempt from having to file a timecard, so the company could avoid having to pay overtime. It was put to a vote, and the union-busting lawyers advised the newspaper to offer employees a bonus if the measure passed: $1,200 for each employee. A majority of our colleagues voted yes. We got our money. Blood money. Michael had his on him—in cash. We'd learned to carry cash from covering the civil war in El Salvador the previous year.

Michael tells me he went to a bank days earlier and exchanged the US $1,200 for hundreds of small bills in Philippine pesos that he stuffed into numerous envelopes. He has just spent the night walking the streets of the slums, giving the entire amount to dozens of beggars.

Hi Dale,

I hope this finds you well. I'd like to ask if you were the journalist who came over to Negros Island in the Philippines at the height of the Marcos dictatorship?

If so, you interviewed my Dad, Emilio. I remember you sent a copy of that article but somehow over the years, we've lost it.

Do you still have a copy of that?

Thank you and hope to hear from you.

This Facebook message from Angelie Yulo arrived on a night in 2021 when the story I had written on her father thirty-six years earlier was stationed on my desk. I turned from looking at the computer screen to the face of Emilio in the picture Michael Williamson took of him in 1985. The message had arrived unprompted, one of those random things in life that makes one believe that perhaps life is not so random.

After responding to Angelie, I learned in follow-up messages that Emilio was now eighty-six and that "he's okay except that he has speech impairment so he has difficulty communicating. But his memory is still good. I talked to him as soon as I got your reply and he remembers you and that you slept in the farm house. He remembers that you sent boxes of used clothing that we distributed to the people and is grateful for that."

Emilio had been elected mayor of the town of Isabela three times. "He was able to improve the financial state of the town. He focused on education and the public schools in Isabela were able to garner achievements through his support. During the Cory [Aquino] administration, we were able to revert all the lands back to sugarcane. Free trade was restored and the farm owners were able to recover with better prices. Yesterday we were talking about the past in relation to the coming elections here in the Philippines."

Angelie was going door-to-door drumming up votes for the "pink power" movement, Leni Robredo's campaign for president in 2022.

When in college, Robredo had been active in the People Power movement that went on to topple Ferdinand Marcos in 1986. She was now vice president of the Philippines. She had been repeatedly savaged by incumbent president Rodrigo Duterte, who had been elected on a separate ballot. Robredo opposed Duterte's brutal drug war.

Robredo's opponent was Ferdinand Marcos Jr., known as "Bongbong." In reality, Robredo was running against Facebook, TikTok, and YouTube vloggers. A typhoon of lies streamed over these platforms. The fabrications against her included accusations of infidelity and promiscuity, and that she belonged to the Communist New People's Army.

The fiction in favor of the latest Marcos: his profound wealth hadn't come from the money stolen by his father; rather, Bongbong was gifted tons of gold by a mysterious royal family; the Marcos years of martial law were a "golden time" for the country; there was a strong economy and massive infrastructure projects.

The reality about the $10 billion ripped off by the elder Marcos was deemed fake news.

It worked. Bongbong won in a landslide.

History was rewritten.

On the day of the election, I wrote an email to Angelie: "For me it seems like the clock has just been turned back, all the energy in the People Power movement forgotten." They were right back where they had started thirty-six years earlier.

"Oh my God! It's disgusting how people can have very short memories," Angelie immediately replied. "Bongbong prepared for this. The disinformation and the attempts at historical revisions are just terrible. In the end, the have-nots will be most affected. Pray for the Philippines."

It didn't take long for history to echo and the American empire to return to the Philippines. In early 2023, a photo ran of US secretary of defense Lloyd Austin III posing with Philippine president Ferdinand Marcos Jr. in Malacañang Palace.

We were looking at the doom loop.

Another US official, another Marcos, and an invitation for the United States to allow American forces access to four Philippine bases, to counter China's increasingly hostile actions in the South China Sea.

# Vietnam Comes Home

Thai Khac Chuyen's job for the US Army's Fifth Special Forces group, the Green Berets, was officially as an interpreter. He was paid $160 per month. In truth he was with a secret unit called B-57, tasked with gathering intelligence in the border regions of Vietnam. A focus of his covert work was inside Laos, to monitor movements of the enemy. South Vietnamese agents like Chuyen were key for the mission of the Green Berets: President John F. Kennedy saw them as the future of American unconventional warfare that relied on counterinsurgency. But in the late spring of 1969, Chuyen's Green Beret "handler" at the Special Forces headquarters—Sergeant Alvin L. Smith Jr.—developed a roll of film captured from a raid of a guerrilla camp in Cambodia. One of the frames was of Chuyen talking to an officer in the North Vietnamese Army. Chuyen was placed under surveillance.

As this investigation was starting, on May 29 a new commander was sent to Vietnam for the 3,500 Green Berets—Colonel Robert Rheault. He wasn't a desk jockey—he knew the terrain. Colonel Rheault had come to Vietnam as a lieutenant colonel in 1964 and roamed all over the country as an executive officer with Special Forces. Returning to command the Green Berets was a dream come true for him—as he said, "To lead the best of the best." He was forty-four but looked older. His gray hair, in a military brush cut, stood straight up; his face was leathery. He smoked a lot. Yet the six foot one, 160-pound

159

soldier could run a mile in six and a half minutes wearing combat boots. Every day, he did a regimen of pushups, sit-ups, chin-ups. He firmly believed that guerrilla tactics were necessary in modern warfare. He relished the new assignment.

On June 11, 1969, Thai Khac Chuyen, age thirty-one, showed up at Camp Goodman, a Special Forces outpost in Saigon. He'd been ordered to go there from Moc Hoa, a town a few miles from the Cambodian border, where he'd been stationed with the Green Berets. At Camp Goodman, he was injected with Sodium Pentothal, a so-called truth serum, and hooked to a polygraph. The next night he was brought home. His house was searched. He was left there with his wife, Phan Kim Lien, and their two children; Phan said to a reporter that her husband was "agitated." It was the last night she would spend with him.

Chuyen went back to Camp Goodman the next day, and from there was flown to Nha Trang, on the South China Sea. He may have been tortured. In the coming days, the Green Berets who were interrogating Chuyen went to the CIA, the agency running the secret war inside Laos fought by Hmong soldiers. The CIA was directing some operations performed by the Green Berets, and in fact that agency may have been Chuyen's main employer. The Green Berets asked the CIA agents what they should do. Numerous accounts say the agents answered that Chuyen was a "Beret problem." The Berets said they were told to "terminate with extreme prejudice." This was a euphemism for "execute."

The Berets protested, but the CIA rebuffed them. On the night of June 20, Captain Leland Brumley injected Chuyen with morphine to knock him out. The Berets carried his limp body to a boat. Out in the South China Sea, Captain Robert F. Marasco shot Chuyen in the head with a pistol. Chuyen's corpse was placed in a bag weighted with a padlocked chain and dropped over the side. The Berets then concocted a cover story: Chuyen had been sent on a dangerous mission deep into Cambodia and vanished. It was backed up with an elaborate ruse—a Green Beret with Asian ancestry was flown to Tan Son Nhut Air Base near Saigon, using Chuyen's ID. Thus the fake

Chuyen was seen publicly embarking on the mission. This fabrication was approved by the new commander: Colonel Rheault.

It would have remained an unknown and unsolved war crime except for Sergeant Alvin Smith, who initially had discovered the photograph of Chuyen with the North Vietnamese officer. On June 30, Smith left his B-57 office in Nha Trang and got into an Army jeep. He drove to the nearby CIA headquarters. There Smith asked for "asylum," saying that the previous night some of the same officers who killed Chuyen had gone on a practice run in the boat as part of a plan to kill Smith, who had protested the execution of Chuyen. Smith said those officers were uneasy and worried that he might go public. Smith told the CIA that they were "a bunch of wild men."

The CIA took this information to General Creighton W. Abrams, the commander of all forces in Vietnam. Seven Green Berets were called in for questioning, and they lied about what had happened. When the cover-up was exposed, General Abrams lost his temper and ordered them arrested on murder charges—including Colonel Rheault.

The case of the Special Forces arrestees was of keen interest to Frank McCulloch, the Saigon bureau chief for Time-Life. While on vacation in Vermont, he saw a newspaper story about them. He recognized the picture of the colonel. Back in 1964, the Special Forces advisers, who were operating in semisecret, had piqued McCulloch's curiosity—he'd wanted to do a story on the Berets. McCulloch was rebuffed by a young lieutenant colonel—Rheault. Later that year, Rheault relented and allowed McCulloch to embed at a Special Forces outpost in Dak Lak province for twelve days.

Two weeks after he put down that newspaper article in Vermont, McCulloch interviewed Colonel Rheault for a story that appeared in *Life* on November 14, 1969. Rheault's face is on the cover of the magazine. His fingers grasp what appears to be a hand-rolled cigarette; smoke rises from it, curling to his squinting left eye. He stares at the camera with a mix of bravado and the diffidence of a man who would rather not be in public view. But here he is. For all the visible male bluster of a soldier, it is offset by something very hippie—a thin gold wrist bracelet that is out of place on such a man. It seems he brandishes it for a reason, a statement; we have to assume this because he dressed for this moment to be photographed by a magazine with a circulation of 8.5 million and seen by tens of millions more in the offices of doctors and dentists. He presents incongruity. There are two decks of type on the *Life* cover over his bristle-brush buzz cut:

> Mailer on the Astronauts
> The Green Beret Colonel

Inside the magazine, the headline over the three-page spread is "A believer in self-reliance and elitism."

Suddenly, the murder charges were dismissed against all eight Green Berets. One gets the sense in reviewing dozens of stories written about the case that the arrests were made only because Sergeant Smith had gone to the CIA terrified for his life; at the time McCulloch did his story, Smith's actions were not yet in the public record. McCulloch could cite only "unexplained reasons" for the CIA's going to General Abrams and the story's making the news.

The case mattered only because a White American soldier was threatened. The war atrocity was not at issue. One analysis suggests that Abrams regretted reacting in anger and ordering the arrests. Once the initial stories died away, Colonel Rheault retired from the military. It was time to move on. Also, a far worse story had simultaneously exploded on the brass. On November 11, 1969, freelance journalist Seymour Hersh broke the news of the My Lai massacre—a mass killing of unarmed Vietnamese civilians by US soldiers in March 1968—in the Associated Press; the next day the *Cleveland Plain Dealer* published the first explicit pictures. As many as five hundred civilians, including infants, had been slain. Women were gang-raped. Bodies were mutilated. It was an orgy of violence.

Amid this, John Milius—a student at the University of Southern California studying film—noticed McCulloch's story on Rheault. In 1967, a professor had commented to the class about how filmmakers had always wanted to make Joseph Conrad's novella *Heart of Darkness* into a movie, but nobody had been able to. "That was like waving a red flag in front of a bull," Milius said to a journalist. He thought the novella would be a great framework for a film about the Vietnam War.

Milius wrote a screenplay based on the novella and, two years later, sold it to Warner Bros. The film was titled *Apocalypse Now* and was to be produced by American Zoetrope, owned by Frances Ford Coppola. Milius's classmate George Lucas was attached as director. Milius was still working on the script, and Frank McCulloch's *Life* magazine article provided inspiration to develop the character of US Army Special Forces Colonel Walter E. Kurtz, a renegade Green Beret fighting his own private war up a fictional Nung River.

Lucas then left the project to make *Star Wars*, and Coppola took over as director. Production was a brutal and long journey—the studio didn't really want a Vietnam War movie when the war was still going on. Filming was done in the Philippines. The US Department of Defense refused to cooperate and allow the use of military aircraft the way it had when John Wayne starred in *The Green Berets*, shot at an Army base in Georgia, complete with several UH-1 "Huey" attack helicopters.

The *Apocalypse Now* filmmakers made friends with Ferdinand Marcos; he authorized the use of Philippine Army helicopters—American-provided Hueys—and other equipment. And the jungles of the Philippines were an apt stand-in for Vietnam: both nations occupy the same latitude on opposite sides of the South China Sea. Once filming began in 1976, the production was beset with cost overruns and other problems, including Martin Sheen's having a heart attack. The film wouldn't hit theater screens until 1979.

Sheen plays US Army captain Benjamin Willard, who is sent on a mission to find Colonel Kurtz and "terminate with extreme prejudice," a quote from McCulloch's article. When Marlon Brando was cast as Kurtz, he got in touch with McCulloch. Brando wanted to know everything about Colonel Rheault so he could fully inhabit the character. They had several long phone conversations. Brando usually called McCulloch late at night.

One hears and feels the Rheault from McCulloch's story in the film. As with the real-life colonel, Kurtz leaves a cushy and high-profile

Pentagon assignment to go back to Vietnam. Like Rheault, Kurtz believes guerrilla methods are needed to fight a war such as the one in Indochina. One can even literally see Rheault in Brando. When Captain Willard is given a black-and-white photograph of Kurtz at the start of *Apocalypse Now*, being sent on his mission to kill the colonel, it uncannily resembles the *Life* magazine cover photograph of Rheault, only in profile.

In 1980, when I began applying for jobs in California, I had a list of big newspapers and contact information for editors that I carefully charted in a file folder. My number-one desire was the *Bee* in Sacramento. I sat at the kitchen table in my parents' house in Ohio and stared at the phone. It was the first call I made. By nature, I'm shy. Even now, over forty years after I began working in the newsroom of the *Gazette*, I hate cold calls. I'm not good at them. I get nervous. I didn't feel on game when I asked to speak with a midlevel editor whose name I'd gotten from a directory of American newspapers at the library. That editor wasn't in. I was transferred to another editor, who must have sensed my nervousness; his voice was deep and kind, and that got me to relax. I forget exactly what we talked about. What I remember is that it was a very long call, nearly thirty minutes. At the end, I apologized for taking so much time and for not catching his name at the start.

"Frank," he said. "Frank McCulloch."

David Halberstam's *The Powers That Be* had just been published, about the rise of major media empires in the United States, and Frank's role in transforming the *Los Angeles Times* between 1960 and 1964 is a key part of the book. Under his watch, the *Times* did deep investigative pieces on the right-wing advocacy group the John Birch Society and shady practices involving the Teamsters Union's pension fund. Halberstam describes McCulloch as "civilized macho," because of his bald head that some said resembled a bullet, and his genteel nature combined with fearlessness. His baldness had caught the attention of President Lyndon Johnson, who was angered by McCulloch's reporting in Vietnam when he returned to Time-Life in 1964. Johnson said that being hatless in the jungle must have affected McCulloch. "He's addled," Johnson said. After leaving Time-Life, McCulloch went to Sacramento in 1975 to lead the newsroom as managing editor.

It's a good thing I didn't know it was Frank McCulloch at the start of the call—I surely would have been starstruck and would have babbled.

I never got to work directly for Frank when the *Bee* hired me later that year. He was moved out of the newsroom and given an office down a long hallway where all the suits worked. He was placed in charge of the McClatchy Company's five newspapers, three of them in California's Central Valley—Sacramento, Modesto, and Fresno. The company had recently purchased papers in Alaska and Washington state. I often made pilgrimages down that long hallway to Frank's place of what felt to me like exile. His door was always open. If he wasn't on the phone, he would wave me in. Frank mentored me about matters concerning journalism, about writing—about life.

Frank was born on a ranch in rural Nevada, and he knew the West, the desolate mountains of eastern Northern California that remain relatively unpeopled to this day. When I began riding freight trains with Michael Williamson for the story on new hobos, which later became our first book, Frank knew all about the Keddie Wye, where the railroad tracks split at the top of the Feather River Canyon. From there, Western Pacific trains that came out of Sacramento either went north through the lava beds country to Klamath Falls, or east to cross the Nevada desert and on to the Roper Yards of Salt Lake City.

Frank would talk about the "faces in the mountains" around Keddie. He understood that haunted landscape, a place of spirits: in a certain light, one does see faces in the sides of mountains there. After serving in the military in World War II, Frank became a police reporter at the *Reno Evening Gazette*. One day he was embedded with police, a story Frank told in exacting detail. (Years later when I looked up Frank's story about it, which ran on November 8, 1947, it was like hearing him tell it to me that day in 1981.)

Frank had trailed officers seeking armed robbery suspects, including eighteen-year-old David Blackwell, to the Carleton Hotel; Frank had been in the room when the officers disarmed one of the suspects. "Capt. Geach and Sgt. Glass proceeded to where Blackwell was lying in bed in an adjoining room," Frank wrote. "As Capt. Geach threw the bed clothing back from Blackwell he was met with numerous blasts from the robbery suspects' .38 caliber super special automatic. He fell to the floor mortally wounded, and Sgt. Glass, standing behind him, was also hit several times and was killed outright." What the story doesn't say: Frank was observing in the doorway directly behind the two officers. He told me that Blackwell had filed down the firing pin of the pistol so that it acted like a machine gun. I asked Frank how he hadn't been hit.

"Pure luck, that's it," Frank said.

I also heard about Howard Hughes, one of the world's richest men, who shunned everyone, especially the press. In the 1950s, once Frank was at *Time* magazine, he reached out to the reclusive Hughes— who, to his surprise, telephoned him back. This led to several stories and numerous phone calls, usually late at night. In 1958, Frank got another phone call, at one in the morning, from Hughes. "[He told me to] drive to the intersection of Olympic and Sepulveda Boulevards, park at the southwest corner, blink my lights twice, and wait for a two-tone, 1954 Mercury sedan to come alongside." This quote comes from a story Frank wrote in 1970, and it's precisely how I remember him telling it to me.

He wrote that he got in a car with that driver sent by Hughes, and once they'd gotten to that intersection, "the driver politely invited me to get in the backseat. We made our way by back roads to the unfinished western end of Los Angeles International Airport. There the driver left me stranded in the middle of an unfinished runway.... Right behind me, looming up in the dark was Boeing's prototype of the 707." The plane was not yet in commercial use.

Hughes summoned Frank aboard, and with Hughes in the pilot's seat, they took off and flew all night, "down the Baja California coast, back up through Arizona, across Las Vegas.... What Howard was trying to show me, though he never articulated it, was that the 707 was a helluva airplane, and if he could just get the money he needed to buy enough of them, he could bail TWA out." They landed at Los Angeles International Airport at dawn.

This was the last interview Hughes ever gave. He never consented to an on-record interview for the remaining two decades of his life. But Hughes occasionally phoned Frank over the years, in off-the-record calls. The final one came in 1976. It was from one of Hughes's assistants, who asked Frank to remain on hold. The assistant then came back on and apologized; Mr. Hughes was suddenly unable to talk. Hughes died the next day.

Frank handed down words of wisdom as he told me these stories. On writing: "Throw your notebook across the room; write the story. Don't look at your notebook." He said that was the mistake of many young writers—you have to get your face out of your notes. First tell the story, he said, then clean up the facts after you fetch the notebook. On how Michael and I were reporting on poverty: "People spend thousands of dollars and travel thousands of miles to cover the things they ignore at home." It was a wise observation; the stories about the working poor that I was finding in Ohio and Texas and other places were the same in Sacramento. On journalists: "It's not that journalists are cynics. They're hopeless idealists."

We young reporters in the newsroom called him Uncle Frank. It seemed he would always be down the hall. But in 1985, our publisher, C. K. McClatchy, told him that it was time for him to retire; he was sixty-five, the age when McClatchy wanted people to leave. This occurred during one of my breakdowns, when I was dealing with the aftermath of El Salvador and other trauma: three years of riding freight trains all over the country; the publication of my book; my collapse in agonizing pain and Hilary Abramson rushing me to the doctor; being on meds for the stress that was wrenching my innards; and being broke because of the time I'd taken off without pay to write the book. I confessed to Frank that I was losing my shit.

For the first time in the four years I'd been visiting his office, Frank got up and closed the door. He sat back down and told about how when he was reporting in the jungles of Vietnam, it meant he wasn't there for his children back in America; his son was troubled and died

167

at an early age. He was emotional and talked with regret about being an absent father. His message: "Take care of yourself." And, though I don't recall the exact words, he essentially said, "Don't do what I did."

In these final days of Frank's tenure at the helm of the McClatchy newspapers, I talked with him about Vietnam. This is when I heard about the nighttime calls from Marlon Brando. The reason I'd asked about the war is that I'd been put on a team assigned to produce a special section for the newspaper on the end of the Vietnam War in April 1975. Our project would be published ten years after the last Americans left Saigon.

There were eighteen thousand people from Indochina in Sacramento, and fourteen thousand of them, many from Laos, were on welfare. They were a mix of mountain and lowland people. What they had in common was that they didn't have a written language. Many didn't even know what a pencil was. They were suffering culture shock in the extreme, and this led to self-destructive behavior and family violence.

Typical was Banh Douangchampa, whom I met on the last day of October 1982. After fleeing Laos in 1975, she lived in a refugee camp in Thailand for six years. She'd been in Sacramento less than one year. She was twenty-six, and her brow was furrowed from fear and confusion. Fahm, her eighteen-month-old boy, had been beaten with a brass lamp by Banh's husband, Chanta. Fahm was in custody of child protective services, and Chanta was in jail on attempted murder charges. Banh wanted her child back. She said that in Laos, the Communists would take children away from parents and there was nothing one could do; she thought it was the same in the US.

No authorities came to talk with her for weeks; and when they did show up, they didn't speak Laotian. The emergency room doctor who was treating the boy's head wounds, Dr. Herbert Ruhs, was baffled and angry enough to talk on the record. This was before the Health Insurance Portability and Accountability Act, HIPAA, was passed, and he was able to speak freely.

"The child is crying constantly" for his mother, Dr. Ruhs said. Fahm was lost in the system. "There should be some way to deal with this, to get children back with a parent or relative...at least a family that can speak Laotian. This whole thing is a big machine that's grinding this family down." The story I wrote about this prompted officials to do something—two days after it ran, Fahm and Banh were reunited. I wrote about that as well.

Just over one year after I met Banh, I was assigned a story on the pain that those on the American side of the war felt. A group of veterans had formed the Viet Vet Center in a small rented house in a low-income neighborhood of North Sacramento, in an area peopled by the descendants of Dust Bowl refugees; the home was surrounded by clandestine meth labs (which I'd mapped out for a different story using police arrest data).

Entering the house was akin to arriving in Vietnam. Some of the guys called the place the "hootch," after the kinds of temporary tents and make-do spaces they'd lived in during the war. Guys wore camos from their tours of duty, surnames sewn on pockets; one vet had a floppy camo hat. The men seemed lost in time, frozen in an experience they couldn't escape. A study by an academic on the center showed that half of the members had not finished high school and were jobless. In 1983, three years after its founding, the center was $8,000 in debt and facing eviction. The story I wrote was published, but I'm not sure if that one was of any help.

I wrote other stories involving Cambodians, Laotians, and American veterans. By early 1985, when an editor put me on the Vietnam project, I was keenly interested based on the reporting I'd already done on the outfall of that war in Sacramento. And there was my long-standing conscious and subconscious fascination with war and US hegemony—I was already doing research on the Philippines, meeting with activists in Sacramento and the Bay Area. (My interest started the previous year, when I did a story on record numbers of Filipinos coming to the US because of Marcos—the newcomers were settled in a community in the South Sacramento area.) But it was also personal. I could explore the unanswered questions from when my friends and I faced being drafted into what seemed to be that never-ending war. One cannot describe the soul-wrenching anxiety that the Vietnam

War caused in young men in that era, the sleepless nights lying in bed worried about what awaited us in a distant jungle.

The project began in the newspaper's morgue, a room next to the sports department where a team of librarians labored at tables, razor knives and straight edges in hand, slicing up copies of that day's Blue Star and final editions. Each story was precisely and tightly folded, some of the longer ones so compactly that the result was akin to origami; glue from a pot was swiped on a yellow, pink, or light green sheaf of paper measuring three and a half inches by eight inches, and the backside of the article was affixed to it.

These were then inserted by order of date into fat manila envelopes just slightly larger than the sheaves of colored paper; the subject was written by hand in heavy black marker at the top of the envelope. Articles were cross-filed by topics, surnames, and bylines. Some were filed six or eight different ways. That meant thousands of daily additions to the library. These were stored in alphabetical rows of gray steel cabinets. It had been done this way for decades. Really old stories, from the 1950s and earlier, were on microfilm. The smell of horse glue and musty yellowed newsprint filled the air when one entered this room.

I went down the row to the "V" cabinet. There were folders about the Vietnam War and the protests against it. I focused on 1968 through 1971. Amid hundreds of clippings, one stood out: at San Juan High School in suburban Sacramento, a fire had been set in the counseling and records office. Whoever ignited the blaze had painted Viet Cong slogans on the walls.

My long investigation into the fire and its fallout at this high school led me to four men, one of them quite difficult to find. Talking with these men transported me back in time to my late teens, and to my demons about that war that I'd missed being drafted into by dint of only a few years of difference in age from the draftees. One couldn't get away with writing in the first person, not at that newspaper or any metro daily of that era, unless there were extraordinary circumstances. But after weeks of reporting and immersion, I came close as possible to it by summing up my quest in the lead, in the existential second person:

It was a time of confusion, those days in the late 1960s. If you were a young man, you had to ask yourself, what am I going to do about Vietnam?

From that cold gray steel cabinet and the faded newsprint in the *Bee*'s morgue emerged the protagonist of this story: Mike Fostar. Mike is one of those rare three-dimensional characters who could reside in the pages of a novel or come alive on the screen. His story is quintessentially postwar American. It begins a decade before his birth, in a small Western Pennsylvania town near Pittsburgh on a hill overlooking the bend of a creek flowing into the Monongahela River, against a backdrop of smoking steel mills in Braddock and Rankin.

It's here where Mike's father, Michael Fostar Sr., was at the age of twenty-one employed as a bearing assembler at Westinghouse Electric before he was spirited off to serve in the US Air Force; he became a senior noncommissioned officer by the end of World War II. This fact is worth mentioning only because of how the war propelled Michael Sr. to change; like so many veterans at the end of World War II, he dreamed of a different life in the prosperity that followed. This meant moving somewhere new, somewhere far from the sulfurous industrial valleys of Pennsylvania: California.

Michael and his wife, Ann, were drawn to an unincorporated area of eastern Sacramento County. This region in 1910 had been subdivided by the real estate company Trainor & Desmond, which sold ten-acre parcels. The company called it Citrus Heights, conjured from imagination. There were no citrus groves. It was rough and dusty land that had been used for cattle grazing, growing wheat and grains, since it had been a Mexican land grant before statehood. The exotic name, however, appears to have inspired the newcomers to plant groves. Citrus Heights actually was soon covered with citrus trees, and in spring the air was scented with the perfume of the orange and lemon blooms.

But like so many California dreams, the newcomers' turned out to be utopian, which never quite work out. The state's extremes of nature are rough on pioneers—in any era. In 1932, a big freeze hit, plunging temperatures to eighteen degrees; most of the citrus trees perished and were left blackened skeletons. The small farms were subdivided after the war; when Michael and Ann Fostar arrived in 1946, the area was starting to become a suburb. One imagines a teenage Joan Didion driving east from midtown Sacramento to the Sierra on the old Lincoln Highway, US 40, looking in horror upon this swarming mass of new boxy little houses.

By the time Michael Fostar Jr. was born in June 1951, Citrus Heights was on its way to having over twenty thousand residents at the end of that decade. Mike had two sisters; their family was typical of the tens of thousands of veterans who lived in the Sacramento region. They were conservative, very White, and very suburban. The majority were working class, employed by the state government, the two US Air Force bases in Sacramento, or at Aerojet General Corporation, which at its peak had twenty thousand workers at its plant in Rancho Cordova, some five miles to the south.

In 1965, Mike entered the freshman class at San Juan High School on Greenback Lane. He was fifteen but looked younger, a geeky kid, a little chubby in the face, with heavy black-rimmed glasses. He was a normal boy for that era, and "normal" for a boy meant joining the junior varsity football team, the Spartans. His position: lineman. In one yearbook picture, he's in the third row amid fifty-four boys seated on the bleacher seats in numbered playing uniforms with the pads squaring their shoulders, making them look bigger and feel tougher; none of the fifty-four are smiling.

In later reflection during an interview, Mike described himself this way: "I believed in all this stuff that our heads were filled up with, that we were 'all in this together' kind of thing. I believed in the coaches and I believed in America." He watched John Wayne movies. He liked football. He felt part of the team. Part of *something bigger*. He was the kind of son Donald Swihart would have loved, and he was evolving into following the life path of his father, who now worked for the National Security Agency, the shadowy and then mostly unknown unit with much of its spy power aimed at the Soviets. It was so secret, it was often referred to as "No Such Agency."

Mike's father was a career military man. There are a lot of them in Sacramento still. Michael Sr. always told his son, "America, right or wrong!"

But something happened the summer before Mike's junior year that began rapidly chipping away at this imprint and made him start connecting the football field off of Greenback Lane to the machines of war that he heard operating to the south, in Rancho Cordova.

During one of the football team's scrimmages, Mike's team member Rich Metz, who was a back, tripped and fell by accident right under the goal post, landing on Mike's leg. Mike went to the emergency room, and his leg was placed in a cast. He came back on crutches and in the ensuing days began hanging around the locker room.

As he tells it:

> I'd been with this team of guys all through my freshman year, through my sophomore year. And the coach came up to me and he said, "You're freaking everybody out. Everybody's beginning to get nervous with you around because they're worried about getting hurt. We don't want anybody second-guessing themselves. We don't want anybody worrying about getting hurt. And there you are sitting on the bench with your crutches and your foot in your cast. You're cheering on the team and all that, but we don't want you here. Why don't you beat it? Get out of here." All of a sudden I was nothing.

Mike was now an outcast. In high school, outsiders often just slink off to the corners and vanish, become the kids no one remembers after graduation; if anyone does recall them, it might be because one sees them a year or two after their senior year bagging groceries at the Safeway or Von's. One might know that kid but have no idea of his name. Outsiders can also become dangerous, and not necessarily in the manner seen decades later of coming back to shoot up the school. These outsiders don't use firearms. They become rebels. Mike had got the impetus to become one from the dean of boys at San Juan High School even before he was told to hobble away from the football team on his crutches.

James K. Conley, the dean of boys, was an unremarkable-looking man, with small, narrow eyes lost in acres of face. His hair was military-style short and slightly blond, and he occasionally wore a plaid jacket that even then was not fashionable. Conley was in his early thirties, but like many adults in that era, appeared to be a decade older.

He had strong ideas about how the boys under his charge should behave. He grew particularly concerned during Mike's sophomore year, in January 1967, when the Rolling Stones released the song "Let's Spend the Night Together." It was some six months before Mike broke his leg. The B-side of the 45 RPM record was "Ruby Tuesday." Conley only paid attention to the A-side. After each physical education class, he had the boys sit in the bleachers, spending about ten minutes with each of the four grades. He didn't quote the lyrics but all the boys knew the song about the protagonist satisfying a woman's needs; in turn that woman satisfying his.

Conley gave a lecture about how this song was improper, saying that the boys should never spend a night with any girl in the school. Conley hated rock music, but "Let's Spend the Night Together" sent him into a new orbit. According to Mike:

> That particular song just drove him crazy. This behavior would lead to unwanted pregnancies. A number of girls got pregnant during the years I was at the school. One right down the street from where I lived. Beautiful girl, named Sue. And when they got pregnant in those days, they were no longer students at our school. They went to continuation high school and had their babies, if they were going to have their babies. They never again showed up. They disappeared.

Mike was disillusioned after he broke the leg and was jettisoned from the football team. The fall of his junior year, 1967, he met Randy Bechtel, a member of the Quill and Scroll honor society and the editor of the school paper, the *Spartan*. Randy, with a jutting chin, carried himself in the manner of a literary man. In photographs from that era he is always brooding. He was a good editor, knew talent, and recognized the outsider in Mike—always the main ingredient of a good journalist. Mike was despondent.

> Randy felt sorry for me. And so he said, "Hey, would you like to be the school photographer?" I had been taking some photography classes, and they had a photography lab. So I became the school photographer.

Mike embraced his new role. He got to meet and photograph everyone. He suddenly shed the label of outsider.

In the wake of his banishment from the jock clique, Mike began chafing at the rigidity of the dean of boys, the clean-cut Conley. Now that Mike was visible and everyone knew who he was, he decided to run for student body president. His platform? Changing the school's conservative dress and appearance codes. As it stood, the boys were all supposed to look like Dean Conley. The girls had to wear dresses.

"I wanted to have the boys be able to have mustaches or sideburns and long hair, and I wanted the girls to be able to wear pants or shorts," Mike says. He ran and he won by a decisive margin. But then: "Conley decided we would have a runoff, which had never been done before." There were four candidates. This time Mike lost by some forty votes.

Amid this, the Citrus Heights community erupted against Mike. He was suddenly seen as a radical.

> My mother received several death threats. This was the period of the John Birch Society, which was really strong in this area. I wasn't a radical at all. But suggesting that long hair was okay on guys, and the girls could wear whatever they wanted, was breaking the authoritarian hold on everyone. They didn't like it. There were rumors going around that if I was made student body president, I would cancel all sporting events. And it was funny because I originally came from the jock world.

As Mike moved into his senior year, his political awakening took him off campus—he volunteered for Robert F. Kennedy's presidential campaign. He worked in a local campaign office and handed out handbills in front of supermarkets. A highlight was being seated up front when Kennedy gave a speech in Sacramento on May 16, 1968.

Conley kept his eye on Mike but watched other students even more keenly. The main focus of Conley's ire was Ethan Aronson, who was close with Mike's sister, Layne. Ethan and Layne were sophomores. Because of this connection, even though the boy was two years younger—a wide gulf at that age—Mike was friends with Ethan and with Ethan's friend Jeff Whitnack. Ethan was far more radical than Mike; he vehemently opposed the war in Vietnam, as did Jeff. They led school walkouts and staged protests against the war.

During this period, the counseling office burned; Viet Cong slogans were scrawled on the walls. At night, someone would run a Viet Cong flag up the pole in front of the school. Conley had suspicions about who was responsible.

Mike didn't take part in the walkouts. And he certainly wasn't one of the students involved in the Viet Cong slogans and flag. He was the opposite of a Communist—in his new position as the school photographer, he saw a way he could monetize his access to the darkroom, with the goal of buying a used car.

"I knew all the cheerleaders, and I knew all the jocks. And I knew they were real big ego hounds," he said. He'd see a couple holding hands and ask if they wanted their picture taken. He'd then run to the photo lab between classes and develop a few glossy eight-by-tens; he'd drop off the images before the end of the school day. He scored ten bucks here, twenty bucks there, and it added up. When he got $700 together from the photo hustle, he made a cash down payment on a 1966 Mustang.

Seven hundred bucks was a lot of money in mid-1968. The Mustang was two-door, beige, with a cream interior. Meantime, the new class president that senior year—the kid who was elected vice president when Mike lost the election junior year—pushed through all the changes that Mike wanted. Boys got to have longer hair; girls were able to wear pants. "It was a big deal. And Conley was choking on it the whole time." Conley seemed to focus his ire on Mike. That fall, Conley saw a chance for payback.

Mike was summoned to the main office. Two Sacramento County sheriff's deputies were present. And Mike's mother. Conley insisted that the deputies arrest Mike. The crime? Selling photos made with school equipment. As he tells it:

> The sheriff's deputies were like, "Why are we here?" He's trying to make a case for theft of school property. The principal came in and was very skeptical. Conley was trying to get me really hard. My mother exploded: "What the hell are you talking about? This is ridiculous."

Ann noted that she'd received death threats when her son ran for school body president. She'd reported those threats to the police,

> "…and nobody did anything about that. But you're worried about him selling pictures?" Everybody was looking up at the ceiling. And the principal said, "Look, I noticed here that you have enough units to graduate midterm. So we're just going to graduate you midterm. Just get on out of here."

This was much bigger than being kicked off the football team. Mike was being kicked out into life. He would turn eighteen that coming June. Prime draft bait. He didn't have plans for college. He had no plan at all. His father was berating him to enter the service. It's what you were supposed to do. It was a working-class community. If you were the son of a veteran, the kids who were football players, you graduated and served your country. You came home and had three children. Those children would then repeat the process.

Until his third year in high school, Mike had been following this de facto plan. Being kicked off the team, then invited to leave school—"Don't let the door hit you in the ass"—made him question going to war. But he wasn't like his sister's friends, Ethan and Jeff. They were certain they wouldn't go. Mike struggled with his decision. He and his dad had intense arguments.

> My father said, "Look, you don't want to become a draft dodger, because that would ruin your life. You'd be a criminal. You'll never

have a good job. And besides, the majority of American military don't go into combat anyway. So it'll be okay."

That New Year's Eve, after he'd left school for good, Mike got together with Randy Bechtel and a few other friends. It was a foggy night. They talked about the kids ahead of them who had died in Vietnam—there were a few each year. "Class after class, from sixty-five to sixty-six, sixty-seven to sixty-eight, they graduate and then *boom*— they're off to Vietnam. And then the couple guys in every class get knocked off. This endless string of guys going off to Vietnam because it's a working-class area." It wasn't like nearby Carmichael, where the upper-class kids lived.

The young men drank and talked about their fears. Randy was set on going—he wanted to write a great American war novel. Someone played The Doors' album *Waiting for the Sun*, released in early 1968, and the song "The Unknown Soldier" about a man killed in war.

What would Mike do if the draft notice came? He'd always answered through his mid–high school years, "I dunno." Now, with his eighteenth birthday nearing, the question grew more acute. "We were saying we were all doomed. We were all going off to Vietnam to be devoured by it."

Fast-forward to the summer of 1985, midway in act two of our story on Mike Fostar. I sign out one of the newspaper's company cars and drive an hour and a half north from Sacramento, through the Central Valley, hot in the July sun, to the town of Paradise, California, in the Sierra foothills. As I come down a forested lane, Mike waits outside to greet me. When I exit the car, we notice a hawk soaring on air currents coming up-canyon. The wind whispers loudly through the pines.

"It's funny," Mike says as we watch the hawk. "This area looks like the highlands of Vietnam. But this is called Paradise. And it really is."

In the end, there was no choice: Mike Fostar went to Vietnam. He went in as a medic, thinking it meant he wouldn't have to kill anyone.

He has war artifacts and pictures displayed inside his home, waiting for me to see. On the table before us: medals, including a Bronze

Star and a Purple Heart. He says that any sense he would not face the violence of war as a medic quickly dissipated. Bombs were soon falling around him. He was told there were two kinds of soldiers: the quick and the dead.

"Combat had a twisting effect on me. I got into it. I went gung-ho. I was just gonzo." He says he quickly forgot the antiwar words of Ethan Aronson and Jeff Whitnack. Their reality was no longer valid. They lived in a past life.

"It got to the point where I was stripped of all other realities. The most bizarre actions were perfectly acceptable. Our unit became the killer force. Our unit was never beaten. We ambushed a lot of people. But we got chopped up in the process. We lost over half our company."

He had to rescue fellow soldiers amid firefights. He describes it as like trying to run to the goal line on a football field with someone in the stands shooting at you.

"You shoot back," he says.

He holds up the Bronze Star. "I got that for pulling five guys out of a burning ammo dump."

There is a picture of him in Vietnam in the fall of 1969. He's eighteen. Shirtless. He wears nerdy glasses, the same kind as when he was a freshman in high school. I look up at the Mike Fostar of today: bearded, with big, owlish glasses and a loud Hawaiian shirt.

Two weeks before his tour of duty was to end, a mortar shell blew up near him. "I was spitting teeth. It was a pretty nasty experience." But he "had a hard time dealing with the civilian world," so he reenlisted. He was stationed in West Germany.

"In 1975, before I got out, Vietnam fell. The colonel came to us and said we weren't beaten. He said we were stabbed in the back by the politicians." He pauses. "That's what the Nazis said."

For him, it all began when he was a member of the Spartans at San Juan High School—he connected his experience with the football team to the war.

"It taught me a valuable lesson, which I took with me into the Army. And when I began to see these team-building concepts going on and realized this is the same. They want you to win the game, take the high ground, destroy the bunker, attack this valley, do whatever was the mission. And we were all going to do this as a team. There was a lot of crossover between the way guys thought of sports and the way guys thought of the military. The same kind of vocabulary, the same kind of attitudes: 'We're all a team. We don't want you to be the last one at the top of the hill; we've all got to get up to that top of the hill together. Right?'"

One thinks of Noam Chomsky's observation on sports: "It's a way of building up irrational attitudes of submission to authority and group cohesion behind leadership elements. In fact it's training in irrational jingoism."

After Mike left the military, the ensuing four years were filled with demons. He has trouble talking about them. He paces the room. He shares memories of the dead. Then he pauses. "I was wild. I went into the *Heart of Darkness* period of my life."

By this, he means he jumped back into the inferno of war. After Vietnam invaded Cambodia at the end of 1978, he read of Cambodians suffering. He decided he had to go in 1979 to help them with his medical skills.

"I went to Cambodia to reverse the karma. It's not good to carry around memories of killing people. I figured I could help instead of kill." What he found was a replay of what had happened a decade earlier. But, he says, "fortunately, their aim wasn't any better."

Mike shows me more pictures. Mike at the operating table. Faces of despair in a Khmer Rouge camp. Lots of blood. Mike with a military rifle. Mike with that same look in his eyes that was in the pictures from 1969. Bombs were falling around him.

"I got to the point where I was going to stay and never come home." He wondered aloud if he was locked in a personal war that would never end.

"Some guys stayed. They're still hanging out in Thailand, mercenaries for whoever will pay. At one point, after eight months, I realized it was time to come home. I drifted for a whole lot of years after the war. I've found rest for myself here. I don't feel screwed up. But I lost a lot of my drive. Vietnam drained me. I'm 'substantial' now—I work for the federal government. I have two kids, nine and sixteen months old. It was an era. I passed through and survived it."

But doctors have told him his liver was damaged by the defoliant Agent Orange that the US sprayed to destroy the jungle cover.

"My liver is slowly destroying itself. It's smashed my overall life expectancy. My father told me, 'You go to war, your country takes care of you.' Yeah. They aren't taking care of me. I'm surprised about the attitude towards Vietnam now. We look back with rose-colored glasses. It was a waste. The people hated or were terrified of us. We were fighting for the oil companies. If they can make war palatable to the Yuppies, we'll be down in Central America with both feet. I hope that doesn't happen."

This is a newspaper interview. I theoretically have time for stories like this—but only so much time. The sun is getting low over the distant Coast Range. I have to head back south. Mike is holding something back. If I stay into the evening and drink with him, I might hear it, but I will leave without getting the full story. That complete version will come thirty-six years later, in act three of the story.

Before I depart, I ask about the other guys. I learn that Ethan Aronson never went to Vietnam.

"Ethan was always radical. It's probably good he didn't go to Nam. He feels the struggle of people more. It would have destroyed him to see people hurting like that."

I next turn to finding James Conley. There is no time to drive to the East Nicolaus school district in Sutter County, north of Sacramento, where he is now superintendent. We talk by phone.

"You never know what surprise you'd have," he tells me of the radical actions of some students at San Juan High School back in the Vietnam War era. "They'd take down the American flag and put up the Viet Cong flag. We'd have to get the fire department out with a cherry picker to bring it down. We didn't fly the American flag for six months so we could foil them."

Conley tells me in this brief phone call that Ethan Aronson was the leader and he had some one dozen hard-core followers. Conley had a mission to get rid of Ethan. He makes it a point to say he kept the FBI informed of the boy's activities. In 1970, Ethan's junior year, Conley tried to expel the boy. The case ended up in Sacramento County Superior Court. A judge ruled that Ethan couldn't be expelled for distributing antiwar literature on campus.

"We should have got combat pay in those days," Conley says. "It was not a pleasant time." Conley thought he'd seen it all, but he says the final shock came when Ethan graduated in 1971. As the boy reached for his diploma, he opened his robe and displayed a Viet Cong flag to the five thousand people in the audience. The crowd hissed and went wild. About thirty students chased after him, screaming that he had ruined their graduation. Ethan would have been "torn apart," Conley says, if he had not intervened. During this melee, Ethan's friend Jeff Whitnack came to his defense. Whitnack was arrested.

Jeff Whitnack is difficult to track down. He's in hiding, not from the American government but from a shadowy left-wing group that recruited him for his medical skills as a respiratory therapist. The leader runs the group like a cult; Jeff describes them as "political Moonies." He has just published a scathing report on the organization.

"I still think the country needs a revolution. But I'm not active with any movement now."

Back then, life changed for him in his early years at San Juan High School.

"At first I felt I would go to Vietnam. I felt we should stop the advance of Communism. Then I found out that it was a hoax, that our troops were doing what the Germans did in World War II." This realization came during his sophomore year, when news of the My Lai massacre broke.

"I became a teenage Weatherman. My attitude then was to bring the war home. I still look down on the people who went to Canada. They should have fought here. If I went, I would have sabotaged the war effort. I would encourage people to do the same thing if we invade Nicaragua. The first year I was eligible, I was lucky. My number was two hundred ninety-three in the draft lottery. They asked me on my papers to put down someone who always knew where I was. I put down J. Edgar Hoover. They had a six-hundred-nineteen-page FBI file on me. It even included my diary."

Jeff's home-front war claimed one victim: his buddy Ralph Patrick Ford, who had been arrested for protesting against the war on the San Juan High School campus. "Of our group, he was the most 'Let's do it' kind of guy. The last time I saw him, he stopped in to see me when I was living in Chico. He was heading for Seattle."

Weeks later, on September 15, 1975, a pipe bomb that Ralph was placing in a Seattle Safeway store exploded prematurely, killing him. It was one of a series of bombings of Safeways in Seattle. The group Ralph belonged to called the stores "Pigways." He believed that the Safeway corporation ripped off poor people and bought nonunion farm produce.

I go into the newspaper's morgue after speaking with Jeff. Ralph is quoted in a 1969 article: "What we're fighting is the system. What we're fighting is the establishment." One assumes there will be extensive reporting on Ralph dying at the hand of his own bomb, but years later all that comes up after a deep database search is a few paragraphs of an Associated Press story. Patty Hearst and the Symbionese Liberation Army were the headline acts at that moment, taking over where the Weather Underground left off, only they were more violent—and short-lived.

Ralph Ford had two misfortunes in his fight against the system: the early detonation, and not being newsworthy in death at the end of an era of left-fringe radicalism. The SLA and the forgotten Ralph were dead-enders in a country that desired to forget everything that had happened in the previous dozen years, especially the fresh pictures of military helicopters being pushed off ships to sink into the South China Sea just a few months earlier; and of people being helicoptered off a roof near the American embassy in Saigon as North Vietnamese troops closed in. We lost. The Weathermen lost. Ralph lost. It was time to move on until enough of the citizenry would forget long enough so that we could enter yet another unneeded war destined to be lost.

Next I go to Randy Bechtel. He tells me he had a burning desire to become a writer, a famous novelist, and he ultimately saw going to war after graduating from San Juan High as a ticket to literary glory.

Randy tried to write his first novel at age thirteen. At sixteen, he and Mike Fostar went to New York City—Randy wanted to see the literary capital of the world. (Mike had told me that "Bechtel was going to be the Hemingway of our group.")

Randy served in 1970 and 1971. He came home with grenade shrapnel in his leg. He was hit on New Year's Eve 1971—exactly two years after he, Mike, and the others drank beer, listening to the music of the Doors, wondering what they were going to do about the war. One might imagine Jim Morrison singing "The End" as the soundtrack to Randy's telling of the next part of his story.

"Civilization is one-half death. In Vietnam there was a double edge. I was never more alive in my life. You never get that sense when you come back here. You smell, taste, feel things that you never do here." He was feeling that lack in his job—he had become a newspaper reporter, covering Fairfield City Hall for the *Daily Republic*, in the small city of Fairfield at the western edge of the Central Valley off Interstate 80.

His is a short interview. Something happened in Vietnam, something he doesn't want to share with anyone. The interview only goes so far because there is not much he wants to say and there is nothing more to discuss. There's no hostility involved—Randy knows the game that we have each played for years. I have walked through my list of structured questions all too fast, and we both realize without uttering any words that it's act three of this interview. We have the kicker. The story ends this way:

"It was a cruel war. Very cruel. As far as Vietnam is concerned, it's dead. I don't talk about it. It's been that way for fifteen years. I prefer to forget it. When I came back, I knew there was no such thing as a great Vietnam War novel. It will never get written by me."

On January 4, 1971, a gala was held at the Sacramento Memorial Auditorium to celebrate the inauguration of Ronald Reagan for his second term as governor of California. Five thousand VIPs went for a show. John Wayne and James Stewart served as co–masters of ceremonies. Frank Sinatra performed thirteen songs, concluding with "My Way." Dean Martin, Buddy Ebsen, and Jack Benny also were onstage. When the event ended and John Wayne exited the building, Ethan Aronson, then a senior at San Juan High School, and a friend unfurled a Viet Cong flag along his path.

"What the *fuck* is that!" Wayne thundered as he lunged at Ethan. Wayne's aid held the actor back. Various news accounts simply say Wayne lectured Ethan and his friend on patriotism and the need for the Vietnam War. We have to imagine the restrained Wayne spitting out these words, fists clenched, ready to land a right just like he did in dozens of his films.

Almost being slugged by John Wayne is the first thing Ethan tells me when I walk into his East Sacramento apartment. It appears to be his proudest moment. I have trouble concentrating on his recounting of that night, because I am overwhelmed by what I see: his apartment is a museum to the Vietnam War. It resembles a hootch, just like the one I saw a few years earlier in North Sacramento, at the Viet Vet Center. Ethan's place is filled with Vietnam-period items, including steel combat helmets. The closet is crammed with vintage US military camos—pants, shirts.

"Look at this coat," Ethan says, reaching into the closet. "Look at the stitching. You can tell it was made in 1967. And look at this shirt. This is 1965 or 1966. The early shirts had exposed buttons." Ethan continues explaining his collection in exacting detail. "Peace, hell. Bomb Hanoi," says a decal, one of dozens he has displayed in cases. He paid fifteen dollars for that decal. The room is littered with dozens of tiny plastic toy soldiers, some firing rifles.

I remark on this, stammering in the journalist's nonaccusatory cop-out third-person question: "This might appear to some people that this is, well…kind of weird. What would you say to them?"

Ethan didn't see it as weird.

"I'm not some peace-freak pacifist. I'm not against the military per se. I grew up believing America should be for the right side. But in

Vietnam, we weren't on the right side. It was the wrong war. If it was World War II, I would have gone. My dad joined right after Pearl Harbor. But we were raised not to blindly respect authority. I just like collecting stuff."

As I absorb this explanation, Ethan tells me that although the draft lottery had him at number nine in 1971, he got a medical deferment for allergies. There was no way he would have ever gone over to fight, he affirms.

"I'm not as radical as I was. I'm working forty hours, paying rent and insurance." He adds that he is now a member of the "death culture" of the middle class he once rebelled against. His demeanor defies this description. Ethan is intense, and has deep-set dark eyes that amplify this intensity. He has twice vacationed in Nicaragua "to study what a revolution looks like. I still go to demonstrations, if they seem worthwhile. Nixon and Reagan are the same thing."

Before showing up at this apartment, I interviewed Ethan's social studies teacher from San Juan High School, Marcia Haley. She is still teaching there. Haley contrasts sharply with James Conley, the former dean of boys. "It was a fun time to teach," she says. "There was a questioning of things. There was more caring for other people. I find these kids today much more passive. They're ten times more conservative. It's awful."

I get the feeling that Ethan fears being judged about his present life as a member of the death culture. Yet he has a motive for talking to me: telling about graduation day at San Juan High School, being attacked by John Wayne, his war on the home front. His glory days. But he wants to speak only so much. He has scheduled this meeting at a time not long before he has to go to work, as a clerk at a video rental store. This timing seems to be no accident.

Ethan tosses on an original Vietnam War US Army cap and coat, one of those he was showing off from the closet. He looks every bit like a soldier seen in newsreels from Vietnam.

"These days, I'd rather see a good John Wayne movie than a Jane Fonda movie. I have more against Jane Fonda and Tom Hayden than I do against John Wayne. They're phonies and sellouts. They're just into power and money. I'm sick of the bullshit about Yuppies and the *Big Chill* generation."

Soldier Ethan stands beneath a poster of Augusto César Sandino, the 1930s Nicaraguan rebellion leader who fought US intervention and was later assassinated. Another poster from El Salvador says, "When history cannot be written with a pen, it must be written with a gun."

"We had a vision of the socialist thing. Of being united. It looked like there would be a minor civil war. It didn't seem that far-fetched. Then, everything changed."

# Snapshots: 1985–1991

I'm with my newspaper colleague Mike Castro covering the vanishing of seven Americans in Guadalajara the previous month. We focus on the disappearance of Vietnam veteran and aspiring novelist John Walker, thirty-six, and Alberto Radelat, thirty-three. They have not been seen since the night of January 30. Their disappearance was preceded by the abduction of US Drug Enforcement Administration agent Enrique Camarena. *Narcotraficantes*—drug dealers—are suspected of killing Camarena.

Mike and I dive into documenting the final movements of Walker and Radelat. Everyone tells us that a brothel and bar called Bellas de Noche, which means "beauties of the night," is key. Friends had told Walker to avoid this place. Way too scary. "If things get ugly, no one can hear you scream," one tells us he warned Walker. "I told him not to go there." But where others saw danger, Walker saw novel fodder.

Walker had moved his family—he and his wife had two girls, ages eight and ten—here from Minneapolis because it was cheaper; he could get by on a $450 monthly military disability pension. (Walker had stepped on a land mine in Vietnam; his legs were severely

188

wounded.) It was paradise—singing birds, subtropical fauna, cool breezes. But he was drawn to the dark side. It was this desire to see the bottom that had lured Walker to Bellas de Noche to observe: like Jack Kerouac, he wanted to wallow in the harsh underbelly of life.

John—I begin calling him by his first name soon after I start investigating, because I quickly relate to him—had been on staff at small daily papers in Iowa and wanted more. He wanted bigger. "His life was affected by Vietnam," says journalist Mike Dorsher, who worked with John at a weekly newspaper. "He'd seen a lot of that side of life and wanted to bring it out. He always went to less-than-pretentious bars in Minneapolis, as opposed to bars where you find ferns. He wasn't a drinker when I knew him."

The directions to Bellas de Noche are told thusly: "When the road ends, keep on going." Mike Castro is driving. He is middle-aged, Mexican American. Mustache. A bit heavy. He wears a gleaming white suit and a white tie. Normally this might be an issue. Who wants to talk with a cop? But the fact that Mike looks exactly like a Mexican federal agent in this moment is an asset. It's 2 a.m., the exact time John and Alberto Radelat came to Bellas a few weeks ago, in what will turn out was their last night on earth.

Cats and gaunt dogs dart from our headlamps as the car bounces down a dirt path. We pass battered 1940s cars and squat adobe buildings. As our car pulls up to Bellas de Noche, men gathered around the door begin whispering nervously. It's a humid seventy degrees, and the air is filled with the sound of crickets and barking dogs.

"*Tienes pistolas?*" asks a bouncer standing just inside the door. He pats us down, seeking guns. He pushes aside a curtain. The chamber is lit with black light, casting an eerie purple glow. The place is packed with well over a hundred people, and the music is throbbing. The shadowy faces of two men at the bar are made visible when they each touch a match to a cigarette. Eyes glower in the brief flashes of light. They clearly want us to see these eyes. I study what I can discern of the women for hire: most are *Salvadoreñas*. A realization: this is an end point for the women held captive in those border camps that Jim Corbett took us to see in the summer of 1984. Elisia? Perhaps she is

189

here. I scan harder. But Mike grabs my arm and pulls me backward out the door; something bad will happen, and it will happen fast, if we remain.

～～～

### Dateline: Mexico City, September 20, 1985.

Michael Williamson is covering the 8.0 earthquake that killed ten thousand. He goes to the Hotel Edison, where we stayed when accompanying Jim Corbett on smuggling runs, and finds the building collapsed to ruin. There is an aftershock the next day; another building comes down right in front of Michael. He and some men hear wails from beneath the rubble. Michael and those men frantically pull aside concrete, bricks, steel. They work all night long. The wails cease. It's morning when they reach the woman. She is dead. Michael slumps on a street curb, head buried in his arms, weeping. A new reporter hired by the big new editor at the *Bee* emerges from her hotel fresh from a good night of rest and, upon seeing Michael like this, is angry. She phones an editor and says, "Michael's losing it. I can't work with him like this. You have to get him out of here."

～～～

### Dateline: a town in the Tarlac province north of Manila, the Philippines, February 7, 1986.

Michael has returned to the Philippines on assignment for *US News & World Report*. The *Bee* doesn't want the story, and he feels compelled to be present, so he has taken vacation time to be there. Michael is with several journalists. They hear that soldiers loyal to President Ferdinand Marcos are stealing ballots. They rush to a plaza and discover troops carrying away ballot boxes.

Later Michael will relate to an interviewer what happens next, before he can even raise his camera:

These suckers just swung around like human gun turrets, lowered their weapons, pulled the triggers, and just opened up. I mean it was like chips of cement flying, bullets everywhere. You don't know if you're hit or not hit, 'cuz your body's gone into freak-out mode. I just *boom!*—hit the deck immediately behind the spot, about a foot tall or so planter. The shit's going over the top of me. I hear, I feel, the chunks of cement landing on my back, 'cuz you can see they're trying to get to me. I have no idea where anybody else went. I really thought Cavendish was dead.

~~~~~

## Dateline: California, September 1986
## Headline: "Need in the Midst of Plenty"

Along with my colleague Nancy Weaver, I had been assigned to lead a six-month investigation into hunger in California. We were the primary reporters on a project that ultimately involved twenty-one writers and photographers working in the field, along with eight editors and graphics staffers. It was one of dozens of stories and projects in the last half of the decade that I worked on to document the growing numbers of hungry and homeless.

We needed to quantify hunger. Food banks were a good measure. When people run out of food near the end of the month, before receiving pay or government support, they turn to charity food. I spent the first weeks gathering data from food banks and pantries in all fifty-eight California counties; these nonprofits kept rigorous information on what they distributed to clients. I didn't count repeat visitors and didn't survey soup kitchens, because there was no way to measure if their numbers duplicated those of food banks. After weeks of data collection, I arrived at a very conservative number of clients: 1 million. With an average of 2.3 people per household in the state, it meant that 2.3 million people, or one out of every ten Californians, were food insecure.

The series, featuring a wide range of hungry people, was published between February 22 and March 29, 1987, taking up a total of twenty-four full newsprint pages.

~~~~~

THE LAUNCH OF THE HUNGER SERIES included a prominent photograph of a young couple, Michelle and David Scott, in the hot and dusty Central Valley town of Taft; population: 5,316. I'd met the couple at the NEEDS Center, a food pantry. They had a son, Davie, age two. They invited me to their home, and I followed them there. Their refrigerator was empty. David, an oil field roustabout, had been laid off. There was no stove. The NEEDS Center food was a big help, but it wasn't enough.

"At the end of the month is when I wonder if we're going to make it," Michelle said. "We make sure Davie is fed. That is what always comes first. My cupboards get bare. It's depressing. I get so I can't even go in the kitchen at that time of the month."

Photographer Jay Mather and I watched as Michelle cooked noodles mixed with tomato paste and a slim portion of fatty ground meat. It would feed them and David's sister and boyfriend, who were visiting. Michelle dished out the food, long on noodles, short on protein. There were no greens. But there was a six-pack of Pepsi on the table, prominent in Jay's photo that was published. During the story conference with all the editors and key reporters, rather than edit it out, I chose to deal with the soda in the article. This sentence appears low in the story:

> A Bay area doctor says many poor people buy expensive soda because they develop a taste for it; it makes them feel as if they've eaten.

The moment I walked into the newsroom on the morning after the story ran, the phone at my desk was ringing. "Don't expect me to feel sorry for them if they can buy Pepsi!" a caller said. The phone wouldn't be back on the receiver for long before it would ring again with more of the same. I asked each caller if they'd read the story and gotten to that sentence; none had.

〜〜〜〜〜

I WAS ONCE AGAIN PLACED on the night cops beat, immediately after returning to the newsroom from a one-year fellowship in May 1988. No reason was given. Near the end of a shift two weeks into this stint, the police scanner at the city desk filled with chatter about a homicide in the east area. As I walked through a cluster of flashing sheriff's cars parked at all angles, I saw a gunshot victim in the street, next to an open car door on the driver's side. A pool of blood had spread across the pavement. It was just before midnight.

Standing over the corpse was Lieutenant Ray Biondi. When he looked up and saw me, he shouted, "Maharidge, who'd you piss off?" I shrugged. There was no explaining the inexplicable. Biondi knew something bad had happened to me, because it was the same with the cops—punishment was being assigned to the shit shift.

〜〜〜〜〜

### Headline: "Life Gets Grim by the Rivers: 125 Homeless Camps on the Waterfront," August 14, 1988.

One of my first stories in Sacramento with photographer Michael Williamson was on what we then called "winos"—alcoholics, mostly men. When they were publicly inebriated, police often would take them to the Volunteers of America Drop-in Center, commonly called the detox center. Some nine hundred hard-core regulars would rotate in and out, using the sixty beds, an official told me at the end of December 1980. Many of them had housing in single-room-occupancy hotels, all of which soon would be torn down or converted to spaces with more lucrative uses.

As for the others, Michael and I counted as best as possible those who, as one man said, "slept in the weeds." They numbered just a few dozen, and most just had sleeping spots, not camps. They comprised the city's homeless. This word wasn't commonly used in 1980. The headline of our story, in fact, called them "winos." The word "homeless" never appeared in the story. It must be remembered that the word "homeless" seldom was seen in the press up to that time.

Seven years after that story ran, I spent one week of afternoons walking and biking the banks of the American and Sacramento Rivers north and west of downtown Sacramento to search for people living in camps. I covered ten miles of bank on both side of the rivers, pushing through tangles of wild bamboo and grape. Now there were 125 active sites. Some were simply pieces of cardboard laid in flattened areas of bushes. But many were elaborate, with huts, firepits, tables, and chairs. This was new.

Some camps were quite hidden. One was on a tall piling of the Interstate 80 bridge in West Sacramento; it required scaling a metal ladder to reach. It belonged to Garner Ellison Wood Jr., and when Michael and I climbed up there, we found the finest camp on the river. It could be called "the Palace." There was a living room, a kitchen (where an American flag was displayed), a bedroom, and even a guest house. The bedroom had wooden shelves that held a library of his *National Geographic* magazines and a Bible. There was a nightstand with a clock, a shirt rack, and posters of women in bathing suits and rock groups. Today this would be a standard homeless encampment. Back then it was quite unusual.

Garner, thirty-one, was struggling to get back into an apartment, keeping himself clean and sober while he looked for work. A radio bandaged with gaffer's tape provided entertainment. "I learned most of this stuff in Boy Scouts," Garner told us, referring to the site's construction. "I did it all with an axe and nails I found [along] the river. A lot of guys call me Grizzly Adams. I'm from a pretty well-bred family, but that doesn't help me here."

He used a broom and rake by the door each day to sweep the sand away. He found it hard to keep the place clean. When he went job hunting, no one ever suspected he didn't have a home.

Upriver we found Robert and Mary Chambers from Oregon, who'd hit the road when the lumber mill where Robert worked was closed. As we talked with the couple, a white truck drove up across a gravel lot. The driver emerged and shouted, "You cannot stay here. This is private land. You got five minutes to leave!" Robert pounded a fist on the roof of his and Mary's car, yelling back: "You think I'd be here in this shithole if I had a job?" But the man in the white truck was already back inside the cab. Police soon came to move the couple on.

The man in the white truck worked for the Raley's Landing Development Project, a twenty-five-acre, $200-million office-and-condominium complex with a five-star hotel, being planned by Thomas Raley, owner of the Raley's supermarket chain. A rice mill and a lot of low-income homes had been razed already.

Provisions should have been made for the displaced poor, said Susan Lindahl, director of the West Sacramento Food Closet. "If you're going to build forty condos, you should build forty low-income housing units," she said when I called for comment. She wondered where the poor would go.

Robert Cutshaw, a spokesman for Raley's Landing, said that his corporation was erasing blight.

"West Sacramento has been treated as a dumping ground. West Sacramento is trying to clean up. It should have happened a long time ago," Cutshaw said. "These people are trespassing. We don't run a campground. Why should we? I have a lot of compassion for people who don't have a home. I have no compassion for those who don't want to have a home. Ninety-eight percent of them are winos and derelicts."

**Dateline: Sacramento, March 5, 1989.**

**Headline: "Between Noon Friday and Noon Saturday, 17 *Sacramento Bee* Reporters and 8 Photographers Traveled From San Diego to Crescent City, From San Francisco to Barstow, Capturing the Faces and Recording the Stories of California's Growing Caste of Homeless, and...They Were Easy to Find"**

~~~~~~

UNPUBLISHED LETTERS SENT to the *Sacramento Bee*, March 1989:

Dear Editor:

The Bee story on the homeless was little more than the "day-in-the-life-of-the-homeless" series that local TV stations run during the ratings sweeps.

In the few areas where the Bee presented facts—rather than the reporter's subjective view—they were grossly inaccurate.... [Y]ou reprinted—without any question—figures given to you by self-appointed "homeless" advocates. It appears that your paper was more interested in advancing their cause than reporting the facts...

John C—
Citrus Heights CA


Letters Editor
The Sacramento Bee
P.O. Box 15779
Sacramento, Ca 95852

Congratulations to Julie Stewart for saying what she thinks (and what many others think also!)

It's about time someone layed [*sic*] the truth on the line. All the milk toast [*sic*] politicians covering their collective backsides is sickening.

Why are these people homeless? Do they have no family? No friends? No education? Whose fault is that? *Theirs*—not society.

Education in this state is *free* for 14 years—12 high school and 2 junior college. O.K.—$100 for that. If people can't get an education in California—shame on THEM! These people must stop whining to the government. The government must stop pandering to them about a situation the homeless themselves are unwilling to do anything about. They must accept responsibility for their situation. It is of their own making.

Signed, Sick of the Whining

Kent M—
Sacramento, CA

Dear Editor

Someone has to have the guts to say it concerning needed housing for the poor. Who are these women having kids all over the place demanding privilege for benefits as opposed to people like me who don't contribute to overpopulation?

We single men are punished worse than lazy state-funded drainers like hit-and-gone fathers who return for more sex-for-drug-babies...just to shoot up. Talk about ignorant legislators in the dark age.

Truly,

Keith S—
Roseville, Ca

~~~~~~

JUST BEFORE FIVE O'CLOCK on April 25, 1989, the phone rang at my desk in the *Bee* newsroom. I always picked up.

"Be at the river, under the I-5 bridge, at six tomorrow morning," the caller said.

"Why?"

"Just be there." Click.

Photographer Dick Schmidt and I were there early. In dawn's half-light, we greeted a very displeased Lieutenant Mike Shaw and his team of officers, who had come to begin what they thought was a secret sweep of the homeless. But Shaw couldn't stop us as we documented the cops as they rousted about a dozen sleeping men, one woman, and a dog.

A group of men sat below a picture depicting Jesus Christ that they had placed on the concrete bridge wall. Police demanded identification and told them that they could no longer camp there. It was the latest nightmare for one of the men, Joe Ortiz. Ortiz, who said the van he was living in had been stolen a week earlier, was slumped on his bed. He sat motionless for the entire hour of the raid, almost in tears. "Now I got nothing…nowhere to go."

We followed the raiding cops. They warned Mike Crawford not to be camped there the next morning. Crawford was confused about where to go. As the officers moved on, one cop announced, "You're free to go wherever you want."

~~~~~

## Headline: "Police 'Sweeps' Continue, Homeless Advocates Charge," June 30, 1990.

Sacramento's police continued sweeping the homeless, as did police in other cities: Santa Barbara, Santa Cruz, San Francisco—fourteen cities in total. Deric Rothe, the editor of *Hard Times*, a Sacramento newspaper about homelessness, said that he believed many cities thought that by applying pressure, they would get the transients to go somewhere else.

# Active Shooter

January 17, 1989, dawned frosty and clear in the city of Stockton, California. At the El Rancho Motel off Highway 99 on the north end of town, Patrick Purdy awakened. The motor-court motel was long past its midcentury heyday as an overnight stop for tourists on their way to or from the Sierra and Tahoe. Purdy's room, number 104, cost ninety-five dollars per week. He'd checked in the day after Christmas, and he was paid up through the 23rd.

The previous few days, the twenty-four-year-old had been pacing the courtyard, usually at night, dressed in military camouflage and a field jacket. A man in the next unit thought Purdy might be a speed freak but had never seen him take drugs. Purdy had been sleeping through most of the days, but on this Tuesday he awakened early. He put on a shirt. On the front was written "PLO" and "Libya" and "earthman." The back: "freedom and Death to the Great 'Satin.'"

He then loaded himself down with two pistols and an AKM rifle with the word "Hezbollah" carved into the wooden stock. The words "freedom," "humanoids," and "evil" were painted on ammunition clips.

He went out to his 1977 Chevrolet station wagon and drove to Cleveland Elementary School north of downtown Stockton. He parked, then lit a cloth wick stuck into a beer bottle filled with gasoline, leaving it on the front seat. In the back were two open containers of gasoline. He turned to students out at play during recess and fired from the hip, spraying rounds in a pattern to hit as many of the four hundred kids as possible. The car exploded in flames behind him. He emptied the seventy-five-shot drum of the AKM with a bayonet affixed to it, and then he fired more from another clip he slammed in—a total of 110 rounds. He then placed the barrel of a Taurus nine-millimeter automatic pistol to his head and pulled the trigger. All this took place in the span of two minutes. Left dead were five children, ages six to nine; thirty other students and a teacher were wounded.

"We'll never know exactly why he did what he did," Captain Dennis Perry of the Stockton police said to a reporter.

The *why* was our job in the newsroom. I was lead rewrite and reported along with my colleagues. No one in authority was going to take apart Purdy's life to attempt coming up with an explanation. Police didn't study motive, at least in these early days of mass shootings. We'd work from Tuesday through the Blue Star deadline on Wednesday, then chase for the final edition after, to make the Thursday morning paper. This is what we did best in a heavily staffed print newsroom of that era: editors piled us on the story. The one I wrote had fifteen top reporters and photographers; other pieces that ran had a similarly deep bench.

Things we learned: Purdy was thrown out of the house by his mother at about the age of fourteen. This began a life of drifting and crime, including purse snatching. He held spotty jobs, often as a welder, and he was occasionally homeless. A 1987 mental health report prepared after Purdy was arrested for shooting guns in El Dorado County described him as suffering from "mild mental retardation" and said that he was "a danger to his health and others."

Purdy had a book on the Aryan Nations, about guns and killing, when he was arrested in that El Dorado County case. He kicked out a window of the police cruiser and said he'd kill anyone who pushed him around. In the late summer of 1988, Purdy paid $349.95 cash for a semiautomatic AKM at Sandy's Trading Post in a small town an hour east of Portland, Oregon. On the required federal forms, he answered no to the question about whether he'd ever been convicted of a felony.

A year before the shooting, Purdy told a coworker at Numeri Tech, a Stockton manufacturing company, that he "hated" Vietnamese immigrants for taking jobs that belonged to Americans. Purdy had attended Cleveland Elementary from kindergarten through the third grade. The school had been predominantly White at the time. It was now 71 percent Asian American—a mix of kids of Cambodian, Vietnamese, and Laotian heritage.

Before leaving the El Rancho hotel to do the killing, Purdy lined up one hundred toy plastic soldiers in battlefield positions. In that room also was a *Calvin and Hobbes* comic, depicting the character Calvin acting out one of his fantasies: destroying his school.

The term "active shooter" had not entered the language at the time of the Stockton mass shooting. It began appearing after 1999, when two teenage boys killed thirteen people and wounded twenty at Columbine High School in Littleton, Colorado. At the time, however, Patrick Purdy's actions made as little sense as those of Michael Swihart, who'd bludgeoned his family to death in Brunswick, Ohio—the first homicide I'd ever covered. There was no feeling in the newsroom that Stockton was a harbinger of things to come. The hunger and poverty projects, not crime, now occupied my workdays.

Yet I was pulled back to the murders of Sabrina Gonsalves and John Riggins in the fall of 1989. I answered a call from a man named Ray Gonzales, who told me he knew of my interest in the case. He had information. Would I like to meet?

I drove across the Tower Bridge to West Sacramento, to its boulevard of flophouse 1940s motor-court hotels with names like Stardust and advertising "Color TV" that still existed beyond the Raley's Landing development. Amid them was a cheap diner. Gonzales was already seated in a booth in the near-empty restaurant when I arrived. He was thin, young, oddly confident, and eager to talk.

He proceeded to tell me that his former brother-in-law, David Hunt—a half-brother of Gerald Gallego's—had been involved in the killing of the Davis couple. Hunt and Gallego had been tight. In 1962 they were convicted of armed robbery. After Gallego was released from prison in 1965, he and Hunt pulled off another robbery. They were again arrested together in 1969 during a bungled armed robbery of a hotel.

Gonzales had contacted Lieutenant Ray Biondi, who met with him in 1987. Gonzales also had been talking with Davis police detective Fred Turner. In July that year, Turner and Gonzales traveled to Los Angeles, where Gonzales had set up a meeting with Richard Thompson, an associate of Hunt, serving a thirty-five-year sentence in San Quentin for kidnapping. Gonzales wore a wire to the downscale bar where the meeting took place. He said Thompson had told him that Hunt had taken part in murdering the college couple to deflect attention from Gallego. In his trial, Gallego tried to use the killing of the Davis couple in his defense—he maintained it was someone else in the sex-slave murder cases. That story didn't work. He was convicted, sentenced to death, and then sent to Nevada to be tried for killings that had happened there.

A problem, Gonzales said, was that the wire malfunctioned. A lot of the conversation was garbled. What was Gonzales's motive for becoming an informant? I never got a clear answer. I only knew that a West Sacramento police dog had been allowed to gnaw on his leg for a long time during an arrest.

On November 14, 1989, I published a front-page story above the fold about arrest warrants in the murder of the Davis couple, issued by the Davis cops for David Hunt, his former cellmate Richard Thompson, and Hunt's wife, Suellen. The Davis police were reluctant to talk until the suspects had been arraigned. I called Ray Biondi for comment.

"This was a theory that surfaced in the early part of 1981, that the crimes may have been a copycat murder to keep the heat off Gerald," Biondi said. "We worked the theory for a while, but we didn't get anywhere with it." Interestingly, his unit was not taking part in the arrests. I sensed that Biondi was skeptical of the case, but he didn't trash the Davis police.

# PART FOUR

# After the 1980s

# Redwood Curtain

came into the unpeopled newsroom at 2 a.m. on February 25, 1991, to clean out my desk and wheel things away when no one was around. I sent out two messages. The first was system-wide to everyone in the building, and in the last sentence I wrote, "It's been nice working with some of you."

I then sent a system message to editor Mike Flanagan.

//maharidge//

For: Mike Flanagan
From: Dale Maharidge
Subject: Resignation
February 25, 1991

Dear Mike:

Effective immediately, please accept my resignation from the Sacramento Bee. As a senior writer, of course, I have the right to schedule my own hours, and as such I am taking vacation leave for two weeks starting today. Consider the attached vacation request form, coupled with one I turned into the desk last week, as advance notice.

You will find in the envelope a key to my desk, a key to my file cabinet in front of business area, my press card, my Bee employee card, and my membership card to the health club. I would appreciate it if you would forward the cards to personnel. I have emptied my desk and cleaned it up so that it is ready for a new tenant. Any files that might be used by staffers in the future are stacked behind the desk, such as the coroner's death records, the police crime data. There are no projects or short term stories that I was working on, so you are not left in any lurch.

As for my remaining checks, you can advise personnel to mail them to my home address. Enclosed you will also find my last expense form.

Pardon the abrupt nature of this. I am sure you will agree it is best for all concerned.

Best,

Dale Maharidge

cc (via computer): H—, J—, B—, P—, F—

My 1980s were over; it was now the mid-1990s. There was no clarity. It wouldn't come for years. History, and life, is like this. It was too soon, and besides, there was too much work to do. To vacate one's mind of the past, there's nothing better than building an off-grid homestead with your own hands miles from utilities. I had been visiting a remote section of the Northern California coast since 1992. In 1995, I purchased thirty-four acres of forest and meadow overlooking the Pacific. It was empty land, off the grid, not in the ha-ha sense of the term but literally. First I had to create a water system, then bring in electric power. It was brutally hard work. To gain a sense of my mindset, this is part of a letter I wrote to a friend:

I am so into this life here that I do not want to emerge. I could see myself remaining here for a year or two and never leaving at this point. I do have to get more outside things done before the winter sets in. My sweat tower is sealed in the bottom and the top is an office/bed with a great ocean view. As you can see by receiving this letter, I have the solar power system going, albeit a bit rudimentary still. But I can use the computer and print things out, all night long, thanks to the batteries.

I've not talked much to anyone this summer, not written letters. I keep up on the news, though, listening to NPR and reading the *New York Times* which arrives by mail anywhere from one to three days late, when I make it down to the p.o. seven miles of bumpass road away.

Outside of the inside of my own head, not a lot to report.

I am going to town tomorrow and so I shall print and send this, or it will be two weeks before I do.

There was no phone. The only cellular tower was a hundred miles north, in Oregon, and it would be years before towers would come to the Coast Range ten miles to the east. The nearest neighbor was a half mile across a canyon. This was my escape from the previous decade. I was broke in every sense of the word. There was no money to hire help. I lived by the sun as I built a home. From the moment it rose enough in the east to strike two eighty-watt photovoltaic panels that I repositioned throughout the day, till it dipped behind the ridge at the top of the meadow, I ran an amp-hungry array of tools. Among them were a circular saw and a drill, neither of which could function on battery power alone. They needed the hot input of live electricity from the panels.

There was a cadence to the long hours of construction. But to call it being in a state of zen would be inaccurate. There was nothing poetic about those years of long days. It was more like an emptiness— not the kind found in nighttime dreams, but rather the nothingness of sedation. There was a purity in the silence when the tools were off, a quiet broken only by the wind pushing through the firs, hawks crying out as they rode thermals, the thunder of surf 1,200 feet below.

In 1995, I emerged from behind the Redwood Curtain after having spent all summer at what I'd eventually call the "ocean house"—low-ercase because it was never given a formal name as I worked to create a homestead with a sweeping view of the Pacific. I drove to Stanford University to start teaching the fall term. The twenty weeks at Stanford paid well enough to allow me to spend the other thirty-two weeks of the year in isolation. Waiting in my mail slot at the university was a questionnaire from Contemporary Authors, a Gale Research, Inc. series of volumes. An editor was asking for commentary on my three books related to poverty. I mailed the reply on September 6. In part, I wrote:

> One sets out to educate Americans about poverty in the hope that in some small way conditions will be changed. Then comes the realization that Americans don't seem to care. This, along with the horror of the lives one documents, takes a toll.... I plan to never again write a nonfiction book about poverty.

The Gale editor had asked about books, but my reply was also rooted in all the stories on hunger and homelessness I had written for the newspaper. My first book, *Journey to Nowhere*, came out of that early 1982 newspaper assignment to ride the rails with the new homeless, who had become hobos in their search for work. Michael and I hoped the book would blow up. We envisioned being part of a new wave of social documentarians, similar to the 1930s American realist writers and photographers whose work and books helped bring about change during the Great Depression. John Steinbeck is of course preeminent among them: *The Grapes of Wrath* flew off shelves by the tens of thousands in its first weeks of publication in 1939.

*Journey to Nowhere* received attention but sales, to understate, were modest. And though a good dozen or so of us were doing this work in those early years, collectively we didn't match the sociopolitical impact of our predecessors.

Why? I could blame Republicans. But that isn't the entire reason. There were plenty of conservatives in the 1930s who dismissed the working class and poor. Not everyone warmly embraced Franklin Roosevelt's New Deal. Conservatives were critical of the Works Progress Administration, which put people to work building walls, bridges, parks, schools, and post offices all around the country. Opponents saw men leaning on shovels, watching others work. Lazy and on the dole. Steinbeck wrote about this in a reflective article on the Great Depression for *Esquire* in 1960.

> I had an uncle who was particularly irritated at shovel-leaning. When he pooh-poohed my contention that shovel-leaning was necessary, I bet him five dollars, which I didn't have, that he couldn't shovel sand for fifteen timed minutes without stopping. He said a man should give a good day's work and grabbed a shovel. At the end of three minutes his face was red, at six he was staggering and before eight minutes were up his wife stopped him to save him from apoplexy. And he never mentioned shovel-leaning again.

I didn't have such an uncle to make shovel. My naysayers in those days before the internet wrote negative letters about the homeless project, or they telephoned in a rage about why a young couple was buying Pepsi to sate hunger. These responses were predictable and expected. What was unexpected was the absence of action or rage in the sociopolitical realm of progressives, ordinary citizens, and Democratic politicians. There was no new New Deal. No call to action to put people to work, to house them, to care for others.

Something had changed with the country, and not simply with conservatives. Much of this decline of interest in the common good was rooted in a reaction to the 1960s, which began to manifest after 1980. In the 1960s, despite the horror of the Vietnam War, and the assassinations of Bobby Kennedy and Martin Luther King Jr., there was a feeling that things were going to turn out okay, that the trajectory of human rights struggles such as the civil rights and women's movements would transform our society.

A strong sense of how things had fallen apart came in 1995 when Jerry Garcia died. Word spread about a pilgrimage to Golden Gate Park in San Francisco. When I arrived, I saw that a throng of hundreds had gathered. It wasn't just Deadheads who showed up. I interviewed a wide range of straight-looking people who'd flown in from everywhere, who told me something had spoken to them about making the journey. They simply had to be present. I witnessed not just a sense of loss of a legend, but a requiem for an era when there was hope for inclusion and a just society.

Journal entry: August 13, 1995

A guy in a bread truck came from Salt Lake. Joe, dressed in a tie-dyed bandanna, tee shirt and pants, said why he dropped everything and drove here.

"He's the hippie God."

The Hippie God was dead. And so were we. The Republicans were now very much in control in the most anti-1960s ways possible. That morning's paper had "Jane Roe" renouncing her pro-abortion stance. There was a picture of her being born-again baptized. The 1960s were an aberration. The Hippie God was able to remind us that it doesn't have to be this way but we knew the illusion of that era was no more solid than the puffs of marijuana smoke rising from the Polo Field, where the drums beat strongly for the dead leader and the women gyrated and danced, and people came to see for the last time, it seemed, the dream.

One morning in August 1997, just as the sun was about to strike the photovoltaic panels in the home I was building, I was setting up boards to cut when the stillness was interrupted by the distant sound of approaching helicopters. One was small; the other, large, black, and mean-looking. They were part of CAMP, the Campaign Against Marijuana Planting, a state and federally funded effort in California. My neighbors were growers, most of them hippies who came in the 1970s, and farmed anywhere from a few dozen to a hundred plants, to earn livings in that wilderness. CAMP had long been their scourge. The helicopters drew closer. My garden grew only cabbages, lettuce, and potatoes. I did worry for my neighbors.

The black helicopter was now right above the meadow, a thousand feet from the ground and dropping. I ran uphill, heart racing. At the crest, five cops in camouflage, sidearms on their hips, jumped out. The chopper, which never actually touched down, lifted and raced off. The five cops were about a hundred feet away. Flashbacks to the Philippines, El Salvador. It was as if I were in the center of one of the third-world conflicts I'd covered in the 1980s. I recalled the people on Mindanao and how they'd looked with fear at the soldiers when we marched into their village.

I wanted to be pissy. But I was a villager. All sorts of bad things could happen. What if someone was growing on my land? It may be difficult to believe, but the terrain was so steep, so rough, so snarled with poison oak that there were several places I'd not seen on those thirty-four acres, and would never see in all the years that I lived there. They might claim it was my grow. Or would they make up some excuse to mess with me?

I greeted them and tried to act casual. The head cop said they'd spotted marijuana nearby and were awaiting orders. "No one is accusing you," the boss cop said in a falsely reassuring way that revealed he often used this line. It was perfect professional cop speak, which translated to the belief that all residents on this coast were growers, that the cops could land and do whatever they want, because everyone there had something to hide. It didn't matter that I made my living as a writer and professor; I was one of "them," the people they flew over.

Orders crackled over the radio. The marijuana was in the canyon, and all five cops suddenly disappeared into the thick brush. I returned to construction. An hour later, the small chopper came back and descended into the canyon; when it reappeared, several large bunches of weed were dangling from a line. It roared overhead to the river bar, where the plants would be burned. The annual income for one of my neighbors, gone. The big black chopper never returned, and it appears the cops were picked up out on the dirt road running along the ridge. Cops dropping in from the sky depressed me for days.

Someone conservative might argue that this is the price paid for living in the Emerald Triangle—at the time the largest cannabis-producing region in the United States—among a legion of outlaws. What did I expect? A liberal could point to the expensive foolishness of antidrug laws. The raid came a few days after California attorney general Dan Lungren, heretofore fiercely antidrug, agreed to a study of the medical use of marijuana, which the state's voters had overwhelmingly approved the previous year. Lungren was running for governor. This support of the study wouldn't win Lungren a lot of the hippie vote, however. One of my otherwise liberal neighbors always voted Republican. His reason: "Because they'll keep weed illegal." His bud was selling for well over $4,000 a pound when he told me this. (Years later, after legalization, the price plummeted to just a few hundred dollars a pound.)

Other disturbing things happened at the ocean house in the following years. On rare warm late-summer nights, when the air was still, I loved walking in the meadow. At the crest, there was a 160-degree view of the Pacific; when there was a moon, it glinted on the sea. On one of these nights, long after midnight when there was a quarter moon, I took a walk after finishing a chapter in a book I was writing. At the summit, there was a glint in the faint moonlight, something shiny on my neighbor's property that hadn't been there before. I clicked on my headlamp. The high beam revealed a pickup truck and two men standing next to it with rifles, some two hundred yards away. They were jacklighters—people who shine a powerful light on deer and shoot them in the dark. This was quite illegal, and these guys had to have cut the fence to get in. I turned off the light and yelled in the best command voice I could muster: "Get the fuck out of here. Now!" I dropped to the ground to lower my profile. Doors slammed. The truck fishtailed as it sped away. At the crest, the guys stopped and popped off three shots over my head.

When I telephoned the county sheriff, the first thing the dispatcher asked: "Is this a grow?" I responded: "No, but why should that matter?" She didn't answer. The unspoken answer being that if it involved a growing operation, it wasn't of concern to law enforcement. Then she asked: "Was anyone shot?" Me: "No." Dispatcher: "We won't come out unless there's a body."

I was on my own.

There was another incident, this one close to the end of my time there: a man parked his motorcycle in front of my gate, blocking it, and went to the house of a neighbor across the canyon who wasn't home. The man ate a meal from the fridge and took a shit on the living room floor. He then walked across my meadow on his way down to the public campground at the beach. Armed with a tire iron, he chased after a woman. He was about to beat her when a man from a nearby campsite shot the attacker in the leg.

Amid incidents like this, Bulgarian mobsters and other gangsters began operating huge grows; killings became more common. People went missing all the time. Bodies were never found. Vehicles burning at the sides of rural roads—roads I had to drive all the time—had corpses inside with gunshot wounds to the head.

What had begun as my place of refuge was now nothing of the sort. At the end, I carried a sidearm when walking the land. When I drove on Highway 101, the revolver sat at the ready on the passenger seat. I'd become a dude with a gun.

Six years have passed since I sold that place in the Emerald Triangle.

But I still have the guns. The weapons are stored deep in a closet in California. Most likely I will never again fire any of them. Yet I can't let them go. (Perhaps there is too much prepper in me after all those years of living off the grid.) I no longer "need" guns because I have the fortune to live in safe neighborhoods on both coasts. Yet it would be arrogant to pronounce that all firearms should be banned. I get hunting. I get skeet and target shooting. (That's fun—a friend and I once "shotgun-pruned" a tree whose towering branches were blocking my ocean view at the off-grid homestead—we called ourselves "bluenecks" and blasted the limbs with shells from five boxes of ammunition till the branches fell.) I get the fact that some people live in dangerous neighborhoods. In doom loop America, everyone seems to have a gun, and in certain places it's crazy not to have one.

What I don't get: AR-15s and one-hundred-shot drums. Open carry. The unrestricted right to pack a concealed piece. Silencers. I know Republicans who feel exactly this way.

# Ray Biondi

I wished to be in conversation with key people from my 1980s, but so many were dead: Bob Forsyth, 1999; Jim Corbett, 2001; Frank McCulloch, 2018; Georgia Lyga, 2019; Ray Biondi, 2020. Biondi wrote several books on serial killers, including Gerald Gallego. I had no idea he'd harbored storytelling ambitions. In searching for Biondi, I discovered something I'd missed because of being so long removed from Sacramento: the conviction of the killer of Sabrina Gonsalves and John Riggins.

After the 1989 arrest of Gallego's half-brother David Hunt; his wife, Suellen; Richard Thompson; and another associate. Ray Gonzales testified at a preliminary hearing in Yolo County Superior Court that Hunt had "wanted to throw the system off" with the killing of Sabrina Gonsalves and John Riggins. This would make it appear that the killer in the sex-slave murders was still at large. Judge James Stevens Jr. set a February 1991 trial date for Hunt and the other three.

In 1980, there had been no evidence of sexual assault on either Sabrina or John. Forensic investigators used the best available technology at the time—swabbing the bodies for an acid phosphatase test, which detects semen. The results were negative. But there was a blue comforter in the van, wrapped as a birthday present for Andrea, Sabrina's sister. It had been opened and cast aside. With advances in science, the blanket was examined eleven years later: semen was discovered, and from it DNA was extracted. It wasn't a match for John Riggins or the three male suspects. Just as the jury was about to be sworn in, the Hunts, Thompson, and the other guy were released.

In 2002, the DNA was entered into a criminal database. There was a match: Richard Hirschfield, in prison in Washington state for child molestation. Hirschfield also had served time in Vacaville prison after a 1975 conviction for robbery and sexual assault in California. He'd been paroled in July 1980.

Strong evidence suggests he may have visited a friend in Davis who lived in the same condominium complex as Sabrina. Joseph Hirschfield, Richard's brother, then lived in Rancho Cordova. In 2002, Joseph was in Oregon. Sacramento detectives went there to question him about his brother; the officers said that he began shaking. The next day, Joseph was found dead in his car from carbon monoxide poisoning. His suicide note read, "I have been living with this horror for 20 years. Richard did commit those murders, but I was there. I didn't kill anyone, but my DNA is still there."

A police sketch artist in 1980 had rendered, from one witness, a drawing of a wild-looking man with an unkempt thistle of a beard—it bore an uncanny resemblance to Richard Hirschfield.

The case didn't go to trial until September 2012. Richard Hirschfield's lawyer tried to invoke the Gallego copycat theory. Lieutenant Ray Biondi testified that he and Davis police detective Fred Turner had spent months working with Ray Gonzales in 1987 on what Biondi called the "Hunt group" angle. Biondi testified: "We weren't getting anywhere with this one." Biondi felt Gonzales wasn't credible. Turner went solo: he forged on with the Hunt group theory. "We thought he had lost his objectivity," Biondi said of Turner.

The jury found Hirschfield guilty, and he was sentenced to death row.

There are several lessons from the case of the "Sweetheart killings"—for police, for the press. Gonzales was believable enough for a while to pull Biondi along, although Biondi testified that he was always wary of informants, and in the end he blew off Gonzales.

Detective Turner came to the opposite conclusion. The Hunt group theory made logical sense. But it had nothing to do with facts.

I wrote my 1989 story dispassionately and never quoted Gonzales. I didn't "convict" any of those four who'd been arrested; I cited court documents and authorities. I'd interviewed Ray Biondi, and he'd expressed doubt. But any reasonable person who read my story would bet folding money that those four were guilty. If that blue blanket had been lost as evidence or if Hirschfield had set the van on fire to destroy it, four people would very likely be on death row or serving life in prison for a crime they did not commit, based on one informant's testimony.

Another lesson has nothing to do with police work or the media: what lies at the core of violence against women is something a shrink I once slept with summed up as "dick don't work," the cause of so many male power issues. Even though I never had a last interview with Biondi, he spoke about this from the beyond when I read his book on Gallego, *All His Father's Sins*. Gallego, he writes:

> ...felt inferior to most people, especially men. It's no wonder Gallego became impotent when he lost a job. And when that happened, his fragile image as a strutting, macho outlaw would shatter. That's when he would inevitably turn to his pedophilia, a sickness that is typical of weak men seeking power over the helpless.... Gradually, Gallego's obsession with his impotence, his sense of social and intellectual inferiority to Charlene, and his... pedophilia created the underpinning for his murderous behavior. The short man who always posed for pictures trying to appear taller, needed to feel like a big man, the type of man who can have any woman he wants at his command."

# Mike Fostar

One can engage in therapy to cope with life's troubles, but I've used journalism to make sense of myself and the world, and by midlife and midcareer, I'd become skilled enough to finally study my own childhood trauma—the most difficult reporting one can undertake. My father's rage and occasional violence were inexplicable. By my late teens, I had suspicions that these were rooted in my father seeing combat as a US Marine in the Pacific during World War II.

After he died, in 2000, I began a quest that resulted in a book, which took eighteen years to complete. I found nearly thirty veterans from L Company, his unit, and through them I learned that my father had suffered blast concussions at least twice, the final incident from being next to the burial tomb on Okinawa that blew up—it was filled with at least one ton of Japanese explosives. He might have had PTSD, but scientists told me he surely had a traumatic brain injury, which irrevocably shatters axons and initiates long-term nerve degeneration. This explains his sometimes erupting in screams. My father fought his impulses, tried not to become the beast we feared, with mixed success. When on his best behavior, most of the time, he was a great dad. When not, it was terrible. At the end of the eighteen years, I came away with both a sense of peace and a feeling of love toward my father.

I made other discoveries on that journey. After I submitted the manuscript, my editor phoned. He told me that he'd been worried that I was going to be antiwar. "You aren't antiwar," he said in a tone of relief. "They are." Some men from my father's unit, L Company, said that if they could turn back the clock, they wouldn't have gone.

Many sons of the veterans of L Company were my age or a bit older. We talked about Vietnam. Some served in that war. Others were like me—they'd come close but didn't have to go. Every so often I recalled my interview with Mike Fostar in 1985, perhaps because he was my avatar for the war I missed.

Now, decades after we first met in 1985, I wondered if Mike was still alive. An internet search turned up a phone number. That didn't mean anything. Many guys from L Company were in the white pages but had been dead for decades; their spouses had never changed the listing. I punched in the number. Mike picked up.

Mike hadn't expected to make it this long. "My friend, a former Marine, always says every time he calls me, 'You're still aboveground, right?'" The Agent Orange exposure had not yet put him below the earth. He had myriad health issues. Bone marrow cancer. His thyroid was gone. Partial loss of vision in one eye. His kidney function had dropped to 22 percent. He now lived on a road called Cripple Creek. The last time we'd met, he'd been in Paradise. The irony was not lost on him.

Our being older made our second meeting much more trenchant. For my part, I wasn't on deadline. There was no rushing the interview. For Mike, he was now seventy. Something about crossing into this decade of life can make one reveal more—in his case, he'd already been very open, yet there was more to learn about the outfall of the violence of war, and about his story. In order to get there, Mike's past must be revisited, the parts I'd missed thirty-six years earlier.

After graduating from high school midterm, forced out for selling pictures, Mike saw no point hanging around Sacramento. It was early 1969, and San Francisco beckoned. The "Summer of Love" was still going on. He couch-surfed with friends. In February Mike met an attractive hippie girl. He followed her home to a commune on a macrobiotic farm in Sebastopol, in Sonoma County, north of San Francisco. The woman was, in fact, a recruiter—her job was to lure hippie boys to the farm. Mike wound up in the "Spring of Free Labor."

He was shown to a barracks and put to work toiling in fields. There were also cows, and a milking barn. Mike had milked cows on his grandmother's farm as a child, and he sold himself to the overworked guy who ran that operation. He began milking. This moved him up in status. He became a commune regular. Now he got to use the redwood hot tubs and eat macrobiotic meals, and he learned eastern philosophy. He fell in love with a woman who called herself Rachel Sunshine.

"I thought I loved Rachel—maybe should marry her—but didn't," Mike said. "I thought she loved me too."

The couple might have figured that out, except that Mike got a notice from the Selective Service System to go for his physical. The draft lottery had not yet begun. Mike wasn't in college. He wasn't married with children. He couldn't claim health issues. Any of these would have given him a deferment.

"I was just a dumb kid. I could have could have come up with all kinds of different things. My mother is Canadian; I have relatives in Canada. I could have gone up there. But my dad and the majority my family were very conservative and all-American. There was just no way I was going to incur the wrath of my dad by not at least going down and taking my physical."

Mike was classified 1-A. It was May. He went back to Rachel Sunshine at the farm, but on June 8, 1969, he was ordered to report to the Oakland Army Induction Center at 1515 Clay Street. He was told to pack a "ditty bag" with two pairs of socks, one pair of underwear, and a toothbrush, and to go to a flophouse hotel across the street. He was given a room number and a food coupon. There were three other guys in the room. The next morning, he ate a greasy breakfast and then walked across Clay Street to line up against the wall of the federal building. Federal marshals walked back and forth to make sure no one left. Inside, the young men filled out forms and then were ushered into a huge room. They were ordered to stand on numbers painted on the floor, making lines. Mike was destined for number ten but held back: eleven had always been his lucky number, so he paused and let another guy take ten.

A US Marine sergeant came in and ordered the men standing on numbers one through ten to fall out and stand against the wall—they'd be sent to Marine boot camp training. It was one of the few times in history that the Marines took draftees, but they'd been decimated by Vietnam casualties. The men against the wall were crying. The Marine sergeant screamed at them to get their asses moving out to a bus.

After those Marine draftees filed out, the rest of the group was given a choice: risk becoming riflemen in Vietnam for two years, or volunteer for a three-year enlistment and pick their jobs. Mike raised his hand to volunteer. The choices were slim: tank or helicopter crew. Still combat jobs. Then he heard "medical corpsman." Mike thought it was like being a nurse, that he'd be working in a hospital.

He was sent to Fort Lewis in Washington state for basic training. From there he went to Fort Sam Houston in San Antonio, Texas, for training as a medic. When he got off the bus in Texas, the men with a college education were separated out—they would become X-ray technicians and other hospital staffers. Guys like Mike with only a high school diploma were destined for battle. Mike noticed that each of the instructors had a Purple Heart. When he asked one about this, he was told: "Oh, you're going to get shot. You're going to get hit."

Mike shipped out of Fort Sam in mid-October 1969. He had a few weeks' leave before going to Vietnam; he went home to Sacramento. Rachel Sunshine had sent him a letter informing him that she was seeing someone else, that she didn't want to be involved with a soldier.

In Vietnam he entered a platoon as an FNG—a fucking new guy. FNGs weren't trusted. He got put through the shit, became trusted, and because of his skill and the high rate of wounded and killed in action, he rose to a top position as a noncommissioned officer in a mechanized infantry unit. He became a company medic, in charge of all the medics in four platoons. His job was to triage, coordinate the deployment of medics, and call in helicopters as needed to retrieve wounded soldiers.

Before the next part of the story, some observations are required:

We are at a table in his kitchen thirty-six years after the last time we talked. Mike's beard is white. He is a bit heavier. Yet it's easy to flash on our first meeting—he essentially looks the same, sounds the same. This conversation is merely an extension of the first. He speaks meticulously, in great detail. Nothing about that has changed. He is once again one thousand feet above, looking down at Mike Fostar seated across from the journalist, a microphone and recording deck between them, cinematically recounting events of that early chapter in his life. He is surrounded by evidence of those years. In the hallway off the kitchen are a number of small pictures from Vietnam arranged under glass in a large frame. On display are over one dozen ribbons and medals, including the Bronze Star and Purple Heart from his time in D Company, First Battalion, Fiftieth Infantry, Mechanized, and from his time in Troop L, Third Battalion, Eleventh Armored Calvary Regiment.

Out the back door, to the right, is what most people would call a shed, made of sheets of cheap pressed-wood board. The studs are exposed; the wood has aged to an orange sheen. This is Mike's "man cave," but it harks to a hootch. Not only has Vietnam remained in his head, but he has created a replica of it in this chamber. Two full-size American flags, one with thirteen stars, the other fifteen, are pinned to the back wall. On top of a pine bookcase to the left, a ceramic human skull wears a dusty faded dark green cap with "Vietnam Veteran" printed on the front. His dusty boots, the ones he was wearing when he got hit with shrapnel from a mortar round, are next to the skull; then on the right a replica Viet Cong National Liberation Front pith helmet with a brass star in the center. Next in line: a miniature brass replica of the statue *Three Soldiers*, by Frederick Hart. The original is at the Vietnam Veterans Memorial in Washington, DC. Other items: a dark green ammo case with yellow writing, "200 cartridges / 7.62 mm"; an Army medic's first-aid field dressing, a bit yellow from age, wrapped and perhaps still sterile; a black flag with a white skull and crossbones; pinned to the pine bookcase, a sergeant's stripes patch, raggedly torn from a coat; a reproduction painting of what appears to be three Thai Nang Ram court dancers, with blacked eyes that look at nothing; a picture of the *Mona Lisa* looking at everything. Books on war abound. Just a few: *After Tet: The Bloodiest Year in Vietnam*, by Ronald H. Spector; *Doc Platoon Medic*, by Daniel E. Evans Jr.; *Red Thunder Tropic Lightning: The World of a Combat Division in Vietnam*, by Eric M. Bergerud.

In a drawer are photo albums of the kind popular in the 1970s— cellophane pages against a self-stick background. These are the albums Mike showed me in 1985, only now I study them more keenly. Mike documented everything when he went back to work as a medic in Southeast Asia. The color snapshots are of Khmer boy soldiers, Mike with medical gear, Mike with an assault rifle. The most striking is an image of a German doctor holding a dying child, his eyes filled with both rage and sorrow. Numerous images are of the young doctors and nurses from around the world struggling to help the refugees amid battle. All of the medical people are beautiful in that very crisp and sharp manner that one takes on in a war zone; their eyes are acutely alert.

Mike had been through bad times when we met in 1985. But more was to come. The 1990s were intense. He got divorced.

"I went through periods of weird stuff at work and really came close to mentally coming unglued. I tried—" He pauses. "I tried to harm myself." He drove to a rural area southeast of Sacramento and stopped on an empty country road. He got out of the car, gun in hand.

"It was dark in one direction," he describes. He stood facing the nothingness. Then something made him turn and look north. "I could see the lights of the city." He realized there were people there who loved him. "I couldn't do this to them." He dropped the gun. It fell to the ground.

"If I hadn't turned away from the dark, I would have shot myself. I ended up taking time off from work. I took a thirty-day leave while I went to a psych center and tried to figure it out."

Mike found help from a US Veterans Administration psychiatrist named Mike Cohen. He saw Cohen between 1999 and 2002. At first, the sessions were twice weekly, then once a week. By the end, it was once per month. Cohen got Mike to practice mindfulness meditation to cope with his post-traumatic stress disorder, or PTSD—it helps rid the mind of negativity.

"I went through this psych stuff. And it really opened me up and cleaned me out in terms of what I was holding in. And what I was concerned about, there was this one experience I had that was really horrible, that I couldn't get over. I kept thinking about it. Thinking about and thinking about it…"

It was April 1970, near the Duc Co Special Forces Camp, west of the town of Pleiku, in Gia Lai Province.

"The way the medical corps was supposed to work was that anybody that had a problem with seeing blood was supposed to be weeded out early. They made them truck drivers, or push a bedpan at the hospital, or some other job where they wouldn't have to deal with blood and guts and gore. But the army is not in any way, shape, or form good at doing everything they're supposed to do, especially with the draft and massive casualties that were happening. So we got this kid in and he was a brand-new medic. I assign him to a platoon, and he goes out and he gets in an engagement. He freezes. The sight of blood freaks him out. He can't function. The platoon sergeant has to do the job, and all the men in the platoon are angry: 'Get this fucker out of here! He is useless to us! He's gutless! He's a chicken!' By that point I'd gotten pretty macho, like everybody else. So I ream this guy out: 'You got to grab your guts and you've got to do your job. You get carried along by the platoon as extra baggage until such time as there is a casualty, and then it's your turn. And you have to deal with the situation.'"

Mike always told his men to be certain they would be covered by suppressive fire before going out to retrieve a wounded soldier. "I said this to the new guy numerous times. So I figured he had the idea. I was keeping a watch over him."

The unit was later engaged in combat. The gunfire and explosions were deafening. "I've got this guy near me. On a leash. He's helping me set up the triage." Another medic was working with them; all three were busy. Mike called in a helicopter to get the wounded.

"All of a sudden, somebody calls out that there's a need for a medic down the line. I've got one good guy working on things while I'm on the radio, and this excess guy. And I said, 'Go get the wounded guy and bring him here, because we've got birds coming in.' Off he goes. I'm thinking, 'Don't forget to ask for covering fire.' But I didn't say that. So off he went. And there's a bunch of fire over there. And then I hear a call for another medic. Fuck. So I went over there. He ran right out into the open and got killed. I felt like he did it on my orders."

Seeing that shrink at the turn of the millennium helped him cope and realize it wasn't his fault, and it lifted some of the burden. There were other terrible things. But there was a big missing piece of the story, something I didn't hear in 1985, about his return in 1979 to Southeast Asia, to the Thai-Cambodia border, and to his "heart of darkness."

*Mike:* The Khmer Rouge were deadly guys. And I remember the very first time I walked into a Khmer camp—

*Me:* How'd you get there?

*Mike:* CIA.

From the *San Francisco Sunday Examiner & Chronicle,* January 6, 1980:

Examiner reporter Ivan Sharpe and photographer Nicole Bengiveno, who have been covering the refugees in Thailand for two months, were with the first Westerners to enter a refugee camp on the Thai-Cambodia border after it was devastated by fighting Friday. Here is their report.

By Ivan Sharpe
Examiner Staff Writer

Nong Samet, Thai-Cambodia border—It was the day after the battle that killed or injured scores of Cambodian refugees, and this once-busy jungle camp was eerily deserted except for groups of guerrilla soldiers and a few looters.

The story mentions continuous automatic gunfire and rocket explosions. The battle was between Khmer Seri factions. Sharpe and Bengiveno brought along three medics who'd hitched a ride in their car—including Mike Fostar. One of those medics waved a "dusty Red Cross banner." Sharpe wrote that this was "scant protection" and they were ready to "dive out of the car...if we came under attack."

They arrived at the hospital. It had been ravaged by the Khmer from the rival camp of Mak Muon.

Michael Fostar, 28, a paramedic also from Sacramento, stared angrily at the looted remains of a $100,000 mobile medical laboratory, which had arrived a few days before. A former U.S. infantryman in Vietnam and Cambodia who left the Army in 1975, he savagely kicked a trash container and said: "I've seen too many wars. But this is disgusting. This place has just been devastated." During Friday's fighting, he had helped get people into the bunker and he had watched the guerrillas battling only 100 yards away.

Mike explains how he ended up back in Indochina with a brief history lesson. The Chinese supported the Khmer Rouge, and the Chinese and the Vietnamese were at odds with each other. Vietnam had invaded Cambodia to push the Khmer Rouge out and install a pro-Vietnamese government.

"But Pol Pot and those guys didn't give up easy, and they kept retreating westward toward Thailand. Ultimately, they retreated into a mountain enclave down in the very southwestern corner of Cambodia, where they set up a little kingdom for themselves."

Media coverage of the crisis and mass starvation "just freaked everybody out. Nowadays we seem to be a lot more immune to starving-baby pictures than we used to be. I think we also felt kind of guilty because of the experience we had leaving that unsettled."

American politicians wanted to extract the nation from Southeast Asia. The CIA worked through private contractors.

"This private contractor called International Medical Teams contacted me," Mike says. The contractor asked if Mike was interested in going back to Southeast Asia "'and making serious money working in this refugee situation. The UN won't go in there. It's too dangerous. But we need to send somebody in there to evaluate what's going on.' And so they hired a dozen or so of us. There's a town called Aranyaprathet right on the Cambodian border on the main highway going toward Phnom Penh. And they park us all there. They gave us vehicles all marked up with 'International Medical Teams' in Thai writing, Cambodian writing. We would drive in three-man teams [into Cambodia].

"Many things told me that the CIA was involved. All the other NGOs thought we were CIA. We had so many top guys working with us, guys who were not so much NGO types and very mysterious people. Translators. One guy who called himself our 'security officer.' We had the full authority of the Pentagon. We had military passes issued that no other NGOs ever got. I would show it to people, Thais, and they would go, 'Oh, is this very good pass.' While tourists could go up and down the tourist corridor between all the tourist spots, you couldn't get off Highway One. As soon as you got off the main highway, you hit a roadblock. This was their way of controlling revolutionaries. But I had a pass allowing me to go anywhere. Anything we needed, we just called guys at the US embassy and *bingo*, we had it. Everything was done in cash—a paymaster came out once a month and paid us out of a briefcase full of cash."

They were the first US medical team on the border, Mike says.

"This was the government's way of being there without officially being there, I believe. Real spooks showed up all the time and stayed with us, and went out with us to the refugee camps to do assessments. Sometimes they would ride out with us, armed—and leave with local guerrillas fighting against the Khmer Rouge, called Khmer Seri. They would disappear for a day or two, and then we would pick them up and take them back. We had medical trucks that had special passes so we were never searched by the Thai soldiers."

Many journalists also stayed there: Morley Safer of *60 Minutes* and his crew; Matthew Naythons of *Time* magazine.

"There was a young guy who introduced me to a number of what he called old hands—old CIA guys from the old wars. One day an old hand named Frank took me and the young guy, who I believe was CIA, to the Grand Prix bar, down in the area of Bangkok known for prostitutes, sex shows. The Grand Prix was a hangout for old CIA guys. I spent several hours buying rounds of drinks while these guys talked about missions into Laos and even into North Vietnam. One guy claimed he had killed a Communist general in Laos. The other guys said he did. They were seriously hard-core."

Front for the CIA or not, Mike was doing medical aid for refugees, in five different camps. But he became involved in some high-level negotiations.

"There ended up being about two million people sitting on the border of Thailand. But the Thais wouldn't let the Cambodians into the country. They kept shooting them—didn't matter if they're women and children. The newspaper guys were getting on that, saying the Thais are murdering these women and children who are just trying to get to safety. The American embassy reached out. I had some military contacts, and the house I was living in was owned by the executive officer of the local border regiment."

Mike's contacts told him about Thai general Prem Tinsulanonda, who controlled the "frontier army." Prem was looking for monetary support. Mike reported back to the embassy, and the information reached US Ambassador Morton Abramowitz.

"Abramowitz arrived in a car with all these security guys, and they took us up to General Prem's headquarters. It was a rainy day, hot as always."

It was a colonial villa. They went into a room with a long table and a fan turning overhead.

"The general was there, the ambassador, and there's one guy who had a briefcase handcuffed to his wrist. He opens up the briefcase, and it's full of American $100 bills—stacks and stacks and stacks of them."

Abramowitz said the US wanted the border opened up to make it safe for the United Nations to set up camps. Prem agreed to a two-mile-wide demilitarized zone where the Cambodians could stay. The money was given to Prem.

I ask: "Was that US government money?"

"Oh hell, yeah. It was probably a couple million. More money than I've ever seen in my life. I became what was called 'field administrator.' I would get a package from the embassy every month, of cash—American cash and Thai cash. Thousands and thousands and thousands of dollars. I would pay all of our staff members. We had drivers and cooks and people who brought truckloads of water and food and stuff out to the camps."

These camps were inside Cambodia, and they were getting shelled.

"The very first time I went to Mak Muon, which is a dangerous camp, filled with these crazy boy soldiers, we arrived and parked our car. Boy soldiers and others gathered around us. We had an interpreter, who was really nervous. We were in Cambodia. We were not in Thailand. Everybody's Khmer, the whole place. And these little people, Khmers, they look up at me like I'm a giant. They were giggling and laughing. We're nervous. I'm just standing there by the truck. And there's about five of these boy soldiers, all with big AKs, and I'm just trying to smile at everybody. I go, *"Tae anak sokhasabbay?"* which is like 'How you doing?' in Cambodian, bad Cambodian. And—*plop*. A Chinese grenade lands right at my feet. I looked down for a minute. My anus is puckering, because I thought, 'Oh, I'm fucked. They're gonna kill me.' And then I realized it was capped. You have to uncap it and pull the pin. The guys are just all looking at me. They have really grim faces. I picked up the grenade. And then I said, 'Here's your grenade back.' They all started laughing. I had some sodas in the back of the truck, Fantas. 'Here, have a couple of sodas, man.' They were like. 'Oh, yum, yum.'"

After that, when Mike went to the Khmer camps, he took stacks of Frisbees and handed them out to the boy soldiers. The air filled with the discs.

"We had to get those camps out of Cambodia, because they kept getting mortared and shelled by artillery."

The United Nations had to get the Khmer Rouge to stop attacking and raiding refugee camps. The Vietnamese were willing to work with the UN.

"The UN put together a team of people and contacted Pol Pot's people. They said, 'Okay, come out and meet with us, and we'll discuss it.' I went on as a security guy. They gave me a nine-millimeter pistol. I said, 'Man, I don't think I really stand a chance. But I'll make a last stand, I guess.' So me and another guy were security."

There were a few United Nations staff with Mark Brown, the chief coordinator for the UN high commissioner for refugees in Thailand. Everyone got into helicopters painted with UN markings and flew to a plantation about two hours south, in hill country.

The plantation was French colonial. It was surrounded by fields and orchards. Mike wondered if they had murdered the original owners. Three women with guitars sang Khmer Rouge propaganda songs.

"They put leis around the necks of the bigwigs. I was with a Dutch guy. And he's looking around, and he goes, 'Look at all these smiling guys. They got so much blood on their hands.' The killing fields. These guys were bloodthirsty. There's the top staff guys; they're all wearing nice shirts and clean clothes. All of a sudden, everybody is nervously looking around. And then, after so many minutes, the door of this house opens up and out walks this little short guy in a porkpie hat. Hawaiian shirt, slacks. He walks over, big smile, shakes hands with the bigwigs and sits down. We're going, 'That's Pol Pot! That's Pol Pot! Right there. This is the guy responsible for all this!' I was close to Pol Pot as I am to you right now. There was something about his eyes. They were, I don't know—reptilian. I mean shifty. He kept looking around the table all the time. Talking and smiling."

Then Mike and the other security guy and staff were seated at a small table about twenty yards from Pol Pot and Mark Brown, at a big table on a porch.

"Finally there was something agreed to at the big table. Everybody got up and was shaking hands. Pol Pot seemed to be enjoying himself—smiling, laughing. We were escorted to our birds, and we flew back. I have no idea what was said. But the guerrilla attacks and raids stopped. It was a such a strange experience. What ended up happening is America, Thailand, China, the Vietnamese, they made a deal if the Khmer Rouge simply stayed in their turf way down in this little corner on the coast, the Chinese could bring supplies to them. Chinese ships were allowed to zip in there and drop off things for Pol Pot. And he kept this thing going for another ten years."

Eventually the UN built Khao I Dang, a camp inside Thailand. At one point it was the largest refugee camp in the world, with over five hundred thousand people.

"I helped build part of it. It's something I am very proud of. The UN boss liked me, and I got things done. I was able to find the few Khmers with education or skills who had not been murdered by the Khmer Rouge, and we worked together to house all the people. It was a huge effort. Most importantly, it was safe. In the movie *The Killing Fields*, at the very end of the movie when they show a UN camp with the UN flag, that's actually Khao I Dang.

"It was ten years after I was inducted, and I was going to change my war karma to peace karma. Seems naïve now, but I wanted to make something good out of all the crazy bad I was feeling regarding the first time I was over there."

Mike was doing medical work, but it got so that he constantly carried a weapon because of the danger. But then he was done with war. Mike went home. It was June 1980.

He was "home." But he had health issues. He was estranged from his father. Mike would not talk with him for ten years, over his anger at his father pressuring him to go to Vietnam. They eventually reconciled.

He landed a job investigating tax cases for the Internal Revenue Service. The job was intense; there were some big cases. One that began with his investigation led to a multiagency operation in the 1990s that brought down an international cocaine-smuggling ring. This iteration of his life involved a lot of cloak but not so much dagger, interviewing people and using computers for investigations. And he married and had his children.

Despite the road's name of Cripple Creek, the area is tranquil and wooded; it feels rural. Wild peacocks roam the neighborhood. Mike spends a lot of time reading. He realized he'd lived through a critical period of American empire, and it prompted him to study history. He read a bunch of books about the Mexican-American War, fought between 1846 and 1848, and General Winfield Scott, who landed at Veracruz and went on to occupy Mexico City. That war ceded California and much of the American West to the United States.

This research became the basis for a novel Mike wrote, titled *Falconer's Long March*. It was divided into three books, with a total of one thousand pages. "It follows one group of Americans from the time they land on the coast all the way to Mexico City. I researched the crap out of it. It was the first time America ever invaded a foreign country." The novel was never published, yet he's still glad he wrote it. It helped him understand America.

"It has to do with being an empire. Empires never learn. Empires eventually fail. That's the sad truth of history. Empires fail because people get set ideas in their heads, like America wants to nation-build all the time. We tried to stop that after Vietnam. A whole bunch of generals wrote books that said, 'Don't nation-build.' Then we went into Iraq. So many of my friends served in the sandbox. I'll never forget [Vice President Dick] Cheney saying, 'We now have the sixth-largest oil reserve in the world; this war will pay for itself.' It didn't. They forgot that they had to get oil out of the ground, pipe it hundreds of miles to refineries. And all it takes is a hand grenade to put a whole bunch of holes in the pipeline. Iraqis were simply driving along the pipeline and throwing grenades about every two hundred yards—destroyed it. There was no way to get the sixth-largest oil reserve to the refineries that were on the coast. So we had this situation where, 'Oh, gosh, what we wanted to happen didn't happen.' Then we were stuck there, occupying the place. We should have just left. But we got into this mindset that we're going to nation-build. We stayed in Afghanistan for twenty years, trying to nation-build. And it didn't work, because those people didn't want us there. America as an empire is really good at fighting its wars. It's really good building up armies. It's really terrible at occupying countries."

I asked: "What's the end game?"

"The end game is collapse."

Mike answers fast, then quickly apologizes for the raw assessment.

"I'm sorry. But if you look at empires, eventually an empire gets stuck in its ways. Gets in a situation where half of the empire wants to progress, and half the empire wants to go backwards. So the two sides can't agree to anything; they can't legislate anymore. Eventually, their grievances become militant. Like the Romans. Most empires that fall apart, they fall apart in wars. Some don't become civil wars. Some, like the British Empire, melted down. People forget that all the little countries that broke off mostly went through their own little civil wars to get to that point. People got tired of being told what to do by the British. Here's America now telling the world how they see the world. And a whole bunch of the people in the world are saying, 'No, thank you.' Our influence is less. And once an empire's influence is less, they just can't manipulate the world as they did before. Just having aircraft carriers doesn't do it anymore. You've got to be able to have people do what you want. And if no one's doing what we want them to, then in fact, we've lost our power. Then we turn in on ourselves. And so we've turned in on ourselves. Lincoln said that a house divided against itself cannot stand."

# Gina

A series of email that began the night of March 25, 2022 and continued over the summer:

Hi,

In a different lifetime, back in the 1980s, I was a reporter at the Sacramento Bee.+

I covered the police in those years and during that time I met a woman named Gina Catania. I'm wondering if you are her. She is a blues singer. If you are, I was thinking about you recently. I was going through a crate of my old reporting files for a book I'm working on…. If you are that person, hello! If you are not, apologies for the email. Either way, I hope you are well!

Best,

Dale Maharidge

+ I'm now a professor at Columbia University in NYC.


Dale!

Of course I remember you, and yes I am that woman. I've Googled you over the years and followed your career. Would you like to talk sometime? Thank you so much for reaching out.

Gina Catania

Hello,

In late 1980, I was hired at the Sacramento Bee, to cover the police and sheriff's departments. I've long since left the newspaper, but now I'm working on a book from that era, and I hope you can help me...a story that has haunted me is a rape that occurred in the early summer of 1981. There was a serial rapist in midtown and I did a very brief story about the incident. Two days later, Gina Catania, the RP, called me and asked that I do a bigger story. I spent two months delving into what happened. Last June, 41 years later, we again met in San Rafael, and I interviewed her to bring the story forward.

I learned from Gina there was another rape by the same suspect, based on his MO, in her unit just a few months earlier.

—Does Sac PD have an information on that previous rape?

—Who would have the rape kit from both incidents? With DNA sequencing, she and I were wondering about the potential for finally catching the perpetrator.

Any help you can provide would be most appreciated!

Sincerely,

Dale Maharidge


Good afternoon Mr. Maharidge,

Thank you for your inquiry. We do not release police reports or specific information regarding a victim's case. That information must be submitted through a Public Records Request. Please follow the link below for information on submitting a public records request for the information you are interested in.

https://pdcityofsacramentoca.nextrequest.com/

Additionally, Detectives would need more information about the offender as there are many variables such as statute of limitations and existing case law that could determine the legal confines in which DNA sequencing would be legal and allowed in court.

We encourage the victim to contact our Investigations Unit at 916-808-0650 and speak to a Sexual Assault Detective who would be able to answer case specific questions.

Please let us know if you need anything else.

Thank you,

SPD PIO Team


Hello,

I see not much has changed with regards to Sac PD and the press, but I appreciate the prompt response. I will soon submit two FOIAs per your guidelines. Thanks.

—Dale Maharidge

A week later this email appeared in my inbox.

Your Sacramento Police Department public records request #23-322 has been closed.

The record you asked for does not exist.

Gina and I had texted over the Signal app to figure out a day for my coming to Marin County. When Gina replied, she wrote that the next day would be "the anniversary" of the rape. It was now only a few days later. I was early for our meeting, seated in an alley outside a hip coffee shop in one of the tony towns north of the Golden Gate Bridge. From behind, there was suddenly Gina's voice, unchanged, and she was recognizable even before I fully turned around.

Our adult lifetimes had transpired since we'd first met, almost exactly to the day, forty-one years earlier. Yet so much was the same. She looked far younger than sixty-one—not that much different, really, than in 1981. She still talked with her hands. We picked up as if only months, not years, had passed, transported back in time to that afternoon on the deck outside the newspaper's cafeteria. It was long gone. The hedge fund that now owned the paper had sold the building to a developer, and the much-diminished newsroom was operating out of a rented suite of offices at another location.

I'd never forgotten Gina. That her story never saw publication had bothered me for years.

"I feel like I let you down. I want to correct that," I told her, adding that she was one of my heroes from all my years of reporting. For her to come forward, especially in that era, was brave.

From that event and others had sprung her life's work. It led to a career as a therapist. In her practice, Gina Catania Bodywork & Intuitive Counseling Services, she specializes in various kinds of trauma, including sexual assault.

Shortly after Gina arrived, I went inside to buy her a coffee. The man ahead in line, a doppelganger for a young Jerry Garcia, used a $100 bill to pay for a $4.50 espresso drink. Not long after I returned, Gina said she'd found that Marin County, a wealthy enclave, was good for her practice, but that it was pretentious.

"And people aren't friendly," she added.

Nearby homes for sale were priced at $1.2 million and way up, reaching $20 million. Gina rents the top back unit of a fourplex, a square postwar building whose most distinguishing feature is a cavernous four-car open garage, with a drive plunging steeply to a busy thoroughfare. She rents an office nearby, located inside another therapist's practice. She lives modestly.

For many years, she said, "I just wanted to have enough work to live and do music." Gina measures life not in the value of owning one of the surrounding homes, but in helping people and finding peace in existing with minimal needs.

In the coming hours I would see her office and her apartment, as she searched for a copy of the story I'd written. I'd forgotten that I'd given her a printout after it was killed by the editors. My own copy was lost when the new editor moved our file cabinets to the basement and then had the contents dumpstered.

A previously forgotten detail: we'd come up with "Gracie" as a pseudonym for the story. Today? "Use my name," Gina said rapidly. There are many reasons for the choice. Among them: it's a different era. And it's a part of her life that she has coped with.

Gina is passionate about her work. She has a steady clientele. While she dug around in files at her office for the copy of the story, I studied notes pinned to a wall. One was thanks from a patient, written on paper rimmed with prints of flowers: "Hi Gina, You are an immense blessing in my life." This online comment was typical: "Her vibe is humble, friendly & very professional…. So caring. And extremely positive. I just love her!"

With the hindsight of decades gone by, Gina believes she would have gotten over the rape "more easily" if not for the childhood sexual abuse, and how she was treated at home.

"There's so many things I blocked out. There are two years that are just gone," she said of her early grade school years. "It's just a 'gift' that keeps on giving—child abuse," she added wryly. As a child, "I thought I was bad. And so that's why these things happened to me."

Then came the rape when she was twenty-one. It wasn't that her parents didn't believe her—they "expected" a rape to happen, because, as they told her, she was "a troublemaker and attracted trouble." As Gina tells me this, I can only imagine the searing impact this had on her mental health. But I could very much relate to Gina's childhood in one way. As in my youth, there was a lot of anger in her house; and like me, she was the middle child. The turmoil focused on her.

"I had a load of trauma and violence from my parents." Her sisters would see Gina getting thrown across the room, or hit, "and they would be like, 'Yeah, she deserves that.' Everybody was aligned about me deserving it."

After Gina told her parents about the rape, she informed her mother that she was talking to me. Her mother got angry.

"'You want people to feel sorry for you,'" she recalled her mother saying. "I just felt like I wanted people to know. And I remember it being easy to talk to you."

This tension continued. In 2000 she wrote a letter to her parents "asking if we could go to therapy because of our past issues that were surfacing in the present." This didn't happen. She broke off contact with them. Her father is deceased, her mother still alive. "I am still not in contact with anyone in my family."

After the rape, there were drugs and booze, but she eventually went sober. About two years after the rape, the landlord settled the suit before going to trial. The evidence was strong—the other rape in Gina's unit just before she moved in, and the fact that she had noted in writing on the rental agreement that she wanted the window lock fixed. The initial settlement offer was $85,000. It ended up being $210,000. A third of the amount went to the lawyer. Gina invested the rest in some kind of real estate trust, and it ended up tanking. She lost most of it.

"But it was a moral victory."

In the wake of those early years, she suffered clinical depression. She lost jobs as she searched for different therapies. "Dysfunctional," she said. "I just knew there was a better way to live, and I was going to find it." Her issues felt larger than herself: "Something wants me to still be here, because so many times I was going to kill myself."

Somatic therapists believe that traumatic events become pent up in the body, manifesting as chronic pain or stress or patterns of behavior that create a feedback loop to the mind. Treatments include making the patient aware of sensations in specific parts of their body; therapists often use sound, touch, and breathwork to do this. Shamanic therapy invokes the spirit world, using trance to direct energies away from the cause of the problem—in Gina's case, PTSD. Gina tried both somatic and shamanic therapies in her late twenties as she struggled to deal with the sexual violence she'd survived. She knew there was a way to heal, and she was determined to find it.

She initially discovered that massage therapy was helpful. In 2000, she was told about a therapist in the city of Napa, California. His methods changed her life, and led her to study and become certified in a variety of therapies. She's had her practice for twenty years.

"Everything I've done, I did it for me first. And then folded it into my work with other people. This has all been intuitive. I was finding my way. Most teachers I found couldn't deal with trauma. [For me] it wasn't like, 'I'm gonna learn this and help others.' It was, 'Oh, man, I'm gonna try not to die.'"

Gina explains the key, and it goes something like this: The biggest lesson she learned over the decades was finding a way to translate trauma into a story that she could live with, "because you're dealing with the part of the self that doesn't know it's over. And you have to go in there very delicately and allow that part of the self to come into the present." The inner self doesn't know the threat no longer exists. It's a survival mechanism. But once one allows oneself to be in the present, it's possible to heal.

Gina is long divorced. We discussed why we both never had children, each attributing it in large part to childhood trauma from the rage in our houses. The conversation became like a therapy session. Gina turned the tables, asking me questions about my youth. I said that in a way, it had helped propel me into journalism. I reminded her that in our first interview, she had a realization that she could be a journalist. Instead she wound up using her listening skills in a different manner. Gina noted one critical difference: "You're helping them in that you're taking their stories going out into the world and you're understanding it, and that is huge."

And then the journalist moves on.

"I get to help them resolve it. Help them fix it. You don't."

This is true. I pointed out that most people I meet vanish, impossible to trace. Among them was a newly homeless man Michael Williamson and I met in St. Louis; in 1983 we rode a freight train with him to Colorado. We tried in vain to find him in 2015. The fate of that man and of so many others remains a mystery. I almost never can reconnect.

"Until now," I said. "You know, I never went to hear you perform," I added, though I may have tried—I went to a bar where she was with friends during the time of the interviews in 1981, and she may have been waiting to sit in and sing with the group that was playing, but didn't. Both of our memories failed on what had happened.

"I stopped performing like ten years ago. It just left me as a desire. It just went away. Have you ever had that? Have your desire for writing just go away for a while?"

The answer was no, but I didn't want to tell Gina this. It's the only thing I've consistently felt certain about in a life of so many other things that have been decidedly uncertain.

I asked Gina about violence—was there anything she felt was peculiar in our culture that was at the root of the rage imbued in Americans?

She let out a deep sigh.

"It's exacerbated in America somehow. But I think there's a systemic issue. If you look at war, how men will conquer a place by violating the women, it just seems part of taking control and power. But I also feel like these guys that are rapists, they have a different kind of sickness and insecurity and need. I don't think it's American. I think it's been going on throughout time. You know, this is not even a need to dominate. It's like a need to annihilate. And I think that these guys are deeply humiliated in some way of their own. And this guy had trouble having an erection unless he was insulting me."

She rhetorically asked if people could really understand violence, adding: "What your father did to you is inside you. His energy is inside of you. You could have activated it. It could have been active in your life, but somehow it's not. It seems that to understand it, we'd have to activate it in ourselves. And I don't think we can afford that. We'd have to unpack something we might not want to unpack, to really understand it."

Gina feared activation. She suppressed the "fight" aspect of the "fight-or-flight" response. She wished she had more fight.

"I think I would be a more whole person if I did embrace that part of myself. Because I'll wimp out. I won't fight for myself when I need to. Or I try to please people instead of standing up. But I don't want to enter into the reality of what my parents did or what other violent people have done."

Gina embraced self-defense, however. She had recently purchased a handgun. "I'm learning how to use it." She was a bit reluctant to reveal this information, perhaps because she thought I might be judgmental or misunderstand. I explained how I'd packed firearms at my off-grid place, become a dude with a gun. And it wasn't just dudes. I related how back in the 1980s, when I was seeing that woman who'd been raped by a man she believed was the Golden State Killer, she would sleep with a revolver on her nightstand. When I wasn't present, the weapon was beneath her pillow. Another ex of mine who never owned a weapon also said she wanted to buy a handgun.

I asked Gina about her own reason for buying a gun: "Was it the rape?"

"It's partly that." It's also where society is headed, she said. "I just think there's so much evil being perpetrated right now."

While Gina rummaged through her office and home files for the printout of the story that afternoon, there was time for me to think about why it felt so satisfying to be connecting with her. Perhaps it was because for so much of the violence I covered in the 1980s, the victims were specters. Hundreds of lost spirits that haunted me. Gina wasn't a ghost. More important: she wasn't a victim—she was a survivor.

Gina didn't want to focus on the darkness. "I don't have depression. But I don't want to be living the way I'm living."

She was exploring how she wanted to spend the last part of her life. It wasn't about the "dying of the light"—it was about running toward something positive. She wanted to live fully, and by this she meant closer to nature. She was talking with some friends about building a tiny home on their land. When I mentioned gardening and my desires for the next phase of my existence, Gina grew excited. "Yes!" she exclaimed. She wanted to be able to put her fingers in soil, create some of the food she eats, in a communal setting.

One year later, when Gina and I spoke again, she was looking into intentional communities, built on teamwork and shared responsibilities. Some of them were off the grid. I mentioned once interviewing a couple who lived in one in Ithaca, New York. Gina knew about it.

"I found that Ithaca one; I turned somebody on to it. She's moving there with her family in a couple of months. Like you, I don't have family. I have to figure it out. What do I want to be when I grow up?"

Curiously, Gina and I both had ended up in the same headspace about the last act of our lives. We wanted to be apart from society yet engaged in our own ways.

For me, this meant emerging to continue writing about the many grave issues facing the world, but having a refuge from the outer world to retreat to for my own sanity and peace. I was done with New York City. A friend and I had just purchased a compound in Southern California, as land partners. We call it The Project, because it's an experiment in a different way of living. Our plan is to make the home carbon-neutral, perhaps even carbon-negative, to grow a lot of food, and to make it a place where a rotating cast of friends can come and go.

For Gina, remaining engaged means continuing her therapy practice, still helping people one on one but living closer to the earth, amid friends.

"For this last part of my life, how do I want to do it?" Gina asked. "How am I going to do the housing part, where I can get someplace where I can grow things and have some animals, and be saved from societal mayhem and be as safe as possible? I'm just going to keep looking till I find that."

# The Investigator

When Gina went to the hospital on the night of the rape in 1981, medical staff took forensic evidence, swabs for semen, and photographs, creating what is now commonly called a "rape kit." Years later, when Gina was in a twelve-step program, her sponsor told her to telephone the Sacramento police to learn if it still existed. It could be part of the healing process—and it could actually give her real closure if the DNA could be used to identify the perpetrator.

"It was so long ago that they didn't even have anything anymore," Gina said.

Was it just Gina's rape kit alone that had been lost?

"Our crime lab does not have rape kits from the 1980s," a spokesperson for the Sacramento County district attorney's office, the keeper of such evidence, wrote in an email. But it wouldn't have mattered anyway. Until 2016, when California governor Jerry Brown signed a bill changing the law, there had been a ten-year statute of limitations on rape. Even if he could have been identified, the man who'd held the gun on Gina and raped her couldn't have been prosecuted.

It was even worse: In 1977, one third of the 389 men convicted of forcible rape in California were put on some kind of probation. And rape using a "foreign object" was treated as a misdemeanor. In 1978, the first time Brown sat in the governor's chair, he signed a bill mandating prison terms for convicted forcible rapists, with a maximum sentence of eight years.

"And so it wasn't until 1978, when Governor Brown signed the legislation, that rape was a prison offense," said Carol Daly, eighty-four, a retired Sacramento County sheriff's detective. Carol had worked for Ray Biondi in homicide. Even with the enhanced sentencing, punishment was minimal. "You could go to prison for three to maybe six years, and then get off for good behavior."

Carol was one of the very few female sheriff's detectives in the 1970s, and given her own interests and the fact that male officers did not want to handle rape crimes, she started specializing in rape cases, before going to homicide. Then, beginning in 1976, a serial rapist began operating in eastern Sacramento County. He became known as the "East Area Rapist," and he struck over thirty times by 1978. The perpetrator stalked victims, and he conducted reconnaissance, sometimes entering homes to take bullets out of guns, so they'd be empty when he came back, or to write down the numbers of landline phones—back then, the numbers were often printed on the phone.

He favored victims with dwellings near creeks, woods, and trails to aid his escape. At first he picked women living alone, then he moved on to couples. He'd break in through a window or sliding glass door, then shine a flashlight on the couple in bed; he'd make the woman tie up her partner before he'd bind her. Men were made to lie face down, and the rapist often stacked dinner plates on the man's back, threatening to kill him if the dishware were to rattle. He'd move the woman to a different room, raping her repeatedly; sometimes he'd eat food and drink beer. Often before he struck, victims received hang-up calls. In one of them, he announced to the woman that he was going to kill her husband. The next day, he attacked. In 2001, one of the victims got a call from a voice she swears was that of the East Area Rapist. He whispered, "Remember when we played?"

The case gripped Sacramento County, each rape getting increasingly massive media coverage. Sheriff's detectives worked hard, identifying and eliminating some six thousand suspects. DNA testing did not then exist. Scores of blood-type tests were done on law officers—investigators believed the rapist was or had been a law officer. Carol was accosted by other deputies in the sheriff's office and derided for not solving the case. It consumed her.

"The most stressful part of my whole career was going to so many rapes and not knowing who it was," Carol said. "Knowing I'm going to interview another victim, who is going to look at me and say, 'If you'd arrested him, I wouldn't have been a victim.'"

After 1978, the crimes ceased in Sacramento County. Detectives believed that the rapist had moved on to another jurisdiction or was in jail somewhere. "I knew within my heart that he was going to kill a victim," Carol said.

Then a series of murders soon began in Southern California. That murderer became known as the Golden State Killer, a name given by investigative journalist and author Michelle McNamara. Fast-forward many years: with DNA, the killer could be identified. But all known crime scene samples had degraded. Investigators combed the state.

The Golden State Killer had raped a woman and then killed both her and her husband in the city of Ventura in 1980. Ventura County medical examiner Claus P. Speth had a practice of producing two rape kits, one for the current investigation and one to be stored, in case it was later needed. The latter kit for this particular rape had gone into the bottom of a freezer and remained there for decades. It was in excellent condition. There was just enough material for one DNA test, and it tied in with the East Area Rapist. A match on a genealogy website led to the 2018 arrest of Joseph DeAngelo in Citrus Heights.

Before the news went public, Sacramento County sheriff Scott Jones asked Carol, by then long retired, to call DeAngelo's victims. Carol had developed friendships with many of them.

"I don't even have credentials anymore for law enforcement. And yet Sheriff Jones recognized that I had such a rapport with them. He said, 'Just start calling.' I've been so vested with all of these survivors. I call them all survivors. And so the first couple, when I called to tell them that the East Area Rapist had been identified, their first comment was: 'We're going to be able to sleep tonight.' For forty years, they barricaded themselves in their house. They moved because they were so scared they were going to be victims again."

When DeAngelo was on his rape spree in Sacramento County, he had threatened to kill the investigating officers.

"Until he was arrested, I didn't walk out my front door until I had looked outside," Carol said. "I would get to my car; I would look in the backseat. I looked for this figure in the shadows that was going to come after the investigators. I did all the things that I had no idea what I was doing. Since he's been arrested, that feeling is totally gone. So I sort of understand the fear the victims had, because they didn't know who he was."

Carol also remained in touch with other rape survivors. What she said about them collectively echoed a lot of what I'd heard from Gina.

"There is still the attitude—I don't care how much has been done for education and everything—there is still an attitude that rape victims probably had a lot of responsibility for their attack," Carol said. Laws are now more stringent, but things have not changed in the cultural sphere. She added that many survivors are shunned by family and friends.

PART FIVE

# Things Noticed

# Parabola

The suburban Sacramento house I bought in 1981 was a three-bedroom ranch, built in 1949, on nearly four-tenths of an acre. The day the title cleared, I walked into the vast backyard and, responding to some primal urge, peed in the center of it. Then I stared at *my* house. *My* house in *California.* I began mowing the lawn. I bought shears to trim the pyracantha hedge. Over time, I became tormented by the invasive and aggressive Bermuda grass that sprouted from cracks in the asphalt driveway, threatening to break up the pavement. All manner of eco-friendly attempts to eradicate it failed. I had to concede defeat and spray herbicide.

Sacramento and its suburbs are not the California of beaches, film stars, and ski slopes. Central Valley towns resemble those in Ohio, with tree-shaded streets on flat land. The only difference is the presence of palm and citrus. Neither of these (to me) exotic species was on my property, but the crowns of Washington and Canary Island palms were visible in the distance.

Some people call Sacramento an ideal location—halfway to the mountains, halfway to San Francisco. It is in the middle in all ways, a very middle-class place for those lucky to have been born at a time when there were jobs that allowed residents to acquire homes in certain choice neighborhoods. These homeowners staffed the many agencies of state government; others of us worked at the newspaper, a very large employer, or at the two military bases.

Yet it wasn't easy to purchase a home at that point. Bank mortgage rates averaged 15 percent. The owner carried paper at 12 percent. I put $18,000 of the $70,000 price down, earned from freelance newspaper writing and grinding industrial tools in my father's shop, at a rate of ten to twenty-five cents per tool over the decade before I left Cleveland. I'd saved this money because my parents didn't charge rent, and they provided meals.

Mortgage rates had reached 15 percent because Paul Volcker, the chair of the US Federal Reserve, was trying to tame rampant inflation. It had three primary causes. One was the collapse of the 1944 Bretton Woods Agreement by forty-four nations, which had based a fixed rate of exchange on the US dollar. Another was that President Lyndon Johnson had chosen to deficit spend and not pursue raising taxes to pay for the Vietnam War and his Great Society programs. The third: the 1973 oil embargo by Middle Eastern nations.

There are much deeper explanations concerning these three reasons—one could nerd out for pages on them—but the key fact is that I bought my house at the beginning of the end of the post–World War II "American Century." Income disparity began increasing in the 1970s and exponentially grew worse starting in the 1980s. This led to an angry electorate, enabling the ascent of Ronald Reagan to the presidency and his "Morning in America" slogan during his 1984 reelection campaign. Reagan was going to take us back to the time when America was booming in the postwar years. Amid this, the so-called freshwater economists told us that the market, not government, would make us all rich.

My house may seem off topic, but today's housing crisis and the epidemic of homelessness have roots in economic policies that began in the 1980s. It's when the impact of America's postwar decline was felt in the sociopolitical realm. To nerd out just a bit, the United States emerged from World War II with about three-fourths of the world's economy, simply because we hadn't been bombed. This wasn't sustainable. The American economy naturally should be around one-fifth of that amount. The 1980s was the beginning of the rest of the world starting to organically reclaim its share.

For years, the Fed had been pumping nearly free money into the financial system, especially after the 2008 financial crisis. Not only did this juice housing prices—low rates allow the value of homes to rise because mortgages become cheaper—but it also gave investors a handout, allowing them to scoop up apartment buildings and homes to create rentals, folding them into the Wall Street casino culture.

Super-low borrowing rates led to rent spikes. This was combined with a NIMBY—"not in my backyard"—culture that froze home and apartment construction out of many communities, especially in expensive East and West Coast markets. These factors made it inevitable that many of those living with housing precarity would lose their homes. Now massive homelessness is so ubiquitous that some young people think it has always existed. A twenty-two-year-old student was disbelieving when I told her that it wasn't always like this, that the word "homeless" hadn't been heard very much before 1980.

I realized I could quantify the homelessness. Until going through my files, I'd forgotten that survey I'd done in 1988 of those living in the weeds and woods along the rivers in Sacramento. The few dozen camps I'd found seven years earlier had grown to 125. When I returned in 2020 during the pandemic, the social services nonprofit Loaves and Fishes estimated that ten thousand people were living without homes in the core inner city area, many in camps along the riverbanks. This meant roughly a 1,000-percent increase in homeless in downtown Sacramento and the surrounding area between 1988 and 2020.

Contrary to what one sees in the most visible of those living on the street, the vast majority of these people don't start out with mental illness. They simply cannot afford to put a roof over their head. In Los Angeles, many homeless people with jobs live in their cars. The idea that someone with a job would be unable to afford rent was unthinkable in 1980.

My first home purchase illustrates how the economic paradigm has shifted and why there is a housing crisis.

Bought in 1981 for $70,000, that house cost almost three times my annual salary of $25,000, which is roughly what the median income was for Sacramento County that year.

Simply adjusted for inflation four decades later, the home's value would be $218,000 and my salary $78,000. The median income in the county today is some $71,000, according to the US Census Bureau.

Zillow estimates that my old house is now worth $546,000. My current proportional wage would have to be $180,000 per year for that house to cost three times my earnings.

Publius Cornelius Tacitus, a first-century orator-turned-historian, wrote about the Roman empire, then in ascension. He observed power, looked back at the conquests of the first half-dozen Roman emperors—the imperialism that included expanding into Britain and sections of Africa and the Middle East. His oft-quoted line about the impact of empire on the Romans: "It belongs to human nature to hate those you have injured." Commentators sometimes apply this concept to contemporary conservatives' attitude toward the working class, the poor, the homeless.

Finding examples isn't difficult. In early 2023, the Republican-supermajority North Dakota state senate rejected a free-school-lunch bill for kids living in poverty. Two weeks later, that same body voted to increase its own meal allowance.

"Yes, I can understand kids going hungry, but is that really the problem…of the state of North Dakota?" Republican senator Mike Wobbema asked in a floor speech. "It's really the problem of parents being negligent with their kids, if their kids are choosing to eat in the first place." Not long after this, Florida governor Ron DeSantis led the effort in the Republican-supermajority state legislature to make housing and hiring undocumented immigrants, as well as transporting them, a felony crime. The proposed bill also would require hospitals to ask patients for their immigration status, which means many people would shun treatment. The bills were interpreted by nonprofit service providers as criminalizing a citizen child driving an undocumented parent, or a landlord renting to a noncitizen.

It should be noted that many undocumented immigrants are doing jobs shunned by native-born Americans, such as working on farms under the hot Florida sun, or as caregivers for the state's numerous retirees.

We simultaneously read news accounts of wealthy and ostensibly liberal New York City suburbs vehemently opposing a plan that Governor Kathy Hochul outlined in January 2023, to create eight hundred thousand new housing units in the state, using strict new laws to override local opposition. Fierce blowback came from communities in Long Island and Westchester County, the latter of which is just north of New York City and three-fourths White; Joe Biden got 67.6 percent of the vote there in 2020. These two areas have blocked construction of new homes for decades, allowing fewer units per capita than suburbs of other major US cities. The plan would have mandated construction if these areas didn't meet quotas, allowing fifty homes per acre within a half-mile of public transit.

Democrats opposed to the plan were smarter than Republican state senator Wobbema—they weren't as blunt. They used code language: "local control." "Overcrowding." "Increased traffic." They said they favored tax and other voluntary incentives for creating new housing. At a rally in support of the bills, state assemblyman Phil Ramos cut through the euphemisms of his fellow Democrats: "It doesn't matter what kind of incentive you give them," he said. "A wealthy community, before they allow Black and brown people in, they'll walk away from any amount of money."

Governor Hochul's plan was defeated in the Democrat-dominated state legislature.

I expect Republicans to be parsimonious and vindictive. As hobo folk singer Utah Phillips once noted, they are like the lightbulb in a refrigerator. Open the door, it comes on. Close it, it goes off. Don't expect anything else to happen.

What has changed is the other spectrum of the electorate. It took me years to begin understanding this. What was impossible to grasp in the 1980s: why weren't Americans and Democratic leaders rallying around the issues of economic equality, housing, the concentration of wealth in the hands of fewer and fewer people? Something has crept into American culture in the past half century. Violence and the berserk in a society aren't measured just by homicide and assault statistics, takeovers of state and federal capitols by angry mobs, and dudes with guns. These can be measured in a disregard for the "other." Tacitus wasn't writing solely about willfully starving children and then hating them. Ignoring them is also a kind of enmity—a quiet and invisible form of violence.

Perhaps it's not the fault of the Democratic Party and its Clintonian wing, which took its cue from my generation, the boomers. Clintonian Democrats merely reflect what has occurred among their voters. When Joan Didion wrote about the "Summer of Love," she talked about the "atomization" of society as she studied the hippies in San Francisco.

"At some point between 1945 and 1967 we had somehow neglected to tell these children the rules of the game we happened to be playing," she wrote in *Slouching Towards Bethlehem*. We were a society cast adrift, and what she witnessed was in reaction to the 1950s. But instead of coalescing around a new paradigm, the children of the 1960s looked backward. We live in opposition or surrender to our parents' lives. The vast majority of the children of the World War II generation surrendered. Many Truman and Eisenhower babies grew up to replicate the 1950s, largely because they were able to. They had the last of legacy pensions, affordable housing, well-paid jobs. And in places like Westchester County and Marin County, the "good liberals" who place Black Lives Matter signs on their lawns want to draw a moat around their private Idahos to keep people unlike them very distant.

These "liberal" places reliably vote to exclude affordable housing—which means modest houses in some California coastal counties priced at $800,000, much less simply affordable apartment units—or create onerous zoning requirements to defy California state law. Thus California has homeless encampments rivaling those of Manila and so-called less-developed Asian cities. NIMBY liberals push lawmakers to crush affordable housing bills in the state legislature. Before, during, and after the pandemic, California state senator Scott Wiener introduced bills that in part would have overridden restrictive local zoning laws that prohibit tall multiunit buildings, and would have increased housing density in transit corridors. Opposition came from both sides: NIMBY liberal "Karens" and Trump conservatives loath to give up local control; they meet shaking hands in the antipoor, pro-tough cop, pro–status quo parabola. We have Clintonism and no FDR because there is no constituency. Lessons were learned in the 1930s—the New Deal—that helped workers in postwar America. But starting in the 1980s, the past was ignored. We aren't even faking trying to help the precariat that has been living in a virtual Great Depression. And we with the ability to act, who have done nothing, wonder why members of this vast underclass are bitter and angry. And why some of them have a lot of guns.

This anger predates conservative commentator Rush Limbaugh; it predates Fox News, which began in 1996. Each emerged to crassly commercialize the discontent. For Limbaugh, it was all an act—at least at the start. In 1988, when Limbaugh left Sacramento to go national, he told journalist Hilary Abramson when she traveled to New York City, "I've always looked at this as entertainment and used my real self for parody and satire, but in Sacramento I was taken seriously. What I do is a shtick—show business."

In the aughts, I met a Fox News staffer at a party in Brooklyn, and she said she was a liberal, as were many people in the Fox newsroom. For her part, she needed a job. We later saw the two-faced cynicism of Tucker Carlson with his wildly differing public and private views of Donald Trump, when emails emerged in court documents in 2023.

Anger feeding on bitterness plays well on radio and television, unlike a liberal message that appeals to logic. The Air America radio network was founded in 2004 to be the answer to Limbaugh, but it shut down in 2010. There are outlets and shows such as MSNBC and Amy Goodman's *Democracy Now!* but their audiences pale in comparison to that of Fox News. Fox, Newsmax, and other conservative media organizations have become like a firestorm in a forest that creates its own weather and lightning bolts to start new fires.

I've long maintained that the United States is divided very roughly into two 40 percent blocks—one is organically liberal, the other naturally conservative. It's the 20 or so percent in the middle that decides elections. In doom loop America, the juggernaut of right-wing media initially spawned to feed the right-wing 40 percent has chipped into this center. Clintonian Democrats, unlike Republicans, don't want to engage in a knife fight. Bernie Sanders did. When I was reporting in Youngstown, Ohio, in 2015 and 2016, a significant percentage of those I interviewed wanted to vote for Bernie. But when the East Coast Democratic Party establishment coronated Hilary Clinton, these people turned to Trump. Bernie might well have won Ohio with the full backing of the Democratic Party.

# Snapshots: War

An email from Mike Fostar, February 11, 2022:

Dale,

Hi, hope all is well.... It was interesting and sort of inner thought provoking, to be interviewed by you in 1985 and 2021—36 years 'tween discussions. How had I changed? Am I someone who has achieved all my personal goals? As many as I could, I suppose, given the hand I was played. Was I "a good man"—as the guy asked at the end of that movie *Saving Private Ryan*? Mostly I guess. How had Vietnam shaped my life to bring me to this point? I have pondered all this a lot. Most every part of my life seems touched by something still linked to Vietnam—my health, the work I did, the people I met. Talking to you. My income is from a job I got because I had a purple heart, and retired from it—the disability pension that helps pay my bills—it's all Nam oriented. The cancer I got—seems to be from Agent Orange. Try as I might in my head—in my life Nam colored just about everything.

I think my dad and his generation were more colored by WW2 than ever I had thought. They did as good a job as they could trying to hide it, but it was there for them also. My father used to talk about my grandfather who was gassed in the Argonne in 1918. He rarely if ever talked about the trench war, according to my dad and uncle, but his health was ruined by the bad lungs and he died young. He was bitter about it was all my dad would say. My dad thought the WW2 vets had it great because they got the GI Bill for college educations and could buy houses and there were Veterans' hospitals. It was so much more than the WW1 vets had been given.

Then we came along with PTSD and Agent Orange and fought a great war that we didn't win. It was so different. America changed. The country didn't like Vietnam vets much. I can still remember the attitudes of people here at home when we came back, and for several decades after the war we were all lumped into a sort of Psycho Killer mode—Hollywood portrayed us like that in many 1970s movies. All that started to change in the 1980s but that was a good 15 to 20 years after our war. In the 1990s people who would never serve in the military started "thanking us" for our service—like we had been serving fast food or something. Often I sensed it was out of guilt. It became so routine—"Here is your receipt—Thank You for Your Service." Like "thanks for killing those yellow people for us. Now move along, nothing to see here."

Many of my brother and sister Nam vets refuse to even talk about what they experienced because of the treatment they received after they got home. War just wasn't a cool thing to talk about. It definitely didn't impress the chicks and many people thought, and still think, military service is for Suckers, as Trump was once quoted as saying.

So this recent interview made me look back at 70 years of living here in the USA. I read that 2/3s of Nam vets are already dead—and that the average age of our segment is 72, we are starting to fade away as a group. I don't think anyone paid much attention to what we did—not militarily or politically—because we did the same stupid nation building/hearts and minds crap in Iraq and Afghanistan and lost there too. So I guess no one learned much.

We will just fade out of memory—like the vets who went before us. I think we were the best our generation had and I guess in the end I am proud to have been part of them. Not proud of the war—But so proud to be one of the Grunts. For all the later suffering I went through, I remained proud of being part of the brotherhood. WE did what was expected of us. We were loyal to each other. All those that never served have no idea what I am even talking about.

America herself has changed, and not for the better. WE passed on the torch and are now fading away. It saddens me to see us divided and at each others' throats. The bad guys of the world would like nothing better than to see America shatter. Our own elites no longer care about us the people. They live like French Aristocrats while the great majority of us suffer like the peasants of old, and they don't care. The Republicans want to end democracy and turn this into an authoritarian police state. Man, things have changed.

I am not in the best shape, so I doubt we can do another interview in 36 or even 26 years. But if you make it that far I hope America makes it too, I have a lot of blood and sweat equity in the Old Gal, and I hope she pulls through. It was a heck of a great democracy— had its problems but it was worth fighting for.

Good luck with your newest project. The Chinese always say Good Fortune. Either one works.

Sincerely
Mike "Doc Mike"

From the Columbia Journalism School website:

Announcing the 2023 Winners of the Mike Berger Award.... The Berger Award, named after the late *New York Times* reporter Meyer "Mike" Berger, is awarded to a reporter(s) for an outstanding example of in-depth human interest reporting.

I co-judged for the awards with my colleagues Professors Joanne Faryon and Meg Kissinger. Columbia's website says that Mike Berger "set the standard for evocative and eloquent human interest reporting" in the 1950s. I was tasked with writing the citation. The concept of empire and the 1980s' American-supported death squads in El Salvador were on my mind as I crafted the press release:

Lynzy Billing is the winner of the 2023 Meyer "Mike" Berger Award for her ProPublica story entitled, "The Night Raids," about CIA-directed death squads called "Zero Units" in Afghanistan that killed countless hundreds. Often raids were based on staggeringly flawed intelligence and resulted in scores of executions—farmers, students, and teachers with no connection to the Taliban.

For over three years, working solo for most of them, Billing did diligent shoeleather reporting across dangerous swaths of Afghanistan. She takes the reader into the shadows of the U.S. war on terrorism that accomplished the opposite of what was intended. "You go on night raids, make more enemies, then you gotta go on more night raids for the more enemies you now have to kill," a member of the U.S. special operations forces told Billing, about his regularly going out with Zero Units.

It began as a personal quest. Billing's mother and twin sister were killed thirty years earlier in a night raid in the civil war that followed the defeat of the Soviet Union in Afghanistan. Her father later died in the conflict. She soon learned about the Zero Units. Billing visited the sites of 30 raids. She interviewed doctors, forensic examiners, eyewitnesses, and family members of civilians shot point-blank. She gained the trust of Afghan commandos who questioned their actions. And she interviewed the former Afghan spy chief who admitted to raids being conducted on flawed intelligence.

Billing's gripping and powerfully written story echoes the CIA-spawned "Phoenix Program" during the Vietnam War that also killed innocents. "The Night Raids" should be read by U.S. citizens so they know what is being done in their name, as well as everyone at the CIA's Langley, Virginia headquarters.

# We Are Devo

Humans don't discern incremental change. We are in fact not like a frog in a pot of water. As the water comes to a boil, the frog will jump out. The frog will not allow itself to be cooked to death. We are not this intelligent. Societal conditions deteriorate, and we learn to live with an ever-increasing dismal reality. I was reminded of this more than forty-one years after starting on the police beat in Sacramento, four and a half years after I sold the off-grid home on that lonely ridge in the Emerald Triangle. I was now living full-time in New York City.

One day, the zipper on my backpack irreparably broke. Not wanting to order a new one online, I walked to a Target, but it was a micro version of the chain and didn't carry backpacks. Across the street was a T.J. Maxx. There was one backpack on display. The tag read:

Trident

BACKPACK

01CARABINER INCLUDED

02CONCEALED CARRY POCKET

As I stood in the checkout line holding the pack, I thought about Patrick Purdy and the dead children in Stockton, California. I couldn't forget that massacre. It would have been unimaginable in 1989 to have seen such a label, or to believe that firearms would become even more entrenched in American culture, so much so that a manufacturer would find it advantageous to design of special pocket in a backpack for a gun and then boldly advertise it on the label.

Twenty-four states now allow anyone to carry a concealed weapon without a permit, and this is merely an expansion on the attitude toward guns I saw in Brunswick, Ohio, when I was on the police beat in 1977. That year, only Vermont allowed residents to carry a concealed firearm without a permit. Just four states back then would unconditionally issue a license to any nonfelon who wanted one; the remaining forty-six states were way more restrictive. In the 1980s, these restrictive laws crumbled after intense lobbying from the National Rifle Association.

And then, in 2022, months after I bought the pack, the US Supreme Court struck down New York City's handgun licensing law, saying citizens have a right to carry firearms in public. By this point, it appears that the citizenry feels helpless to do anything to stop the increasing leniency regarding firearms. Pressuring members of Congress would be futile with Republicans adamantly opposed to restrictive gun laws. Reluctantly or with a sense of despair, we have learned to accept mass shootings as a given fact of American life.

In the fall term of 1991, I was an assistant professor at the Columbia University Graduate School of Journalism in New York City, teaching a boot-camp course called Reporting and Writing the News. My mandate was to put sixteen students through the rigorous paces of learning how to report, which meant covering crime, courts, and cops. This included deadline drills that replicated actual newsroom rewrite experience. I crafted one exercise based on the Stockton schoolyard massacre.

Portrait of a Killer—Patrick Edward Purdy

It's the day after Patrick Edward Purdy, 25, stormed the playground of the Cleveland Elementary School in Stockton,

California. Five children are dead and 30 children and a teacher are injured....

[S]omeone else is writing the main story. Your job is to find out who this guy was. The story is guaranteed for A-1....

You know you are going to have a tough time. You are responsible for fielding eight reporters who are working to feed you from southern California to Oregon, and then rewrite all their notes into a compelling and comprehensive story. You have run property, driver's license records, and have checked phone directories for Purdy's friends and relatives. From this information you have dispatched the reporters to key addresses. You are essentially a nerve center for all these reporters—a combination editor/reporter/rewrite man/woman. All day you have done phone work tracking down leads. There has been no time to write anything. You know from experience the notes from the field reporters won't start coming in until 1-1/2 hours before your deadline. It is now 1:45 before deadline.

My students sat at computers facing the walls of the long rectangular room. Over the course of the next hour and forty-five minutes, I passed out "feeds" of new information from field reporters, keeping the deadline parallel with what it actually had been but in a much truncated form. I paced the room, looking over the shoulders of students in professor/drill sergeant mode. One European student was extremely anxious, perhaps channeling my stress. After all, not even three years had passed since I'd done this one for real. I'm sure I exuded the sweat-dripping intensity from being on that kind of deadline, on that kind of story.

Ann Belser was one of those sixteen students. She'd come to the journalism school after being a reporter at two newspapers, including the *Winthrop Sun-Transcript*, covering its namesake Boston suburb. In 1986, she went to her first homicide, of a man who appeared to have been stabbed to death. Most students didn't have this experience, but covering violence is part of the job. So I had them gain exposure to police and homicides, then plentiful in New York City. This further immersion was helpful for Ann.

After graduation, she was hired at the *Pittsburgh Post-Gazette* as a night police reporter. She went to numerous gruesome crime scenes. At one, she stepped around a body the police had not yet discovered. She reported about an innocent kid killed by a gang and interviewed the victim's mother; that woman would later be stabbed to death by her son's father.

"When I covered homicides," Ann later wrote, "I was always able to distance myself. None were in my neighborhood." When she wanted to buy a house, "my criterion was to look only in neighborhoods where I had not been sent to cover crime."

In 1995, she bought a house in the Pittsburgh neighborhood of Squirrel Hill, home to many Jewish people. Ann came from a Jewish family, but her upbringing had been secular. Her father questioned Ann before the sale closed. Why would she buy in a Jewish neighborhood? He worried about anti-Semites. "They will know where to find you," Ann recalled her father saying.

On the morning of October 27, 2018, Ann was walking Fred, her Corgi puppy, about four hundred feet from her house, passing in front of the Tree of Life synagogue. There were five loud sounds. Ann thought boxes inside a passing UPS truck had fallen. The dog sensed danger and pulled her away. She got home, and her son said there was shooting going on inside the temple.

"I grabbed my camera and ran towards the synagogue. It's a short block. And suddenly, the door at the top popped open, and all the smoke started to come out. Smoke from the gunfire from the shooting. The police had automatic weapons; there were just hundreds of rounds fired."

The shooter, a heavyset White man, yelled, "All Jews must die!" He was armed with an AR-15 and three handguns. Eleven people were killed and six wounded.

Ann didn't remember the Patrick Purdy exercise. And in fact, I eventually stopped using it because it was a *Groundhog Day* of PTSD for a lot of the violence I covered in the 1980s. Ann had her share of PTSD even before the eleven gun deaths four hundred feet from her house.

"Back when I was a police reporter, I tried to just say that the tragedies I was seeing—shootings, fires, that sort of thing—were other people's tragedies, not mine. It was totally a matter of staying sane not to take in all of the grief from what I was seeing."

Ann, no longer at the daily newspaper, is now a one-woman operation—writer, photographer, layout person, publisher—putting out a hard-copy newspaper, *Print*, "Pittsburgh's East End Newspaper."

Not long after we talked, Ann wrote an editorial about guns.

Now, as I write this on the 99th day of the year, there have been 145 mass shootings in the U.S. in 2023. It is time to scare the pro-gun lobby into common sense gun measures including renewing the ban on assault rifles...People across the country want to see regulations adopted, or in the case of assault-style rifles, reinstated.

Ann came to find hope in how young people are mobilizing—a grassroots movement that could grow and have impact.

"I want the assault ban back in place," Ann said. "For people who already have assault-style rifles, they can keep them but cannot transport them or transfer ownership. I want real penalties on anyone whose gun is found by a child who then uses it to injure or kill themselves or another. I know prosecutors go easy on parents who have lost a child, but it has happened way too many times. Of course I also want to get rid of bump stocks and large magazines, but anytime anyone proposes gun control, it is like Black Friday at Walmart with all the people who race out to buy guns."

I'd go further. As someone who once hunted, I understand having rifles. But one cannot legally use a hundred-shot drum to hunt deer. Military-grade weapons should be outright banned, existing ones made illegal. Just as local police have handgun buyback programs, there could be a national one for AR-15s and other assault rifles.

It was a country on edge. A country with a paranoid and heavily armed populace. In the two years following the start of the pandemic in 2020, one in five Americans bought a firearm. Thirty states have enacted "stand your ground" laws that essentially allow people to shoot first and ask questions later. It is a country where simply being lost or confused about an address can get you maimed or killed in a hail of bullets. The following events happened within a five-day period in the spring of 2023:

> Kansas City, Missouri: A sixteen-year-old Black youth is shot for ringing the doorbell of the wrong home when he came to pick up his younger siblings; an octogenarian White man opens fire through a glass door.

> Hebron, Upstate New York: Two carloads of young people seeking a party at a friend's house in this rural town pull into the wrong driveway. They begin to leave when the homeowner comes out with a gun blazing. A twenty-year-old woman is killed.

> Elgin, Texas: Two teenage cheerleaders get into the wrong car after practice in a supermarket parking lot. It looks exactly like theirs. A twenty-five-year-old man gets out of the car after the women exit and shoots them.

Unhinged incidents spike. People attack cabin crew on jetliners. Waitstaff in restaurants are punched. I visited a friend in Sacramento after leaving Gina in the Bay Area. In the morning, I took some trash to the curbside waste barrel waiting for pickup. A neighbor across the street began screaming, so crazily it was impossible to discern the cause of her anger. It slowly became clear that she was accusing me of placing waste in her barrel. I'd never been closer to her barrel than I was at that moment, a half-block away, but there was no way to communicate my innocence over her screams. Her face was bright red and seemed full of homicidal intent; it's easy to imagine that if she'd had a gun in hand, she'd have started firing.

California Highway Patrol data shows an increase in violence over the past two years. In 2019, there were 210 reported shootings on the state's roads; in 2021, 411. Authorities have no idea why shootings doubled in those two years. About a quarter of the incidents involved identified road rage; a small fraction were gang-related. Who knows about the others? Perhaps it was the pandemic. But much of this anger predates COVID. It began with the growing economic insecurity starting in the 1980s. As a young journalist, I saw rage simmering in places such as Peoria and Flint and Youngstown, cities on the front lines of the end of the American Century.

From Sacramento I took a road trip, driving on US Highway 50, dubbed by *Life* magazine as the "loneliest road in America," from Lake Tahoe into the rural desert of central Nevada. A storefront church covered in placards: "Trust Jesus" and "Warning/Repent/Luke 13:3. Your country in Peril/Your liberty at Risk/Wake Up America." On other road trips in Iowa and Nebraska: antiabortion billboards featuring pictures of fetuses. And everywhere: "Make America Great Again!"

You stop and talk to the people who own these printed gesticulations—in their churches, bars, feed lots. You are a human, they are a human, and you have a pleasant interaction 99 percent of the time. Once you drive away and return to a distant home near salt water, however, you are no longer a human; you are a lizard with a tail to be vilified on Twitter, now named X, Truth Social, Reddit, Facebook. The divide is profound.

The reality is that you feel alien among them, and they among you if they visit where you live, with your "liberal" friends who revile them on social media. The liberal lizards with tails are called pedophiles by the far right. This dehumanization reminds one of wartime. In order to kill or harm another person, the enemy must be made less than human. In World War I, Germans were Huns in cartoons; in World War II, the Japanese buck-toothed monkeys. In modern times, QAnon and other right-wing groups have taken a cue from Putin's Russia, where opponents are often set up on false charges of pedophilia, with incriminating evidence planted on them. In America, the far right has invented a child-sex-slave dungeon beneath a Washington, DC, pizza joint that is mythically frequented by famous Democrats; left-wing opponents are "groomers"; "save the children" a mantra; Hollywood elites harvest migrant children at the border for their sexual pleasures. The message: these things make violence against Democrats, liberals, and other perceived enemies acceptable; it's open season on "pedophiles."

The big-city coastals don't get off easy, especially those in Congress. When factories, steel mills, and mines began closing by the score in the early 1980s, throwing hundreds of thousands out of well-paid jobs, there were some lame "retraining" programs funded by Congress. They failed. The Democratic Party dumped the working class and embraced the neoliberal free market. The party partook in the negative feedback loop of descent by embracing the ideas of Republican/ Libertarian economists. Al Gore was among them. I knew he was going to lose the 2000 election after I reported in his hometown of Carthage, Tennessee, that summer.

Gore supported the North American Free Trade Agreement of 1994, which had caused a hemorrhaging of jobs to Mexico. Clothing manufacturer OshKosh B'Gosh had a huge plant in Carthage. It was shut down, and thousands of jobs were sent to factories south of the border. Of NAFTA, Gore said he was "proud of what we've achieved" and that the agreement had created nineteen million new jobs.

Elizabeth Boles, fifty-five, was among those former OshKosh workers who got one of these new jobs—at a Rite Aid drugstore. Her old job at the shuttered OshKosh paid up to $14 per hour. Her new wage in the free market economy: $5.15 an hour.

"People in Washington look at the papers and see you're working," Elizabeth said. She was raising her twelve-year-old son alone, trying to get by on the reduced wages. "On paper you're working. I don't have stock. Or a bank account. I'm just surviving." She added of Gore: "He's not stupid. He knows. He's a small-town boy from Carthage. He knows the new economy is not helping working-class people."

I found many others like Boles, helping explain why Gore lost his home state in the 2000 election. It wasn't that the downsized workers voted Republican. Many simply didn't vote at all. Who knows how many people from places like Carthage were eventually lured to rage radio and Fox television while Democrats turned Republican-lite in the post-Reagan 1980s. Neoliberal free market Democrats helped create the political doom loop. Republicans, for their part, continued to focus on social issues, all the while ignoring the plight of the working class in red states while handing Wall Street and billionaires more tax cuts. Wacky conspiracy theories are taken as fact—many Republicans label what's in the *New York Times* "fake news," while embracing crazy ideas tweeted by Russian trolls or broadcast on Fox or Newsmax.

We get here because Gina is right. War—for some men—means rape. But the deeper need, as Gina says, is to annihilate. It explains the actions of so many mass shooters, like the one in Las Vegas who in 2017 opened fire on a music festival from the thirty-second floor of the Mandalay Bay resort and casino. A (legal) bump stock made his weapon act like a machine gun—sixty were killed and hundreds injured. The shooter was going for numbers. Las Vegas police concluded after investigating that there was no clear motive. But the police missed the point: the driving force, racial animus or not, connecting mass shootings is annihilation. Killing the enemy is what war is all about. And the United States is now a war zone, with public mass shootings occurring at an all-time-record rate of one every six days in 2023.

To understand this juncture, we have to return to the dawn of the 1980s. For me, it's that day after the 1980 presidential election when Bob Forsyth told me he had good news and bad news. Reagan becoming president marks the beginning of the ascent of the extreme right. Reagan was made possible because of Richard Nixon's post–Barry Goldwater "Southern Strategy," which preyed upon White racial fear—including resentment over school busing to achieve integration—to pull voters away from the Democratic Party. Reagan mastered this message, using mythical "welfare queens" driving Cadillacs as a nemesis. But he took things to a new level.

Reagan's mantra began in his Inauguration Day speech: "Government is not the solution to our problem; government is the problem." The tone was set to prime White resentment against federal authority, and in the coming decades it became a mantra of the far right. Nixon was necessary for Reagan; in turn, Reagan led to the first Bush, then the second Bush; ultimately, this long descent led to Trump.

In the weeks after Bob hired me, I wrote in letters to friends that landing the gig the day after Reagan became president portended something. I wasn't sure exactly where things would land. I knew only that it was a very good time to be a journalist in cutting-edge California. It was the start of a journey that resulted in my spending almost all of the 1990s researching and writing *The Coming White Minority: California, Multiculturalism, and the Nation's Future*. (The original hardback subtitle contained the word "eruptions"—far more accurate.)

I began this work before the 1991 Los Angeles riots. In 1996, Whites fell below half the population of California, yet they still made up 80 percent of voters. When Republican governor Pete Wilson ran for president in this era, it was on an anti-immigrant, anti–affirmative action platform. He supported Propositions 187 and 229, which targeted immigrants and affirmative action. Pandering to White rage won Wilson two terms in office. But it was a doomed strategy for Republicans in California. As older White voters died off and Whites continued to shrink as a percentage of the population, the state became solidly blue.

A then-dominant White electorate in the 1990s passed those propositions. In the book, I describe it as a "white riot" at the ballot box. The book, published in 1996, was meant to be a cautionary tale for the United States. "History has shown that when California erupts, America does, too," I wrote. "The growing hostility toward non-whites that is being spawned in California presents a grave threat as the nation becomes increasingly non-white."

Being early with a prediction doesn't mean one will have an impact. Pioneers get arrows in their backs. It was easy to envision the White riot at the ballot box in the 2016 election, yet I was the man in the dream watching that figure shimmying out onto the rotting limb, yelling at him to turn back. What couldn't be augured was an escalation of mass shootings, which are cumulatively vastly more violent in terms of casualties than the urban riots of the inner city in the 1960s and the 1991 riot in Los Angeles, which fueled White fear. We've entered an era of an actual White riot/war on the streets and in shopping malls, movie theaters, synagogues, and classrooms, with White mass shooters often wearing tactical gear, emulating soldiers.

It's as if there's a symbiotic relationship between these dudes with guns and Republican members of Congress, an inversion of what I saw in the Philippines, with the leftist Philippines National Democratic Front representing the political dimension and the New People's Army the warring arm. Republicans take care of the street wing by blocking any and all efforts at gun control, offering only thoughts and prayers after each episode of carnage. The warring branch, a disparate irregular army, finds inspiration in Timothy McVeigh, who parked a Ryder rental truck full of explosives in front of a federal building in Oklahoma City in 1995; the explosion killed 168 and injured 680. McVeigh had hoped his actions would start a war against the federal government; it was a call to arms echoed by many subsequent mass shooters. Amid this, Republicans continue to stoke White resentment, "rioting" in office by being the party of "no," figuratively burning down the US government.

Meantime, nothing is being done for struggling people in places like Carthage and Youngstown. Many on the left vilify Appalachia, stereotyping its residents as crackers, hicks, hillbillies, racists, rubes, rednecks, white trash—"deplorables"—to be laughed at. Sure, the left isn't gunning them down. But they end up dead in other ways—from poor health, from opioid overdoses. Negative branding justifies ignoring these people, and this is a form of violence.

We get here because Mike Fostar is correct: this is how an empire ends.

When the decline began is open to debate. Perhaps it doesn't matter. But it's reasonable to argue that a starting point emerged on May 4, 1970. Mark Mothersbaugh and Gerald Casale were literature and art students at Kent State University. Casale was out on campus that day. "I watched Guardsmen shoot with M1 rifles," he told an interviewer. "I watched an exit wound as big as a softball come out of the back of Allison Krause. I saw Jeffrey Miller lying in quarts of blood. I knew them both. No Guardsmen were in danger."

The men were shaken. In the wake of the massacre, they concluded that humanity was no longer evolving. It was devolving—de-evolution. DEVO. It became the name of a band they formed in 1972. The group struggled. At gigs, audiences hated them. In 1978, they put out their first album: *Q: Are We Not Men? A: We Are DEVO!* The premise of the song "Jocko Homo" is that humankind is going backward to an ape-man state. It has a catchy refrain: "Are we not men? We are DEVO! D-E-V-O."

Avant-garde musician Brian Eno produced that album, and David Bowie presciently deemed DEVO "the band of the future." John Lennon was a fan. Yet in its early years, the group, which performed wearing plastic flower pots on their heads, was reviled by critics and much of the public until their 1980 hit "Whip It." The group intended the song to convey the emptiness of striving for the American dream; many listeners thought it was about sadomasochism. The band embraced the misunderstanding as more evidence of devolution.

It was music made for the dawn of the 1980s, and it became a soundtrack for the decades that followed.

When living at home with my parents in the late 1970s, I wrote at night to music on WKSU, the college station out of nearby Kent State University. Two of my favorite shows were *The Industrial Wasteland* and *Fresh Air.* DJs played DEVO and 15-60-75, also called the Numbers Band, which Gerald Casale had been in before DEVO. The concept of devolution was captivating yet abstract at that time. In later interviews, Casale said that devolution went beyond violent acts like the Kent State shootings.

"The gene pool has been corrupted by masses of morons... who can't think," he told a journalist in 2004. "They can't process information. It's like a big Jerry Springer world, where every fact has as much importance as every other fact." He also said devolution was about corporate power and consumerism.

We have to understand that we now all are DEVO.

D-E-V-O.

# CODA

# "So Good to Be Alive When the Eulogy Is Read"

For several months in 1986 after Michael Williamson's and my role in smuggling that El Salvadoran family came up in federal court, I worried that US attorney Don Reno would charge us. I thought he would at least go after Michael for allegedly lifting that fence off the back of Sandra as she set foot on American soil. But as it turned out, everything about that trial was a stage set. We had nothing to fear.

There's a long history of political theater in the United States, of elected officials grandstanding to advance careers and agendas. There were the infamous Palmer raids following the First World War, pushed by President Woodrow Wilson, to arrest people on charges of socialism and subversion. Three thousand Jewish intellectuals and Italian immigrants were jailed. In 1947, Congressman J. Parnell Thomas, chairman of the House Un-American Activities Committee, went literal in his quest for political theater by attacking Hollywood for supposedly being infested with Communists.

In the initial hearing, friendly witnesses were called to the stand, among them Walt Disney, who was happy to testify. Disney blamed Communists for a 1941 strike at his studio during the production of *Dumbo*. The animators were merely underpaid and wanted a raise—they didn't want to start a revolution. The first hostile witness was writer John Howard Lawson. Among his many credits were the World War II movies *Sahara* and *Action in the North Atlantic*, both from 1943 and starring Humphrey Bogart. Lawson defied the committee, citing the free speech afforded all Americans; he refused to cooperate.

"It's unfortunate and tragic that I have to teach this committee the basic principles of Americanism," he declared. Parnell persisted in asking, "Have you ever been a member of the Communist Party?" When Lawson continued citing his constitutional rights, Parnell hammered the gavel and ordered officers to take Lawson away. A succession of screenwriters, producers, and one director refused to cooperate. Ten of them were sentenced to one year in prison. None of the "Hollywood Ten" was a threat to the United States, but their being sent behind bars fueled the careers of congressmen on the committee.

In the 1950s, three hundred film industry members were blacklisted, which meant they couldn't work. Those banned included Charlie Chaplin, Orson Welles, and Paul Robeson, the African American singer and actor who tried to get laws passed to prevent Blacks from being lynched in the South. The committee was followed by Senator Joe McCarthy, who went after the military, college professors, and others with unfounded claims of Communist infiltration.

There were smaller acts of political theater in later years, among them one by Alabama governor George Wallace. When the University of Alabama was integrated in 1963 and Black students were allowed to enroll, Wallace stood in the doorway of Foster Auditorium, blocking the access of Black students—as seen in film footage. Nicholas Katzenbach, the deputy assistant attorney general at the time, asked Wallace to step aside, and Wallace complied. What is not commonly known is that Wallace struck a deal with the Justice Department beforehand, allowing him to put on the show of defiance for his constituency, with the promise that he would submit to federal authority in the end.

Conservatives have dominated the use of aggressive theater in the courts and Congress. Perhaps it's because liberals do better in the theater of smaller moments. We think of Abbie Hoffman when he "levitated" the Pentagon in protest against the Vietnam War, or when he went to the New York Stock Exchange with demonstrators who threw one-dollar bills down onto the trading floor; the traders acted greedily, as predicted, and scrambled for the money. In more recent years, when a video surfaced of US representative Alexandria Ocasio-Cortez dancing in college, conservatives tried to use it against her. AOC's response was to dance in front of the US House of Representatives.

In the case of the Sanctuary movement, President Ronald Reagan's Justice Department appeared to have history on its side with the theater of arrest and trial when it indicted priests, nuns, and laypeople. Just as in other eras, the heavy hand of a conservative government would at least for a while crush the left while simultaneously helping the reelection prospects of Republicans. The US Justice Department ignored internal warnings. A Border Patrol agent wrote a memo to his bosses:

> A ploy is going to be..."baiting" in order to demonstrate to the public that the U.S. Government thinks nothing of breaking down the doors of their churches to drag Jesus Christ out to be tortured and murdered.... [A]ll political implications should be considered before any further action is taken toward this group.

Another memo from an immigration investigator said arrests would make movement members into "martyrs." No matter. Prosecutors needed to make a point of standing up to these religious radicals. It must be remembered that in the 1980s, conservatives had few targets, because there wasn't much overt activism. There was the AIDS Coalition to Unleash Power, whose members chained themselves inside the New York Stock Exchange in 1989, to protest the cost of drugs to treat HIV. The Sanctuary movement was just about the only other civil disobedience happening in that decade. The theater of the moment compelled conservatives to go after Sanctuary, the biggest game in town.

Perhaps the reason Don Reno was so obsessed with Michael's and my immersion is that we were not playing our assigned roles as members of the press in this performance. We'd gone off script. We weren't meant to get inside; our part in this show was supposed be restricted to observing from a distance, just like the press had done with the House Un-American Activities Committee, McCarthy's crusade, and all the other political theater of the past. Reno couldn't indict me, and he chose not to press charges against Michael. But he could, it appears, hope to shame us in the media.

Neither the bust nor the shaming ever came. There were just brief mentions in daily stories. Those worries were the least of my problems anyway.

Crime and violence defined much of my life in the 1980s. I also spent the decade in the West with job-seeking hobos, in the Deep South with former sharecroppers, in the steel town necropolises with downsized workers. If I showed up at your door in those days, your life had been marked by epic tragedy. In writing for newspapers and books, I closely witnessed one thousand shattered lives, which is to say I retain one thousand demons from that decade.

For years, I had nightmares about the El Salvador project and other experiences. Many people I'd met had died, like "No Thumbs," the hobo who taught me how to ride the rails—murdered in his camp. But the fate of most remained a mystery. I had to move on. Over time, the demons came less often to rattle their chains.

An email I received on April 2, 2007:

Escape From El Salvador

You may not remember me, but I have a slight hunch that you will. In 1984 you and a photographer, Michael Williamson, helped me and my family escape El Salvador, via underground. You may remember me as Beatrice Flores and my parents as Ramon and Victoria Flores, or my father as Francisco Nunez, I think in 1989 my father went by Francisco Nieto when we lived in New Jersey. I now go by my real name, Lil Beatriz Calderon-Huezo and am an American citizen and have been since 1994, two years after the peace treaty was signed in El Salvador. I'm 25 now and live in Sacramento, which is what brought on this whole search. You were so young, I can't say I would ever do what you and Michael and many others involved did for me and my family. My older sister, younger, brother and mother still live in Kalamazoo, Michigan and my father lives in El Salvador for the time being with his mother. He missed his father's passing in 1988.... I'm writing you this email because I would really love to talk to you and maybe get together and talk. I would love to hear your side of our journey, I've heard my parents for years. And if this email is all I have and never get a response...please note I will always have a special part for you in my heart.

Dear Lil,

How incredible and wonderful to hear from you...a very special voice from the past. The El Salvador project has haunted me. I wrote about this a bit in my most recent book, *Denison, Iowa*. I lived in that small Iowa town, about 1/3 Latino, in 2003 and 2004 and ended up tutoring a class of ESL learners 3 nights a week. My table was all Salvadorans. I had lots of flashbacks to 1984 while there. Now, as you know, the country is in sad shape and I really bonded with those folks at my table. El Salvador holds a place in my soul.

Of course I remember you, though you were tiny back then! Thank you for your kind words—they mean a lot...

Best,

Dale

That June I waited at a coffeehouse in the Oak Park neighborhood of Sacramento. I was a bit nervous. Lil appeared and was instantly disarming, a happy young woman. We melted away an hour learning of each other's lives. Lil had just moved to Sacramento and was planning to go to college. The next hour was therapy for us. Lil grew up with anxiety attacks.

"I was scared of the dark," she said of the legacy of her youth. "I still have the TV on when I sleep. I need the noise."

She needed to fathom her journey to becoming an American, why she felt like an outsider. Across the gulf between writer and subject, smuggler and "smugglee," we were trying to make sense of who we were. I admitted that if she'd emailed a few years earlier, when I was in deep-hideout mode at my off-grid place, I might not have responded. I didn't know until this very afternoon that I needed to meet Lil, to see the good end of something from my 1980s.

I noted that so much could have gone wrong—the panel wagon's breaking down out in the hot desert fatal miles from anywhere, being caught. We laughed, the kind one seldom hears—a from-the-soul, glad-to-be-alive laugh that drew odd looks from coffeehouse patrons.

I quoted the late folk singer Phil Ochs: "So good to be alive when the eulogy is read." We high-fived.

# Gina

Last words go to Gina.

Four decades after that day we sat on the third-floor deck of the *Sacramento Bee*'s cafeteria, I finished writing this book. I did something very unusual: I mailed Gina a printout of the manuscript. I wanted to get it right, wanted to make certain she was okay with the way her story was told so long after the editors had killed it. Gina needed to be my first reader—not just of her story but of everything—in part because she had been there at the start of my journey into American violence. In an email after she received the manuscript, Gina didn't ask for any changes, but had one request—that she could say where she had landed after her travels down that long road:

> Wow.... One of the reasons I felt drawn to being in the book is that I have a message: I want people with PTSD and other challenging life issues to REALLY GET THAT THE SUFFERING CAN END AND LIFE CAN BE SOOOO GOOD!
>
> And.... It's not possible to do it alone. I needed a guide, many guides. It's imperative. It took me a long time to find my way. But I was fortunate enough to find a guide into those darkest places, those impossible places, who walked down in with me and walked me back out.

I get to do that now. I am that guide.

—Gina Catania, CC, CMT

**—Dale Maharidge**
NEW YORK CITY September 22, 2023

# Notes

Memory is, of course, imprecise. I minimized its use. I relied on those footlockers filled with ephemera from the era documented in this book. I also had nearly twenty-three hours of interview tapes of myself and Michael S. Williamson, conducted by Jan Haag and recorded by Richard Schmidt. These multiday sessions began on June 25, 1991, and continued into early July.

"We had gathered for the interviews for two reasons: to provide material for my master's thesis on writers and photographers as journalistic teams; and to allow Dale and Michael the chance to capture on tape, for the first time, their memories of working together," Jan wrote in this thesis. Contained in the transcripts is a significant portion of my 1980s work at a time when my memory was fresher, with the advantage of Michael's recollections. And original newspaper stories provide the core of material for this book; the *Sacramento Bee* more or less allowed its writers to infuse their stories with details more commonly found in magazines, although one had to often push back hard to do this.

I'm not footnoting those *Bee* stories authored by me. They are too numerous and in many places these chapters are a combination of those stories, notes, memories, and files. Most of this book is drawn from my archives. In most cases where this is not the case, I attribute sources in the text. Other source material is noted below.

It's inevitable after producing a number of books that include one's lived experience that there will be crossover. I've written in a truncated manner about moving to California and included some of my early homeless reporting in *Someplace Like America: Tales from the New Great Depression;* that material is vastly expanded here. And a brief description of the El Salvador project appears in *Denison, Iowa: Searching for the Soul of America Through the Secrets of a Midwest Town;* that also is told here in much expanded form. On the other hand, I've greatly condensed in this volume the mentions of my childhood and my father in *Bringing Mulligan Home: The Other Side of the Good War* and material from *The Coming White Minority: California, Multiculturalism, and the Nation's Future.*

## Epigraph

*Bringing Mulligan Home: The Other Side of the Good War*, Dale Maharidge, PublicAffairs, 2013.

## River Styx Road

"Federal Policy on Homelessness Becomes New Target of the Right," Jason DeParle, *New York Times*, June 20, 2023.

"In Mississippi, poverty but not homelessness; Greater Jackson's unhoused rate is far better than L.A. County's, showing the power of cheap dwellings to keep people off the streets," "Mississippi Has Problems, But It's Handling Homelessness Better Than L.A.," Noah Bierman, *Los Angeles Times*, August 23, 2023.

"Toward a New Understanding: The California Statewide Study of People Experiencing Homelessness," University of California San Francisco Benioff Homelessness and Housing Initiative, June 2023.

Gun Violence Archive, https://www.gunviolencearchive.org/The Violence Project, https://www.theviolenceproject.org/methodology/

"Why Women Mass Shooters Are a Rare Occurrence," Terry Collins and Grace Hauck, USA Today, March 27, 2023.

## Copshop

"KKK Paint Job Angers Brunswick Couple," Wilhelmina Ingram, *Call & Post*, March 14, 1985.

"Holloway served travelers, covered crime beat," Obituary, *Sacramento Bee*, October 13, 2012.

## Snapshots: 1980–1982

*Every Secret Thing*, Patricia Campbell Hearst with Alvin Moscow, Doubleday, 1982.

"Rush Explains Rio Linda," *The Rush Limbaugh Show*, transcript, April 20, 2007, https://www.rushlimbaugh.com/daily/2007/04/20/rush_explains_rio_linda/.

## Good Cop/Bad Cop

"A California Town Is Able to Kill a Watt in Its War on Waste," *Wall Street Journal*, May 17, 1978.

"Davis, California: Darling of the Conservationists," Deborah Hand, *Christian Science Monitor*, January 2, 1980.

Led Zeppelin tape: This story can now be told because all principle characters are dead.

*The Dracula Killer: The True Story of California's Vampire Killer*, Ray Biondi and Walt Hecox, Titan Books Ltd., 1992.

## The *Pogo* Factor

"California Town Says Mountain Lions Don't Stop Housing After All," Maria Cramer and Alan Yuhas, *New York Times*, February 7, 2022.

## Shithole

"2 Facing Death Throw Acid on Jailer, Escape," Associated Press, September 11, 1954.

"They Stalked the Frat Party," Steven A. Capps, *San Francisco Examiner*, November 9, 1980.

"Prosecutor's Grim Picture of Killing of Young Couple," Jennifer Foote, *San Francisco Examiner*, December 14, 1982.

"Book on Gallego Murders Sparks Sales, Memories," Bob Sylva, *Sacramento Bee*, December 8, 1987.

"The Sex Slave Murders," R. Barri Flowers, *Cosmopolitan*, January 1997.

## El Camino High School

"History of the California Cadet Corps as Viewed Through Primary Source Documents 1911–2015," California Military Department History Office, Installation Support Unit Camp, San Luis Obispo Second Edition, July 1, 2015.

*Every Secret Thing*, Patricia Campbell Hearst with Alvin Moscow, Doubleday, 1982.

## Kent State

"Michael Douglas, as Villain, Hits It Big on 'Wall Street,'" Helen Dudar, *New York Times*, December 6, 1987.

"Greed Will Go On—With 'Money Never Sleeps,' Oliver Stone Tries to Make Peace with His Unholiest Creation: Gordon Gekko," Reed Tucker, *New York Post*, September 19, 2010.

## Escape From El Salvador

"God and Caesar at the Rio Grande: The Sanctuary Movement and the Politicization of Religion in the United States," M. Hilary Cunningham, dissertation, Yale University, 1992.

*United States of America, Plaintiff, v. Maria del Socoro Pardo de Aguilar, et al.*, defendants. Trial proceedings, vols. 49–50, January 30–31, 1986.

## Empire: The Philippines

Tax records: author's collection of his parents' 1040 forms.

"The Ballad of Barry Sadler," Bob Sipchen, *Los Angeles Times*, January 27, 1989.

"'Green Berets' Singer Barry Sadler Dies at 49," Associated Press, November 7, 1989.

"Senate Aide Calls Base Security Lax," Bill Keller, *New York Times*, September 12, 1985.

## Vietnam Comes Home

"Beret Victim Low Level," Robert G. Kaiser, *Washington Post*, August 19, 1969.

"C.I.A. Tells of Beret Case, Saying It Opposed Slaying," Benjamin Welles, *New York Times*, August 29, 1969.

"New Jersey Green Beret Named by Army as Slayer," *New York Times*, September 27, 1969.

"N.J. Captain Is Named as Beret Case Gunman," *Newsday*, September 27, 1969.

"The Message Came Too Late," Tom Lambert, *Los Angeles Times*, November 10, 1969.

"Abrams Orders Jail for Col Rheault's Unit," Tom Lambert, *Los Angeles Times*, November 11, 1969.

Frank McCulloch told me about these phone calls from Marlon Brando during several talks in McCulloch's office.

"A Midnight Ride with Howard Hughes," Frank McCulloch, *Time*, December 21, 1970.

"Conrad, Vietnam, Meet in 'Apocalypse,'" Charles Champlin, *Los Angeles Times*, May 22, 1979.

"Robert Rheault, Green Beret Ensnared in Vietnam Murder Case, Dies at 87," Paul Vitello, *New York Times*, November 2, 2013.

*A Historical Overview of the Evolution of Citrus Heights, 1850–1997*, Leonard Davis and James Van Maren, Citrus Heights Historical Society, 1998.

"The 1988 CBC Massey Lectures, 'Necessary Illusions,'" Noam Chomsky, CBC Radio, November 6, 1988.

"Experts Seek Clues in 3 Explosions," Associated Press, January 2, 1976.

"Duke Goes Gunnin' for Demonstrators," Associated Press, January 6, 1971.

"War Reporter and Onetime Editor at *Times*," Associated Press, obituary for Frank McCulloch, May 17, 2018.

### Ray Biondi

"Couple Will Stand Trial in Double Slaying Case," Associated Press, August 22, 1990.

"Riggins/Gonsalves Investigators Detail Evidence in Case," Lauren Keene, *Davis Enterprise*, September 25, 2012.

"Family's Relief after Sexual Predator Is Finally Convicted of Killing Teen Couple 32 Years after Their Bodies Were Found in California Ravine," *Daily Mail*, September 30, 2013.

### Mike Fostar

*Bringing Mulligan Home: The Other Side of the Good War*, Dale Maharidge, PublicAffairs, 2013.

### The Investigator

"Mandatory Jail Term for Rape Passes," *Oakland Post*, August 18, 1978.

"From Guns to Sex Crimes to Texting, the New Laws Affecting California in 2017," Jeremy B. White, *Sacramento Bee*, December 30, 2016.

"To Catch a Killer: A Fake Profile on a DNA Site and a Pristine Sample," Tim Arango, Adam Goldman, and Thomas Fuller, *New York Times*, April 27, 2018.

"Frozen in Time: The DNA Sample that Led to the Arrest of Joseph DeAngelo," Becca Habegger, ABC 10 News, June 29, 2020.

## Parabola

*The Agricola*, Tacitus, translated by Alfred John Church and William Jackson Brodribb, Macmillan, 1877.

"North Dakota Republican Blames 'Parents Being Negligent with Their Kids' for Students Going Hungry," Brandon Gage, AlterNet, March 29, 2023.

"Why the Suburbs Are the Center of New York's Housing Debate," Mihir Zaveri, *New York Times*, April 3, 2023.

California State Senator Scott Wiener, interview with the author.

"The Rush Is On—But It's a Slow Start: After Two Months in NY, Limbaugh is Happy, Hopeful," Hilary Abramson, *Sacramento Bee*, August 31, 1988.

## We Are DEVO

*Bound in the Bond of Life: Pittsburgh Writers Reflect on the Tree of Life Tragedy*, "The News Next Door" chapter, Ann Belser, University of Pittsburgh Press, 2020.

"In a Nation Armed to the Teeth, These Tiny Missteps Led to Tragedy," Jack Healy, Glenn Thrush, Eliza Fawcett, and Susan C. Beachy, *New York Times*, April 20, 2023.

"This American Is Hungry," Dale Maharidge, *George*, October 2000.

Gun Violence Archive, https://www.gunviolencearchive.org/The Violence Project, https://www.theviolenceproject.org/methodology/

"Nowhere Is Safe: California Highway Shootings Double in Two Years, Data Reveals," Abené Clayton, *The Guardian*, August 8, 2022.

"Are They Not Spudboys? No, They Are DEVO," John Beifuss, *The Commercial Appeal*, June 30, 2000.

"DEVO'S Gerald Casale on Why the Band's 'Original' Sound Deserves The Hall of Fame's Recognition," Jason Brow, *Hollywood Life*, April 13, 2022.

**"So Good to Be Alive When the Eulogy Is Read"**

"The One-Man March; James Hood Returns to the Door He Opened 32 Years Ago," William Booth, *Washington Post*, November 1, 1995.

"God and Caesar at the Rio Grande: The Sanctuary Movement and the Politicization of Religion in the United States," Mary Hilary Cunningham, dissertation, Yale University, 1993.

"Escape from El Salvador," Dale Maharidge, *New York Times Magazine*, August 19, 2007.

# Acknowledgments

I am indebted to the newspaper journalists and editors who mentored and guided me. In the 1970s: Sarah Crump, Jim Dudas, Stephanie Nano, and Ken Rosenbaum at the *Cleveland Press*; Ed Noga at the Medina *Gazette*; Norma Conaway, Judith Haynes, and the late Bob Roach at the *Cleveland Plain Dealer*. Judith in particular was a mensch when she was my editor for the paper's *Sunday Magazine*. In the 1980s at the *Sacramento Bee*: Diane Alters, Steve Green, Terry Hennessy, Bill Moore, and Eleanor Shaw; the late Mort Saltzman, Bob Forsyth, Mike Flanagan, and Frank McCulloch. The late Paul Avery, an outstanding reporter who sometimes filled in as an editor, but he always was a role model in either capacity. At the Nieman Foundation: the late Howard Simons, the curator and onetime *Washington Post* managing editor, who was my final mentor.

Thanks to the University of Arizona Libraries, Special Collections, for access during the time of pandemic.

I am grateful to the *Sacramento Bee* for its policy in my time at the paper of allowing reported material to be used in this and my earlier books.

I couldn't have gone through the 1980s without Michael Williamson; so much of that journey happened with this blood brother. I'm indebted to Jan Haag and Dick Schmidt for the interview and recording sessions. Deskmate Hilary Abramson at the *Sacramento Bee* kept me sane with bawdy conversation and cheap cigars.

On the publishing side: thanks to Gretchen Young, founder and publisher of Regalo Press. And as always, Jennifer Lyons, of The Jennifer Lyons Literary Agency, LLC.